Student Companion to

Thomas
HARDY

Recent Titles in
Student Companions to Classic Writers

Student Companion to
Thomas Hardy

Rosemarie Morgan

Student Companions to Classic Writers

GREENWOOD PRESS
Westport, Connecticut • London

Library of Congress Cataloging-in-Publication Data

Morgan, Rosemarie.
   Student companion to Thomas Hardy / Rosemarie Morgan.
       p. cm. — (Student companions to classic writers, ISSN 1522–7979)
   Includes bibliographical references and index.
   ISBN 0–313–33396–3 (alk. paper)
   1. Hardy, Thomas, 1840–1928—Criticism and interpretation.   2. Hardy, Thomas, 1840–1928—Examinations—Study guides.   I. Title.
   PR4754.M58   2007
   823'.8—dc22   2006031758

British Library Cataloguing in Publication Data is available.

Library of Congress Catalog Card Number: 2006031758
ISBN: 0–313–33396–3
ISSN: 1522–7979

First published in 2007

Greenwood Press, 88 Post Road West, Westport, CT 06881
An imprint of Greenwood Publishing Group, Inc.
www.greenwood.com

Printed in the United States of America

The paper used in this book complies with the
Permanent Paper Standard issued by the National
Information Standards Organization (Z39.48–1984).

10 9 8 7 6 5 4 3 2 1

Contents

Series Foreword

This series has been designed to meet the needs of students and general readers for accessible literary criticism on the American and world writers most frequently studied and read in the secondary school, community college, and four-year college classrooms. Unlike other works of literary criticism that are written for the specialist and graduate student, or that feature a variety of reprinted scholarly essays on sometimes obscure aspects of the writer's work, the Student Companions to Classic Writers series is carefully crafted to examine each writer's major works fully and in a systematic way, at the level of the nonspecialist and general reader. The objective is to enable the reader to gain a deeper understanding of the work and to apply critical thinking skills to the act of reading. The proven format for the volumes in this series was developed by an advisory board of teachers and librarians for a successful series published by Greenwood Press, Critical Companions to Popular Contemporary Writers. Responding to their request for easy-to-use and yet challenging literary criticism for students and adult library patrons, Greenwood Press developed a systematic format that is not intimidating but helps the reader to develop the ability to analyze literature.

How does this work? Each volume in the Student Companions to Classic Writers series is written by a subject specialist, an academic who understands students' needs for basic and yet challenging examination of the writer's canon. Each volume begins with a biographical chapter, drawn from published sources, biographies, and autobiographies, that relates the writer's life to his or her work. The next chapter examines the writer's literary heritage, tracing the literary influences of other writers on that writer and explaining and discussing the literary genres into which the writer's work falls. Each of the following chapters examines a major work by the writer, those works most frequently read and studied by high school and college students. Depending on the writer's canon, generally between four and eight major works are examined, each in an individual chapter. The discussion of each work is organized into separate sections on plot development, character development, and major themes. Literary devices and style, narrative point of view, and historical setting are also discussed in turn if pertinent to the work. Each chapter concludes with an alternate critical perspective from which to read the work, such as a psychological or feminist criticism. The critical theory is defined briefly in easy, comprehensible language for the student. Looking at the literature from the point of view of a particular critical approach will help the reader to understand and apply critical theory to the act of reading and analyzing literature.

Of particular value in each volume is the bibliography, which includes a complete bibliography of the writer's works, a selected bibliography of biographical and critical works suitable for students, and lists of reviews of each work examined in the companion, both from the time the literature was originally published and from contemporary sources, all of which will be helpful to readers, teachers, and librarians who would like to consult additional sources.

As a source of literary criticism for the student or for the general reader, this series will help the reader to gain understanding of the writer's work and skill in critical reading.

Preface

This book is designed primarily for students of every stripe, from high school to college and beyond but with lay readers, teachers, and scholars also in mind—those seeking either a classroom tool or a perspective on areas previously unexplored in Hardy's prose and poetry. There are various useful, informational handbooks on Hardy, from *Notes* booklets to Sarah Bird Wright's A–Z, but none provides critical analyses and insights into Hardy's fiction and poetry. The *Oxford Reader's Companion to Hardy* (2000) supplies excellent overviews of Hardy's life and work, but these range from notes to surveys with considerable overlap of material and some scholarly inconsistency, inevitably the consequence of entries coming from 40 different contributors.

This Hardy companion seeks to fill the gap between the informative and the specialized text, offering—with the benefit of current scholarly research—received interpretations augmented by new perceptions of Hardy's life and career, exemplary critiques of four major novels, and easily accessible approaches to his poems—that is to say, ways of thinking and talking about his poems that are jargon free and devoid of the changing fashions in critical theory.

Hardy is matchless among writers in English. His uniqueness lies first and foremost in achieving greatness in two separate genres—fiction and poetry. Additionally, his life and work spanned two contrasting ages, the Victorian and the modern, beginning (as a teenager) as a poet and ending as the Grand Old Man of English Letters 70 years later with more than a thousand poems, 14 novels, and the epic drama *The Dynasts* to his name.

Predictably, Hardy's following is broad, wide, and global. To encompass his achievements in one single volume where the work of scholars extends to thousands of publications is an enormous challenge. I have sought to meet that challenge by focusing on selectivity of material and close readings. I have not attempted to include any background of literary influence (Shelley, Greek dramatists, etc.), although I have devoted time and space to the historical, social, and cultural contexts of his work (as reflected, for instance, in his use of allusions). Cultural context also takes into account the publishing scene of the day—an especially important element in Hardy's literary life and one that forcibly shaped his career (notably censorship and the opinion of critics) and embattled him personally for all his days. The extensive bibliography at the end of this book, which provides the most up-to-date, comprehensive list of modern critical works currently in existence, will more than adequately serve those who wish to pursue their interest in Hardy beyond these pages.

"Selectivity" means, for my own purposes, three things. First, it means the particular rather than the general. That is to say that the four major novels and the numerous poems I have reserved for closer scrutiny represent a unique aspect of Hardy's achievement as opposed to a general representation of his work. *The Woodlanders*, for example, was Hardy's favorite novel: structurally, thematically, and poetically it pleased him. With great reluctance I decided not to include it, despite its accomplished symmetries, because these symmetries remain, in general, a feature of all his novels, albeit in varying degrees of accomplishment.

Take, for example, Hardy's other great pastoral novel, *Far From the Madding Crowd*. This may not possess an aesthetic of comparable excellence, but it is in many ways more innovative. Here, Hardy experiments for the very first time with the trials and tribulations of a young woman entering the world of work—a world made for men by men, as Bathsheba puts it; she will be followed, in Hardy's oeuvre, by Tess (*Tess of the d'Urbervilles*) and Sue (*Jude the Obscure*) and also by her antithetical counterpart, Eustacia (*The Return of the Native*), who, in common with countless middle-class women in the real world, remains trapped in a "do-nothing" existence with no opportunities for work or action of any kind. At a different level of innovation, *Far From the Madding Crowd* sees the inception of Wessex. It also marks Hardy's first major success in his career as a novelist.

Hardy learned much from this first experience with the serialization of *Far From the Madding Crowd*, and enthusiasts will be able to trace his artistic progress in close detail by means of the prefatory passages I have prepared for each novel and volume of poems. Indeed, if readers so choose, they could trace Hardy's entire career via these prefatory passages; alternatively, they could focus solely on, say, his characterization of female protagonists or on his settings—each segment being completely self-contained as well as constituting part of the larger picture.

Biographical details are kept to a minimum and have been incorporated into prefatory material only where they play an important part in his literary career. Again, a comprehensive list of biographical publications is provided in the bibliography for readers wishing to venture further. Hardy's literary career is, in fact, a fascinating one, full of pitfalls and challenges. Given his autodidacticism (being self-taught) and lack of university education, his achievement is not only extraordinary, artistically as well as in terms of courage and fortitude, but an inspiration to aspiring writers everywhere.

The second tier to "selectivity" reflects my commitment to a preferred course. I know full well I cannot do justice to Hardy's entire canon, but I do know where I can do justice to his great distinction as poet and novelist. This is one reason for choosing, say, *The Return of the Native* over *The Mayor of Casterbridge*. The latter makes for a far more entertaining movie, but it is, structurally, artistically, and philosophically, the less ingenious of the two novels. Likewise, the poem "A Trampwoman's Tragedy," with its subtle fusion of form and content (another of Hardy's favorites), takes precedence, in my view, over a similar balladic verse, "The Revisitation," which displays Hardy's metrical ingenuity with lesser distinction.

And third, "selectivity" points to the peerless and the inestimable in worth. In the case of the four major novels, *Far From the Madding Crowd*, *The Return of the Native*, *Tess of the d'Urbervilles*, and *Jude the Obscure*, time has proven their literary and cultural preeminence. *Far From the Madding Crowd* probably remains the most popular of Hardy's novels among lay readers, and the three others are standard texts in British General Certificate of Secondary Education (GCSE), A-Level, and college courses and in equivalent courses in the United States. Of the four novels, *Tess* and *Jude* remain the most controversial—notably in their relevance to issues of self-responsibility, consensual sex, crimes of passion, sexual equality, and class division.

Ideally, a thousand poems created by one of the most important poets in the English language warrants a separate book altogether. Readers will, I hope, forgive the compression of so many preeminent pieces into so short a space as this book affords. One Hardy critic once spoke of Hardy's poems as a mansion one could live in forever. I have supplied but a floor plan to the mansion and have tried to let in as much air as possible—enough, I hope, to breathe in if not enough to sustain a "life."

In terms of the poems I have foregrounded, there is a mix of the popular and the exemplary. Incidentally, speaking of popular, I heard, quite by chance, Garrison Keillor on public radio recently, who not only picked Hardy as his poet of choice but also read verses that, to my surprise, coincided with some of my own highlights but which I had actually considered unusual choices; and when American poet laureate Robert Pinski chose "The Darkling Thrush" to herald the millennium year, he was speaking to thousands already familiar with this much-loved poem. Then, too, as I mention later in the poetry section, the newest Cunard liner, Queen Mary II, has Hardy's "Embarcation" engraved on its starboard walls. These instances of "popular" are but the tip of the iceberg. As the Thomas Hardy Association's forum discussion group bears witness, the popularity of Hardy's poetry increases each year as the postmodern age relinquishes its hold on conventional forms and embraces the experimental and often deviant forms of the Father of English Poetry. "Popular" thus points to the oft-quoted, oft-read, and oft-anthologized Hardy poems and not, of course, to their alignment with popular culture.

More often than not, I provide no gloss on the better-known poems; the bibliography in this book lists numerous sources for critical commentary in this area. Contrariwise, I have reserved my brief comments for works I consider neglected or, if popular, in some way overlooked in aspect or design. It is the case, for instance, that whereas Hardy considered the aforementioned "A Trampwoman's Tragedy" one of his finest poems, many scholars have demurred, so I have offered some considerations on their behalf.

In terms of the exemplary, there is probably no such uniformity or representativeness of form as this word implies in Hardy's poetic oeuvre, unless we can speak of examples of iconoclasm and broken conventions. Even his balladic forms tend to break the rules. So, by "exemplary" I really mean examples of a thematic line here (say, the anti-God or antiwar poems), or a peculiarly Hardyan technique there (of, say, making the outer world a "talking text" or "speaking dead"). Among the exemplary are poems of irony, satire, love, tragedy, humor, social comment, and philosophy, as well as verses memorializing great men and women from Catullus to the Victorian artist Helen Paterson, right down to the humblest Wessex laborer, "Drummer Hodge."

I have not endeavored to discuss metrical arrangements or deep structures. It seems to me that a poem should first and foremost be *read*, preferably aloud. Then, when the sounds, rhythms, and images have stirred the senses, when the haunting echoes of vowels and syllables have created their own magic, and when the words juxtaposed with ideas or starts of ill-fittingness and ugly clefts have left their mark, when all of this has roused the reader's sensibility to a readiness of cognition, then and only then might the time be ripe for asking how and why it is done.

Hardy might say, "The bird knows the song." It might be raucous or driven or mellifluous. All that matters is that it is received, that the listener hears it, senses it, feels it. This book is not designed for career theorists but for listeners and readers. Hardy only ever had these individuals in mind, and he would have made no distinction between the "birds," that is, their theoretical classification or hypothetical attributes, only their songs. Each song is a thing in itself, and, as "The Darkling Thrush" evinces, it may be accessible to the senses but not necessarily to explanation. Knowledge is not always amenable to analysis, and poems are not always best appreciated by application of theory.

With this in mind, I have assembled Hardy's poems much as he himself arranged them. Frequently his poems talk to one another, so this remains an important part of my own rationale. I have, however, tried to group the poems in each volume according to a rough thematic—"rough" because no one poem is about any one thing. To this end, I have created subheadings and grouped together those poems that share certain themes or topics. Hardy's poetry resists categorization, so these subheading are simply signposts, not classifications. He does, however, on rare occasions provide his own subheadings (*Wessex Poems* is arranged under composition dates, for example), and these authorial subheadings have been followed in all cases. Sorting by chronology is possibly the least satisfactory method because it gives readers no idea of topic or theme, but it is Hardy's chosen method in *Wessex Poems* and thus it suffices.

This Hardy companion is arranged for ease of access. The chapters are autonomous, divided into subheadings by topic, theme, or characterization, and can be taken as single entities or read interactively and progressively. Many of the early ideas are developed in later sections, and many stand alone. As Hardy once said, there can be more in a book than the author consciously puts there. You, the reader, will supply the "more."

1

The Life of Thomas Hardy

CHILDHOOD AND FAMILY

On a "thyme-scented, bird-singing"[1] June morning in 1840 in the tiny Dorsetshire hamlet of Higher Bockhampton, a son was born to Jemima Hardy and Thomas Hardy Sr. Married barely five months, they discreetly called the birth premature, and indeed, the infant was fragile and, sadly, laid aside as dead. However, of the many strong women who were to later shape Thomas Hardy's life, the local midwife, Lizzy Downton, was the first. She revived the frail infant and nurtured him with gentle care. And it was she who subsequently cherished him throughout his early childhood—as he later recalls, "the smallest and feeblest ... / Weak from my baptism of pain" ("In Tenebris, III").

Hardy's birthplace, situated a few miles from the county town and market center of Dorchester, is a picturesque thatched cottage set in the heart of rural Dorset. He records, in an early poem, "Domicilium," adopting the narrative voice of his paternal grandmother:

> Our house stood quite alone, and those tall firs
> And beeches were not planted. Snakes and efts
> Swarmed in the summer days, and nightly bats
> Would fly about our bedrooms. Heathcroppers
> Lived on the hills, and were our only friends;
> So wild it was when we first settled here.

Hardy never forsook his homeland ("Domicilium"). When he later built himself a house, where he lived until the day he died, it was within walking distance of his birthplace.

The second, and most important, strong woman in Hardy's life was his mother, Jemima. She had worked her way up from humble beginnings as a housemaid to develop remarkably cultivated tastes. She had become an omnivorous reader, well versed in the classics, and was later fiercely ambitious for her children—Mary (1841), Henry (1851), and Katherine (1856). It was Jemima who encouraged her frail firstborn's interest in books and music. Said to be reading (somewhat precociously) at three years old and, at seven, the eager recipient of Dryden's *Virgil* and Johnson's *Rasselas* from his mother, the young Hardy also played the violin, occasionally accompanying his father, who performed at country-house balls. Little more than a child, Hardy would not only play the fiddle but would also dance the night away, stepping to reels, waltzes, and jigs. His passion for music and dance remained with him all his days.

Thomas Hardy Sr. had come from a long line of instrumentalists, leading choirs and musical services at the parish church "much as described," says his literary son, "in *Under the Greenwood Tree* ... though ... personages, incidents, manners etc." were all invented.[2] Well, they had to be invented! These music makers and their assemblies had already disbanded by the time Hardy the younger was a year old. By trade, Thomas Hardy Sr. was a small-scale, unambitious stonemason of genial temperament, maintaining several men in his employ in the building trade (and a reputation as a womanizer).

The third of the strong women, Hardy's paternal grandmother, who also lived at the Bockhampton cottage, died when he was 17. Her influence on the young, budding poet was immeasurable. A vital source of songs and stories, she would transport her rapt listener back to the distant past with vivid tales of old Dorset, recalling events as far back as the Napoleonic threats of invasion (1805–15). Possibly it was as an unspoken tribute to "Granny" that Hardy embarked, in his thirties, upon the work of his lifetime—his Napoleonic epic drama, *The Dynasts*. When he was seven he had found, in a closet, copies of his grandfather's collection of contemporary issues of *A History of the Wars* (Napoleonic) and had pored over pictures of crossed bayonets, serried ranks of soldiers, and slain bodies. In a sense, Napoleon came alive for him at a very tender age.

Although Hardy started research for *The Dynasts* in the 1860s, he did not complete it until he reached *his* sixties in 1908—hence the distant past was with him always, throughout his entire career as a novelist, to be invoked by a variety of different voices in his prose and in many of his poems. *The Trumpet-Major* (1880) may be the only novel to go as far back as the Napoleonic period, but the voices from the past are omnipresent elsewhere, from Granfer Cantle's tales of the "Bang-Up Locals" (based on stories of the local Volunteer Light Infantry) in *The Return of the Native* (1878), to the internal setting of *The Mayor of Caster-bridge* (1886), which returns to the period when Hardy himself was born.

During his childhood and teenage years, Hardy's most intimate companion was his sister Mary, one of the strongest of them all. She remained, at all times, his chief confidante. The empathetic Hardy felt that her "unusual" disposition—solitary, tomboyish, artistic (a skilled painter), and wholly indifferent to opinion—ill-suited her for the teaching career she embarked on. It was an age when few professions were open to women. She was, he said wryly, "doomed to school-teaching"—not unlike her fictional counterpart, Sue Bridehead in *Jude the Obscure* (1895). No doubt "tomboy" Mary inspired Hardy at several levels of creation. Certainly her passing comment to her brother that there is a fashion in women's faces just as there is in haute couture sounds very much like the kind of remark Sue might have lobbed at Jude.

Significantly, intimate sibling relationships, frequently transferred to cousin-lovers, feature strongly in his fiction, from *Desperate Remedies* to *The Return of the Native* and beyond. Hardy's deep understanding of women, physical and emotional, originated in his bond with Mary—after all, they shared a bedroom in the tiny Bockhampton cottage for most of their formative years. So close were they that their mother once expressed the wish that all her children should remain forever together instead of marrying "out" of the family.

When Mary died in 1915 Hardy became deeply depressed. For three months he scarcely left the house. During that desolate winter he wrote a poem, "Logs on the Hearth," in which the speaker, dreaming into the dying embers of the fireside, reifies the burning logs into their former existence as an apple tree. This ancient fruit tree "bloomed and bore striped apples ... / Till its last hour," as also bearing upon its "bending limbs" a laughing girl, his sister, "her foot near mine," waving "her young brown hand." The Edenic symbolism of the apple tree (singled out for the axe in both cases, symbolically and literally), the evocation of innocence and happiness, the Eve figure plucking at will the fruit she desires, and even the placement of her foot upon the bough where the Satanic snake would have lurked in the Genesis story all combine, powerfully, to subvert the biblical myth. In place of guilt and punishment, this sister, "Eve," exercises free will, free desire, and free, shameless pleasure in her young body. A splendid tribute indeed!

SCHOOLING AND APPRENTICESHIP

Hardy called himself "rather an idle schoolboy" (*LW*, 27). At eight years old he was strong enough to attend the village school, at nine, a Dorchester day school—walking into town every day through woods and fields. At 14, he won a Latin prize and found a special satisfaction in numbers, "a certain poetry in the rule for the extraction of the cube-root, owing to its rhythm" (*LW*, 29). And, at 15, he became a teacher in Sunday school while, with unfailing regularity, losing his heart to pretty girls (including his own beautiful cousins). In 1856, when he was 16, he was articled to a successful Dorchester architect, Mr. John Hicks. Still the avid scholar—in reality, far from idle—he now added Greek to his accomplishments in French, Latin, and German.

Working next door to a school owned by the Dorset dialect poet William Barnes, the young apprentice would sneak out of the architect's office from time to time in search of philological arguments with his venerable neighbor. Roaming farther afield, he would also spend many free hours in the meadows, walking and talking with his eminent literary companion and cherished friend, Horace Moule of Queen's College, Cambridge. When the talking ceased and the philosophy waned, he would go watercolor painting with Horace Moule's brother, Henry—later to become the vicar of the church at Fordington, Dorchester. Thus the young architect grew to manhood, intellectually inquisitive, artistically gifted, mentally precocious but, in his own mind, physically immature—"a youth till he was five-and-twenty" (*LW*, 37). He continued to play his fiddle in the evenings when he was not writing poetry or chasing girls or dancing until dawn.

ARCHITECTURE OR LITERATURE?

A few months before starting in Hicks's office, Hardy had published his very first piece of prose, "an anonymous skit in a Dorchester paper on the disappearance of the Alms-House clock." For the narrator, the 16-year-old Hardy picked the ghost of the Alms-House Clock, who then sets about berating all the town clocks for being in a "constant state of doubt and perplexity." While "the Trinity Clock scorns the society of its neighbour … and obstinately refuses to keep company with it," the ghost complains, "the South Street Clock has infinite contempt for both, and keeps its own course."[3]

This small piece of juvenilia employs three characteristically Hardyan techniques. First is the adoption of the voice of the ghost as speaker; second, the use of irony to lighten the weight of the piece. And third, absurdity. Absurdity invites readers to smile—in this instance at the irresponsibility of clocks and their reprehensible failure of duty. These three techniques were to become distinctive Hardyan traits—later, the signature of his literary art.

At 21, Hardy migrated to London with little more than the clothes he was wearing and a return ticket in his pocket. He feared he was countrified, pink faced, and unprepossessing. Was it then his mischievous sense of humor and gentle sensitivity that charmed people? For even upon first meeting, they would go out of their way for him. And many were to become his lifelong friends. One such was the celebrated architect Mr. Arthur Blomfield. Within a few weeks of their meeting, the "pink-faced" apprentice from Dorset had been appointed architectural assistant to the great man, and they remained firm friends ever since.

Meanwhile, with Moule's constant encouragement, Hardy's thoughts turned increasingly to writing. So influential was Moule that he managed to persuade Hardy to read soon-to-be Cardinal Newman's masterpiece of religious autobiography, *Apologia pro vita sua* (1864)—a weighty tome that Moule "like[d] … so much" (*LW*, 50). Try as he might, Hardy did not like him "so much." He found, what he rather superciliously called, Newman's "gentle childish faith in revelation" (*LW*, 51) charming but his religious reasoning unconvincing. This is an interesting detail because it is commonly held that Hardy's agnosticism was mainly inspired, later in his thirties, by the influence of his famous editor, Leslie Stephen (father of Virginia Woolf), who suffered his own crisis of faith in the early 1870s. Not so. The disappearance of God, for Hardy, and what he calls his "revolutionary fervour"—his socialist leanings—were already insurgent in the 1860s.

Hardy was now keeping a literary notebook, and with a poet's feel for shapes and designs, he would play with words, truncating syllables, fragmenting consonants, and introducing odd accidentals, much as composers allow their hands to roam randomly over disconnected chords and broken arpeggios. The following lipogram, revealing that even at this young age he was experimenting with onomatopoeia,[4] reflects a young man's turn of mind as "sweet ache of n—k, l—p, s—l" conveys the physical sensation of kissing (the consonant's lipping of tongue and lips). For Hardy, this play on the sensations, on the feel of language, was the foundational stuff of poetry—never less than physical and invariably palpable.

Back in the world of work, what Hardy's biographers and commentators tend to elide is the sheer courage it must have taken for one so young and inexperienced to forge ahead, alone and unaided, in the world's largest city at the time. Breaking through the rigid class barriers alone was daunting. Coming as he did from the artisan, rural underclass with no university education and a Dorset brogue to hinder him at every turn, he was beset by the class struggle from day one. For Hardy, then as later, throughout his 20-year career as a novelist, this remained a battle.

Sexual discrimination and the subordination of women also deeply concerned him. And, no doubt, his mother and sisters played an educative part in this. Hardy was nothing if not empathetic. It was, though, his own sensitivity and impressionability that sharpened his profound understanding of the social conflict—he was deeply vulnerable to class oppression, to the perpetual defensiveness of his own position, and to the constant repression of his sense of injustice at the belittlement of his person and of his work.

Transferred to the novel-writing process, these factors, in turn, sensitized him to censorship and to the restriction on free self-expression. Fortunately, he possessed the ability to summon transference of thought, feeling, and ideas and what Keats called "negative capability" to objects both animate and inanimate. Armed, then, with a rare set of skills, Hardy settled down to become a writer—and, first and foremost, to battle issues of class and sex discrimination. It was this battle that shaped his first novel, *The Poor Man and the Lady,* and that doomed it.

The year is now 1865, and Hardy, 25 years old, produces his second minor publication, "How I Built Myself a House," which was published in *Chamber's Journal* (March 1865). London life, however, was taking its toll on his health, and within two years he was back home, temporarily at work in his old office in Dorchester. Walking to work over hill and dale every day slowly restored his vigor.

The Poor Man and the Lady (PML, 1868) was rejected by publishers primarily for its overzealous attack on the upper classes. George Meredith, an editorial reader, had, however, found signs of literary promise underlying Hardy's class diatribe and suggested he try his hand at a sensation novel; he should focus on artistic purposes (not sociopolitical issues) and work on a more complicated (intriguing) plot. The aptly titled *Desperate Remedies* was the result (DR, 1871, Tinsley Brothers). This novel, published in volume form, combines mystery, entanglement, elements of surprise, and what Hardy called "moral obliquity," enhanced by a vividly drawn local setting.

Hardy had now moved to the Dorset port town of Weymouth, later the model for Budmouth in his novels. Again, as in *PML*, the protagonist in *DR* is an architect, and those diverse touches of salt-of-the-earth dialect, philosophical interest, class struggle, psychological insight, and ironic situations, for which he would later become famous, are subtly infused into the crime-fiction plot.

Hardy was encouraged by these modest beginnings. And within the year he had followed up with *Under the Greenwood Tree* (*UGT*, 1872, Tinsley Brothers), published in volume form. This is a pastoral story of poetic color and narrative charm, both comic and serious, alternately vital and reposeful—the least controversial book he ever wrote. *A Pair of Blue Eyes* (*PBE*, 1872–73) followed within the year, serialized in *Tinsley's Magazine*. This was the first of his novels to show his name on the title page. *DR* had not only been anonymous but Hardy also had to subsidize the cost of publishing it. *UGT*, also anonymous, had received good reviews but had not sold well. *PBE*, benefiting from periodical serialization and thus a far wider readership, was his first all-around success.

COURTSHIP AND MARRIAGE

Hardy was now on his way—and in more ways than one. In 1870, he had been sent on architectural business to supervise the restoration of the church in St. Juliot in Cornwall. At the rectory, he met Emma Gifford, the woman who would be his wife. Hardy, who fell in love easily and was instantly attracted to strong, independent women, was captivated.

The Emma he met in 1870 was lively and intellectually keen. Additionally, she was a skilled horsewoman, enthusiastic painter, and aspiring writer. According to some accounts, she feared she was already "on the shelf" when, at 29 years old, she met Hardy. Four years later there was still no firm marriage plan. The story goes that she then feigned a pregnancy (which means, of course, that they were sexually active)—like her fictional counterpart, Arabella, in *Jude the Obscure* (1895). Critics have assumed that her rage at that novel and her attempts to block it from publication were linked to the prevailing "Jude the Obscene" controversy. However, that it might have been Arabella's characterization that enraged her has not yet been fully examined (certainly there is a physical resemblance to her own buxom, hair-coiled self).

Be that as it may, the Hardy marriage took place without ceremony (no members of his family attended) in London in September 1874, and the couple remained childless thereafter, much to Hardy's disappointment. Indeed, neither of them sustained in matrimony the joys and affinities they had dreamed of in the Cornwall days. Despite Emma's strong encouragement of Hardy's literary career, her invaluable role as amanuensis, and their shared devotion to their many cats and dogs, the tensions born of temperamental difference, domestic disagreements, and no doubt the suppressed envy of the aspiring writer and the sexual jealousy of the neglected wife increased with the years. Emma's bitterness and resentment and Hardy's evident inability to assuage her troubles were exacerbated by her snobbish sense of her own class superiority and, more tragically, by the emotional disorders and mental instability that appear to have run in the Gifford family.

When Emma died in November 1912, following many years of domestic alienation, Hardy's bereavement shock propelled him back to the Cornwall days of their courtship. Psychologically driven and poetically inspired to reify the youthful Emma he had once dreamed of loving, and merging aspects of time past with the chimeras born of memory and imagination, he created, in verse, "Emma" figurations representing various forms of the beloved: the lost prize, the plaintive lover, combine with phantom figures of mind and spirit infusing loss, desire, misunderstanding, grief, and so on, into the poems. Thus the great collection of "Emma" poems was born (notably the "Poems of 1912–13"). As in his novels of the 1870–90s, in which Hardy had formed a half-dream, half-real world called Wessex—in psychoanalytic terms "recovering" the lost natal land of his birth, reinventing it, reliving time past, and bringing it all into the present moment of creation—so, too, there are strong elements of reification, invention, and recovery in the "Emma" poems.

FAME AND FORTUNE

Embarking on a career as novelist following marriage to Emma and the publication of the highly acclaimed *Far From the Madding Crowd* (1874) did not mean, for Hardy, an end of architecture. On the contrary, his literary work is replete with architectural details and complex motifs of structural restoration. The youth who had apprenticed to Hicks in Dorchester at the tender age of 16 was bound to have internalized the whole experience—the challenge, the learning, and the new love. Hardy was deeply impressionable. He never lost the wonder and fervent interest of the architect's apprentice—as evidenced in his prose fiction right through to his last poems.

In a composition from his late years, "The Church and the Wedding," a bridegroom-architect promises his bride that he will "restore this old church for our marriage"—an ironic restoration as it happens because, meanwhile, the parallel structure, the union of woman and man itself breaks. Alternatively, in Hardy's last novel, *Jude the Obscure*, the young protagonist yearns to embrace and be embraced by an alma mater (bountiful mother), the medieval university at Christminster. Instead, he ends up as a stonemason. This, in real life, was the trade of Hardy's father. It is worth noting that these invisible "parents," embedded in the text, function as an extended metaphor within an internal landscape of solid architectural artifacts—a city marginalized on the very edge of Wessex. Tragically, the actual parents in *Jude* will suffer more than marginalization: their children and indeed their own lives will be entirely obliterated.

There were, in fact, very few childhood incidents that did not indelibly mark the oversensitive Hardy. Perhaps the most haunting was the public hanging of Martha Brown for the murder of her husband. Standing close to the gallows in the crowd of several thousand, Hardy experienced, possibly for the first time in his young life, that disturbing sensation called algolagnia—an adrenaline reaction to violence characterized by sensations of pleasure fused with pain. With the distance of hindsight, he writes: "I remember what a fine figure she showed against the sky as she hung in the misty rain, & how the tight black silk gown set off her shape as she wheeled half round and back." And then, as her face was covered, "I saw—they had put a cloth over the face—how, as the cloth got wet, *her features came through it.*"[5] Evidently, he is half fascinated and half repelled; his later image of Tess's hanging appears, by contrast, stupefying and remote. Perhaps reinventing the experience but erasing its terrible nearness was a psychological burial of a kind.

By the time of *Tess of the d'Urbervilles* (1891), Hardy's fame and fortune was ensured. He didn't see it quite like that, however. Every novel from *Far From the Madding Crowd* onward had involved battles with editors. Every passing year, which generally saw the advent of another novel (16 in all), had brought periods of depression and intermittent thoughts of suicide. His work had been persistently cut, bowdlerized, and even rejected outright by several publishing houses simultaneously. Occasionally, he was forced to bowdlerize his novels himself, if he was to gain a publisher at all. Then, at the other end of the production, when in those days copyright law was in its infancy, there were the literary pirates. And finally there were the critics, who could be and were exceedingly harsh. In fact, when Hardy finally abandoned novel writing in the 1890s, he felt only a madman would continue to battle on as he had done. Enough was enough, and he quit.

The problem with editors and critics was that Hardy was strong on candor and on subverting puritanical Victorian sociosexual codes, whereas editors and critics were strong on Mrs. Grundy. Mrs. Grundy was a powerful icon, but unlike Britannia or Uncle Sam, she embodied not pride or fealty but censure. Accordingly, no Young British Person should be faced with reading material that might cause a blush (to wit, arousal). Hardy should write, editor Leslie Stephen once told him, as if for the parson's daughter—and, inevitably, for her pious father. Hardy found this code of ethics frustrating, suffocating, false, and hypocritical. But he also wanted to sell his books.

Part of Hardy's genius is the manner in which he circumnavigated Mrs. Grundy. He was able to develop prose techniques that defied the literal mind of his more censorious reader. One way of achieving this, as an early influential poet-critic, Coventry Patmore, was quick to notice, is to infuse poetry into the prose. Hardy's iconoclasm subverts the literal by embedding unpalatable truths or injudicious material in figurative forms; explicit delineations of sexuality, say, are rendered implicit—couched in figures of speech, extended metaphors, synecdoche, and so on. As early as *A Pair of Blue Eyes*, Hardy was employing these techniques, although he still had much to learn—his portrayals of taboo subjects, such as illegitimacy, were still far too explicit. Nevertheless, he was most definitely finding his way to a method.

The troubled editor still had to maintain strict vigilance, especially when critics complained, as they did, constantly, of sacrilege on the one hand and a distinct voluptuousness (sexual pleasure) in the heroine on the other—which, infuriatingly, they couldn't always pinpoint. We need to remind ourselves that "nice" women, including fictional models (who had considerable influence as models, as do celebrities today), should display no sexual interest or even a sexual consciousness, no "knowledge," no pleasure, no desire whatsoever, and should most certainly not have physical contact with men (a good example of this was when editor Leslie Stephen replaced Bathsheba's touching of Gabriel Oak's arm with "sleeve").

Part of Hardy's purpose was to restore to middle-class women their pride and delight in their bodies and their enjoyment of sexuality. He deplored the sexual double standard whereby men could be sexual and still retain their social status, their reputation, their integrity, and self-esteem—all denied to the sexually active woman. Female sexuality spelled shame, and in Hardy's book, this was cruel, oppressive, and counterproductive in a society working toward sexual equality. And indeed, despite the wrath of a puritanical brigade—the Grundyans—he succeeded in breaking a good many Victorian codes and conventions, thus opening the way for a more liberated readership.[6]

Nevertheless, his relationship with editors and many professional reviewers remained severely strained during this period. Those who acclaimed his work enthusiastically had to be balanced against those who declaimed harshly. The vitriolic attack inevitably made a deeper impact than did the eulogy, and Hardy often found it too much to bear. Fame and fortune were now at his door, but so too were psychological anguish and depression. Thus it was, following the publication of the polemical *Jude the Obscure,* when the bishop of Wakefield publicly declared the book suitable only for burning and ceremoniously threw it into the fire that Hardy ended his novel-writing career forever.

THE GRAND OLD MAN OF ENGLISH LETTERS

In the later years of their marriage, Emma, estranged and unhappy, moved up to the attic at Max Gate, the house Hardy had designed and built in Dorchester in the 1880s. This meant that whereas his domestic life was lonesome and sad, his life among London's literati and society women was relatively unencumbered. Of course, visitors to Max Gate were plenty, and entertaining them appears to have given Hardy (and his guests) considerable pleasure (in his earlier years at any rate, before old age got the better of him). Meanwhile, his London life grew even more involved. Among his most intimate friends, the aspiring writer Florence Henniker (wife of Major Henniker) secured a special place in his heart. Rarely a day passed, especially in the 1890s, when the couple did not meet for lunch or theater or dinner parties. In between these encounters they would write notes to each other, sometimes two or three times a day.

Just as Hardy had drawn inspiration and strength from Horace Moule in his younger days, when he was still undecided about whether to pursue a career in architecture or in writing, and before Moule's tragic suicide in the 1870s had left him agonizingly bereft, he now turned to Florence Henniker. He had met her at the crossroads in his life when the novelist was dying and the poet had yet to survive his stillbirth (he had been composing verses all his life but had never succeeded in publishing them). Florence helped him sustain his faith in himself during this appallingly difficult period when he was at his most lonely and depressed. So low were his spirits at this time that he feared to go out in the London streets at night, imagining his more savage critics creeping up to bludgeon him in some dark alley.

No doubt his father's death in 1892 deepened his sense of morbidity. At a less traumatic level there was also the burden of making revisions to the Wessex novels. The first collected edition, demanding copious revisions, was to come out in 1895–96 (Osgood-McIlvaine), and this intensified his ongoing anxiety. He felt the task of revising and refashioning his Wessex construct to be a despairing one: the first flush of creativity could never be revived, yet publishers were clamoring. The commercial value of "Wessex" was rising—the work had to be done.

The concept of Wessex had materialized relatively late—being but a casual allusion in his fourth published novel, *Far From the Madding Crowd,* and taking shape slowly over the years, novel by novel, as imagination fired and as readers demanded more (Wessex was one aspect of his novels that never ceased to charm and delight). Hence, revisions were complicated and arduous: he now had to construct a coherent Wessex "universe," novel by novel, step by step, pathway by pathway, from topographical details that didn't always add up. In some cases he failed, as in coordinating the distance between manor house and church in *Far From the Madding Crowd.* Enlarging the acreage, he accidentally rendered Bathsheba's sighting of children playing in the churchyard a feat worthy only of a telephoto lens. But ultimately he achieved his goal without too many disasters of this kind, and Wessex was now as mimetically real as it would ever be.

Meantime, Florence Henniker was also rising. She and Hardy had started collaborating on a book, *The Spectre of the Real* (1894). Thereafter they sustained, for many, many years, an emotional and intellectual intimacy of exceptional depth. That there was also a sexual dimension to the friendship seems probable, but the evidence is nowhere to be found.[7] Be that as it may, Hardy's creative flame was now rekindled after the bleak misery of the *Jude* scandal, and in 1898 he published *Wessex Poems and Other Verses.* He had never really stopped writing poetry, and several of the *Wessex* verses had been conceived years before. But now, possessing economic security from the novels and a kindred spirit with whom he could share his feelings and ideas, the poet came fully into being. *Wessex Poems* was well received, and *Poems of the Past and the Present* followed shortly afterward in 1901.

When Hardy's mother, the single most important influence in his life, died in 1904, she would have had the satisfaction of knowing her son had finally found his place in the world. He was now in his literary prime—immersed in part 1 of his magnum opus, the Napoleonic drama *The Dynasts,* which he had begun 40 years earlier and had continually worked on ever since. Part 1 of this epic drama was published in the year of her death. Parts 2 and 3 were completed and published in 1906 and 1908, respectively. It must have been deeply satisfying to Hardy that the Oxford University Dramatic Society chose *The Dynasts* (over Shakespeare) when, with the end of World War I, it resumed its annual dramatic productions.

Hardy's third volume of verse, *Time's Laughingstocks and Other Verses*, came out the following year, in 1909, and at this point, the Grand Old Man of English Letters, the Father of Modern Poetry, came face to face with a ranking he had once thought his family had owned in medieval times and had lost forever. This was a knighthood. Hardy had always thought, whimsically or otherwise, that his family stemmed from ancient noble stock, long since fallen from grace. Now Prime Minister Asquith offered him a knighthood, and—in common with fellow writer John Galsworthy—he turned it down. Well, to be precise, he didn't quite know how to refuse Asquith. He seemed embarrassed at refusing and stumbled around in several circular sentences saying, in the end, that he couldn't accept it at this time.

Knighthood was latterly accorded to the nobility, but in more recent years has been offered as a reward for services rendered to crown and country. This honor may have suited Hardy's idea of ancestry but not his idea of modern literary prizes (unlike the Nobel Prize, for example). Subsequently, however, he accepted the Order of Merit and became Thomas Hardy, O.M. This reward, in his view, was acceptable.

In the year following his mother's death, Hardy met Florence Dugdale. She became his secretary, and two years after Emma died in 1912, he married her. Florence managed Hardy's household and secretarial work at Max Gate with expert care, if not always with integrity and truthfulness. She was young and insecure and tended to inflate her needy ego with gossip mongering, deceitful stories, and manipulative behavior. Hardy remained, as ever, deeply loyal, although his mind was usually elsewhere and his heart still roamed.

Notwithstanding his ripe old age (now in his eighties), he could still be stirred by womanly charms. It was at this time that he wrote a note in the margins of his copy of *Jude* about Arabella's amplitudes, adding a comment from Browning on "her breasts' superb abundance." Hardy's passions would take instant possession of his mind and heart. Florence was devastated by his adoration of Gertrude Bugler (the actor who played Tess in 1924) and did everything in her power to keep the beautiful woman away from her infatuated husband.

While the death of Hardy's sister Mary in 1915 had plunged him into months of deep depression, news from the war front (1914–18) intensified his anguish. Man's inhumanity to man appalled him, and the utter powerlessness of all living creatures in the face of an indifferent God reduced him to despair. His anti-God poems are prolific and constitute a major theme in his verse, expressing as much protest and sense of cosmic injustice as unconcealed ridicule and contempt.

Hardy was highly productive during the war years. *Satires of Circumstance: Lyrics and Reveries with Miscellaneous Pieces* came out in 1914, as did *The Dynasts: Prologue and Epilogue*. His iconoclastic poems baffled some of his critics and drew admiration from others. Added to his unconventional (heterodox) choice of topics, there was the difficulty, for traditionalists, of his metrical experimentation—nowadays regarded as heralding the modernist movement—stylistically, far ahead of his time. But in the main, while lay readers might have found him challenging, fellow poets adulated him.

Hardy was delighted by positive criticism, bemused by his detractors, and unlike Hardy the novelist, often diffident about his poetry reviewers. He did grow weary of pessimism charges, seeing his mission as finding a way to a betterment of the human condition, but he shrugged these off—readers simply did not understand! Thus, undeterred, he forged ahead. *Selected Poems* arrived on the scene in 1916, *Moments of Vision and Miscellaneous Verses* in 1917, *Late Lyrics and Earlier with Many Other Verses* in 1922, *Human Shows, Far Phantasies, Songs and Trifles* in 1925, and *Winter Words in Various Moods and Metres* in 1928 (posthumously). During these late years he also brought out another volume of short stories, having published three collections in the 1880s and 1890s. *A Changed Man and Other Tales* came out in 1913. *The Famous Tragedy of the Queen of Cornwall*, a drama, appeared in 1923.

By 1923 tributes and accolades were flowing in, although Hardy's modesty, like the simplicity of his lifestyle and close identification with the rural life of his beloved Dorset, remained unaltered. On one especially modest occasion, when it had been suggested that the holograph manuscript of *Far From the Madding Crowd* be sold off at Sothebys to raise war funds for the Red Cross, he was pleased with the idea but wondered, to his publisher, whether anyone would want to bid on it. Another time, he observed to Middleton Murray (poet and editor of *The Athenaeum*) that he felt "a sad sense of shortcoming at your good opinion of my writings & myself. I fear you do not know what a feeble person I really am." And when he subsequently found a poem for Murray, "The Maid of Keinton-Mandeville," he seems to have felt quite abashed at his choice saying, apologetically, "since you wrote kindly asking me for another poem I have found some verses which at first I thought would only suit publication in a *daily* paper." A daily paper would be, of course, a nonliterary publication.[8]

There was one literary endeavor that did, however, test his humility to the utmost. It was the Thomas Hardy "biography." Journalists trying to gain access to Max Gate to write up their gossip columns, literary bounty hunters seeking spicy tidbits, and scholars masquerading as best friends and then publishing detailed accounts of his life and art—these events drove him crazy. Life as a celebrity was abhorrent to him in the respect that it stole his privacy, misrepresented his ideas, and violated his most cherished concerns. To alleviate the perennial frustration and anger these unlicensed "biographers" caused him, he set about in his later years preparing notes, collecting anecdotes, rereading old letters, and, in sum, creating his own account of his life that he then dictated to Florence to be published pseudonymously in her name. Pseudonymous autobiographies have a very respectable lineage. Contrary to the occasional critic's snide suggestion that this was nothing less than a deception perpetrated by Hardy, self-writing of this kind is commonplace and laudably creative in the annals of biographical history. Naturally, Hardy didn't broadcast this exercise—only a handful of people knew of it. But one thing is certain, he was not going to leave this world without raising his Hardyan fist at those who sought to appropriate his life. If anyone was going to appropriate it, it would be Thomas Hardy.

Hardy's sight was rapidly failing at this time (making something of an irony of his title, *Moments of Vision*), but this did not stop him from enjoying the huge spate of dramatizations of his works. He had always relished the theater, and these performances gave him the deepest pleasure, especially when they took place at Max Gate. One such event was a production of *Tess* given by the Garrick Theatre in the winter of 1925. The entire company of West End actors arrived laden with theatrical props and transformed Hardy's living room into an instant theater. He was thrilled.

The following winter he returned to the place of his birth, at Bockhampton, where he had visited his mother every Sunday until the day she died, to take care of the garden and trees. He was not to know that this would be the very last time he would see his childhood home. One night, some weeks later on January 11, 1928, he suffered a heart attack at Max Gate and did not live to see the morning.

There is one passage in his autobiographical *Life* that he never read: "The dawn … rose in almost unparalleled splendour. Flaming and magnificent the sky stretched its banners over the dark pines that stood sentinel" (*LW*, 481).[9] But the great Hardy was dead.

NOTES

1. The phrase is from Thomas Hardy's *Tess of the d'Urbervilles*, edited by Tim Dolin (London: Penguin Books, 1998), 101.

2. See Thomas Hardy, *The Life and Work of Thomas Hardy*, edited by Michael Millgate (London: Macmillan, 1984), 17 (hereafter cited in text as *LW*). *Under the Greenwood Tree* (1872) is Hardy's second published novel.

3. *Thomas Hardy's Public Voice: The Essays, Speeches, and Miscellaneous Prose*, edited by Michael Millgate (Oxford: Clarendon Press, 2001), 1. An almshouse, funded by charity, provides housing relief for the poor.

4. Words that imitate sounds, such as "crackle" or "ooze."

5. Hardy's italics. See Michael Millgate, *Thomas Hardy: A Biography Revisited* (Oxford: Oxford University Press, 2004), 62–63.

6. In the political arena, feminists were already agitating for equal rights in the workplace, in education, and in the franchise—the vote was finally accorded to them some 25 years later. In the family planning arena, upon which women's liberation partly rested, Dr. Marie Stopes (who corresponded with Hardy) made her voice felt at the turn of the century just as Hardy was abandoning the novel and returning to poetry. Hardy's 20 years as a novelist witnessed radical social changes, and he was assuredly a factor in raising the sociopolitical consciousness.

7. Many letters were destroyed. This probability is largely determined by the varying inclination of Hardy's biographers. Some have him sexually timid, fearful, even impotent; others have him spirited, explorative, and adventurous—to the extent of fathering a child with his cousin. His letters are, inevitably, formal and reserved, but the sheer volume of confidences that passed between Florence and Hardy suggests an intense intimacy that is unlikely to have ceased upon a mere handshake.

8. Thomas Hardy, *The Collected Letters of Thomas Hardy,* 7 vols., edited by Richard Little Purdy and Michael Millgate (Oxford: Clarendon Press, 1978–88), vol. 6, pp. 2, 12 (hereafter cited as *Letters*).

9. This last entry was made by Florence Emily Hardy, who was designated the official biographer of Hardy's pseudonymous *Life.* Hardy was buried in Poet's Corner at Westminster Abbey, and his heart was taken to the church at Stinsford, Dorset, where it was placed in Emma's grave.

2

Hardy's Career and Contribution to World Literature

EAST OF WESSEX: HARDY'S LITERARY ENDOWMENT

The very first Thomas Hardy Society was established not in England but in Japan, some decades before Hardy's homeland followed suit in the 1960s. Why Japan? Curious as this may seem, the reasons for it are neither complex nor arcane but purely pragmatic. The discussion that follows will offer some explanations and ideas while, at the same time, providing some insight into Hardy's reputation and influence in general.

Perhaps the first point to consider is genre. Hardy's oeuvre spans three different genres—prose fiction, drama, and poetry—or to be completely accurate, *four*: the short story has recently qualified as a genre in its own right. This is an important point because there is no other writer in the English language, aside from Shakespeare, who possesses this multiple-genre distinction. Second, and aligned with genre, is the mastery of creative writing itself. Now, an important factor here is the lack of works of the imagination in Japanese culture. Popular works of fiction are a relatively new development. This gives us the opportunity to examine Hardy in a completely new light—as filling a very real cultural need.

Ancient prose forms did exist in Japan, albeit rare and mostly episodic, but it is the forms of verse (Hokku) from the Edo period (1600–1868) that are of interest here. These forms were reformed in 1892 (Hardy's heyday) to a more independent and more popular form known as Haiku: herein lie two points of relevance concerning the rise of the novel in Japan and Hardy's rise in particular. Both points of relevance are concerned with literary form. The first is that the most valuable quality recommended by the reformers of Haiku is realism (sometimes called verisimilitude). Realism, broadly speaking, means conveying a sense of the everyday world and keeping true to life. For Haiku writers, realism is best conveyed when there is no center of interest in the poem (no major theme or plot). The second point of relevance is that the poet should aim for first impressions of subjects taken from everyday life, adding local color wherever possible to create a sense of freshness.

These literary considerations are closely linked to Hardy's popularity and influence. It is not difficult to see that the first contingency of avoiding a center of interest in Haiku poetry opens up vast new potential for readers and writers wishing to experience that very thing—a center of interest in the story. What is a center of interest? In short, it is a well-realized characterization that develops throughout the story, coupled with compelling themes that engage the reader at various levels of philosophy, ethics, social problems, and so on, and an intriguing plot designed to hold the reader's attention over several hundred pages. So, what happens when those readers discover a contemporary writer who offers the widest scope of central interest in terms of characterization, themes, and motifs, and who also happens to fulfill the second condition of featuring everyday lives and the freshness of local color? This is where Hardy enters the scene.[1]

Some examples from the Wessex novels will show how and where Hardy's point of entry lies. At the risk of oversimplification of his plots (or themes and characterizations), there is, for example, his focus on the dilemma facing one rare and beautiful woman farmer in coping with the simultaneous courtship of three very different men, as in *Far From the Madding Crowd*. Alternatively, there is the exploitation of women and the sexual double standard in *Tess of the d'Urbervilles*, the rise of the underdog in the social hierarchy in *The Mayor of Casterbridge*, the love of an older, married woman for a much younger man in *Two on a Tower*, the clash of town and country values in *The Woodlanders*, and the unfulfilled ambitions for higher learning, kinship, and love in *Jude the Obscure*.

There are 14 Wessex novels altogether and many more short stories, but for now let's simply take note of these themes. How universal they are! Despite their regional settings, their *center of interest* mirrors the human condition everywhere. And with Hardy at the peak of his novel-writing career when the East was increasing its contact with the West and, at that time, drawing eagerly on Western culture in order to develop much of its own, time and circumstance combined to meet a fast-growing need—most auspiciously for Hardy.

Equally auspicious for the postindustrial rising middle classes of the period, and indeed of the centuries to follow, is the detailing of ordinary, everyday lives and the vibrancy of local village culture in Hardy's novels. It may be superstitious beliefs, community relations, economic struggles, private passions, ethnic rituals, issues of employment and labor, the enchantment of pastoral scenes, sexual and social relationships, the interplay of the natural environment, and the habitat of all living things—whatever the shades of concern might be, Hardy's vivid, localized evocations lure readers into deep and subtle levels of engagement. Even young readers today experience an intense identification and, no less intensely, a contraidentification with character and circumstance in Hardy (contraidentification is when readers identify against themselves, as in sympathizing with Michael Henchard in *The Mayor of Casterbridge* even when he's being horribly overbearing with his daughter). In short, the relevance of Hardy's novels is personal and acute.

Using the Japanese experience as a paradigm, then, as a model or pattern of universal significance, there is one last point to consider, which should appeal to anyone pursuing a spiritual path. In some respects this also addresses the perennial question, why do we read novels? Lacking the wealth of imaginative literature that Europe had enjoyed for many centuries and has always taken for granted as its birthright (while, in turn, endowing this wealth to the New World), Japan welcomed the nineteenth-century novel as an agency of enlightenment and sheer enlargement of life. As we have seen, it was a time when the infiltration of new stories, new ideas, new values, new cultural practices, and so on, were surging in from the West—a time ripe for the novel, in all senses of the word. A literary work of the imagination, imaginative vision itself, was and is, "novel"—it is new and unusual. Transformation of the ordinary, everyday world and its re-creation in another form, made manifest by the splendor of language, defies rational explanation (in terms of empirical science). Not surprisingly, to the tabula rasa (new and unused) mind, such a manifestation resembles something more than "novel"—something almost magical—a transference of knowledge and understanding as if by revelation. Revelation, historically speaking, is the truth bearer; it is canonical, the word of an inspired writer, holy writ. Indeed, a book is so sacred object in India and related Hindu/Buddhist cultures that to accidentally touch it with your foot may require a ritual act of cleansing. Revelation also bears many secrets and mysteries. "How," one mystified student at Kansai University asked me, "did Hardy imagine Tess?"

THE LEGACY OF WESSEX

Born into the Victorian era, raised in a village community, and largely self-educated, this seemingly ordinary young man writes a novel called *Tess of the d'Urbervilles*, and a sensitive young woman, pure and lovely in mind and body, vivid in her shining intelligence—existentially vital, possessing a consciousness uniquely her own—comes into being and *lives* in the cultural imagination. The aspect of authorial vision thus transfers from writer to reader, and if, on the one hand, the tabula rasa mind, open and innocent, seizes upon this as revelation, as a pathway to enlightenment, seasoned readers, on the other hand, are seized *by* it—the individual consciousness has been possessed by and in turn possesses the vision and is enlarged thereby.

It is true to say that once an imaginative concept enters the public domain the cultural imagination is changed forever. Whether it is the concept of Eden, or of the Martin Luther King "Dream" of racial parity, or something as psychologically recidivistic (relapsing into previous behavior) as Peter Pan's Never

Never Land, or as paradigmatic as Hardy's Wessex, the cultural imagination is changed by absorption of it. Thus, students from Kansai cross the world to search the southwest territory of England for dairy houses where Tess milks her cows, where Fanny Robin dies in the workhouse, and where Henchard confronts the grotesque image of himself floating down the river. And the pilgrimage is not for imaginative scenes alone, it is also for artifacts: the newly invented Victorian steam threshing machine that drives Tess to exhaustion, the Bronze Age burial mounds on barrow summits where beacon fires burn (as does Eustacia, emotionally speaking), the dead eyes of trilobites that gaze at Henry Knight on the Cliff With No Name. Imaginative scenes, artifacts, and pilgrimages are for dreaming on.

There is, in the process of cultural absorption, the cyclical consequence that where one story ends, another begins. Hardy's stories may come to closure but not to finality. Was the characterization of Tess partly inspired by his adored cousin Tryphena Sparks? If so, let's search for Tryphena (at least six books have been written on Hardy and Tryphena and their purported illegitimate son). New stories are born from the old, frequently in the form of paratexts, meaning those that take on an existence separate from their originating texts (*paratexts* is a word also used nowadays to describe electronic texts on the Internet). In turn, Hardy's half-real, half-dream country of Wessex (a name he revived from the ancient pagan kingdom of the Anglo-Saxon Heptarchy A.D. 650) materializes to become an actual place with numerous Wessex ramifications—in modern times there is the Wessex Water Board, the Wessex Railway, and, by recent appointment to the queen, the Countess of Wessex. Even at the level of the royal household, life imitates art.

Yet, when Hardy embarked on his career as a novelist at 28 years old, he had not conceived of a "Wessex." First, there was one failed novel, *The Poor Man and the Lady* (1868; declined by every publisher he approached for being too scathing in its attacks on class). Next, on the advice of the publishers that declined *The Poor Man and the Lady*, there was a Wilkie Collins–type melodrama, *Desperate Remedies* (1871; which one critic called a desperate remedy for a desperate purse, Wilkie Collins was a best-selling writer of sensation fiction, or, page-turner murder mysteries and intrigue). Then there was the rural idyll, *Under the Greenwood Tree* (1872; unique among Hardy's novels for not inflaming the censors). And then there was the serialized novel, *A Pair of Blue Eyes* (1873; regarded by the popular poet Coventry Patmore as a prose work better suited to poetry).

Only at this point in his literary career does Hardy frame a tentative topography—a detailed description of the natural or artificial surface features of a region or place. This frame first enters his fiction in 1874, near the end of his fourth published novel, *Far From the Madding Crowd*, where the name "Wessex" is casually dropped into the Greenhill Fair scene, almost as an afterthought. Meanwhile, the scene features the main characters in isolation, disconnected. This is conceptually ironic because the symbolic and literal function of the fair is to bring people together. Hundreds of people gather at fairs, within and beyond the novel, to engage in trade, to be entertained, to meet old friends, and to connect with others, but not, as here, to find themselves oddly disengaged from fellow citizens and loved ones or, as in Bathsheba's case, vulnerable and threatened.

The irony of the situation is compounded by the advent of Wessex at this point given that this inaugurates a twenty-year endeavor on Hardy's part to create a coherent topographical construct. Wessex is initiated at a point of unsettlement—better described as destabilization. This is the kind of conceptual irony at which Hardy is past master. As readers grow more and more familiar with his works, the better they are able to pick up on these subtle shades of meaning that ultimately enhance an appreciation of his art.

The overall patterning of Wessex illustrates the intrinsic irony of its construction. As it evolves over 20 years, this universe in miniature, this microcosm, will provide not only pastoral settings for the novels but also, in its various aspects, a paradigm for all manners of human struggles, divisions, and conflicts. Unions between kin and lovers are particularly fragile. Wessex performs in various configurations as an "external correlative," where the natural world correlates to the human condition. It will embody a psychological terrain mirroring a variety of situations and conditions including, say, the struggle of individual lives in an indifferent universe, infantilized states resisting completion of the separation from childhood, unresolvable conflicts of sexual and class inequality, or as nurturing/nonnurturing terrain, the abandoned/abandoning maternal body and the once-upon-a-time world of rural simplicity and freshness—the lost ancestral village so nostalgically mourned by Victorians overwhelmed by the onrush of industrialization.

Repeatedly, this microcosmic universe unleashes both the source and the absence of nurture (*Tess of the d'Urbervilles*, 1891), just as it highlights the anguishing loss of roots and homeland in Hardy's last novel, *Jude the Obscure* (1895). Significantly, the Wessex homeland remains, in all its natural loveliness and pristine beauty, a place of alienation and lost love. In this sense, its configuration maps the psychological territory of the perpetually searching human soul. The regenerative powers of nature offer solace and emotional reinvigoration, as does the experience of beauty and art. But with all things sustaining and replenishing, there is the inevitability of their passing. Hence the ultimate irony: one unified construct, Wessex, functions as the arena of dysfunction in the human communities it enfolds; it is the embodiment of one disunited world.

Perhaps the ultimate irony is that Wessex is sought out as both physical terrain and fictional universe by thousands of devotees every single year. But returning to literary influence, there is the aspect of genre, the effect of Wessex on the regional novel. Hardy's microcosmic universe puts the whole concept of regionalism to the test. Regionalism is characterized by a fidelity to a geographical area accurately representing regional culture—notably dialect, customs, history, folklore, and beliefs. The regional novel relies on unifying its center of interest: action and principals cannot be removed without major loss or distortion to any other geographical setting (Brontë's Heathcliffe, for example, cannot be removed without distortion to Wordsworth's Lake District).

This is where Hardy breaks the rules. Dialect aside, which in his case is peculiar to England's southwest region, the center of interest in two major novels has been located in separate (foreign) regions. These were subsequently and rather craftily designated by Hardy in his efforts at unification Off Wessex (Endelstow/St. Juliot, Cornwall in *A Pair of Blue Eyes*, and the university city of Christminster/Oxford in *Jude the Obscure*).

To illustrate the universality (as opposed to the regionality) of Hardy's Wessex, his works have been adapted—back to the paratext—to the geographical settings of "foreign" lands (Ireland, in the case of Ronan Scanlan, *The Mayor of Castlebridge*). Moving to another medium, film adaptations of Hardy's fiction have successfully relocated his settings to the Canadian Rockies (*The Claim*, based on *The Mayor of Casterbridge*) and to northern France (Roman Polanski's *Tess of the d'Urbervilles*). This relocation would be difficult to achieve without considerable distortion to the regional novels of, say, Jane Austen and the Brontës.

As far as regionalism goes, in these Hardy adaptations and transpositions, local color is sustained insofar as this affects the temperament of the characters and their roles, private and public. Geographical settings alone have been changed. Hardy would, I think, have welcomed these innovations. Expanding its boundaries beyond the original Dorset land of his birth, and even beyond the Off Wessex of his own expanded boundaries, would, no doubt, have charmed and intrigued him. In developing his Wessex construct, he had in mind a microcosmic, Homeric universe right down—topographically speaking—to the southernmost tip of Wessex, which he named the Pillars of Hercules. The model for these pillars is located on the Dorset coast, west of Lulworth Cove, in a tiny bay where natural arches have formed in the Portland and basal Purbeck limestones. The ancient mythological name, the Pillars of Hercules, derives from promontories flanking the east entrance to the Straits of Gibraltar—the rock of Gibraltar on the European side and Mt. Acha at Ceuta on the African side. They are also referred to as the Gates of Hercules, once believed to mark the edge of the world (where, as we now know, the Atlantic begins).

HARDY'S DIVIDED CAREER

Part 1: The Novels

In the mid-1890s, after a furor with critics and the enraged bishop of Wakefield—he couldn't burn the man, quipped Hardy, so he burned the book—the Wessex novels came to an end. *The Well-Beloved* appeared in 1897, but this was a revised book version of *The Pursuit of the Well-Beloved* serialized in *The Illustrated London News* in 1892. For more than 20 years, since the advent of his first published novel, *Desperate Remedies*, Hardy had braved hostile reviewers who frequently left him feeling suicidal—unfavorable reviews invariably tending, in his mind, to eclipse the favorable. And fastidious editors were almost as depressing. Beginning with his fourth published novel, *Far From the Madding Crowd* (1874)—commissioned by *Cornhill* editor Leslie Stephen—editors had persistently excised and censored Hardy's work when they did not reject it outright, often unseen.

Stephen was the first of many censors. In the early 1870s he had read only the rural idyll, *Under the Greenwood Tree*, which had thoroughly delighted him, and knew nothing about the anonymous Hardy. Hoping for yet another rural idyll, he was quick to grab his editorial pencil as chapters of *Far From the Madding Crowd* arrived on his desk and he discovered he was getting rather more than he had bargained for. Month by month Hardy's installments arrived, and month by month Stephen assiduously cut words and passages, even sizable chunks of the manuscript, scouring the script with a fine-tooth comb. He missed nothing. He couldn't even risk the word "buttocks," so he struck it and replaced it with the word "backs." Hardy's offending word had not, as readers might think, pruriently breached the privacy of the bedroom, the dressing room, or the boudoir but had simply ventured into the local stables, where there "were to be seen at this time the buttocks and tails of half a dozen warm and contented horses standing in their stalls" (xviii). The word "buttocks"—equine or otherwise—was not to be uttered in polite company.[2] Serialization in literary journals was the most prestigious mode of publication in Hardy's day. The only Wessex novels not serialized prior to volume publication were his first two, *Desperate Remedies* and *Under the Greenwood Tree*. Serialization had the advantage of ensuring that the work reached a mass, educated readership. The disadvantage was of having to write against the clock on a month-to-month basis. An added hazard for avante-garde writers such as Hardy was the public nature of the literary journal. Unlike a book that engages a reader in total privacy, the literary journal started and ended life in the Victorian middle-class drawing room, or the public reading room or the club lounge, and was often read aloud in company. The judicious discretion of the editor was therefore of paramount importance. In Stephen's case, his overzealous prudery in behalf of his readers was outmoded by the mid-1870s, and the *Cornhill* rapidly lost readers to less conservative publications.

Inexperienced, unused, given to candor and what he called "revolutionary fervour," Hardy, at this early stage of his career, was often mystified and sometimes indignant in the face of Stephen's censorship, but after protesting, he would comply—albeit temporarily. He assured his prudish editor that he simply wanted to become a "good hand at a serial," although it is revealing that he immediately restored his moments of candor to the subsequent volume edition at the first opportunity. However, by the time of *The Mayor of Casterbridge* (MC) in 1886 he had become miserably accustomed to rejection slips as also to the bowdlerization of his novels. Leslie Stephen had by now refused to publish him.

What is emerging from this troubled history is twofold. The world of publishing is being severely challenged. Leslie Stephen's prestigious *Cornhill* is rapidly losing readers under his puritanic al editorship and Hardy is fast learning how to circumnavigate his censors—embodied by the iconic Mrs. Grundy. Certainly the commissioning editors of *The Mayor of Casterbridge* felt the challenge and decided to exercise caution. They felt constrained to delay periodical publication until Hardy had completed the entire manuscript and to this end they extended their deadlines to leaven the customary practice of writing-against-the-clock. Hardy now had leisure enough to make many modifications to his urban-based plot, muting the so-called "unsuitable" part (his inevitable slips into impropriety) and transferring much of the embedded erotica to the female principals. This effectively endowed Lucetta and Elizabeth-Jane with a sexuality that did not risk censure. Sensual contact between women transgressed no moral boundaries; it was not understood to be sexual; physical contact between the opposite sexes remained, by contrast, strictly circumscribed and boundaried.

But at the same time Hardy was itching to write at his own imaginative, energetic pace. He found the release from installment writing and the lack of relentless deadlines to be a clamp on his attention and focus. *The Mayor of Casterbridge* was, he feared, either strained and forced or loose and unkempt as a result of his felt inertia. So, to pick up some of the slack, he began composing the first chapters of *The Woodlanders* (1887), revisiting, in his imagination, his natal land, the world of *Under the Green Tree*—his birthplace. Here again, Hardy transfers much of the erotic interest to the female principals.

Frisson for frisson, there is nothing that quite matches the erotica of the night meeting in the woods between Grace and Felice. But this aspect of female sexuality remained invisible to the censors who were looking in an entirely different direction. Once more, Hardy achieves his purpose of creating a heroine who is fully sexualized.

Hardy had long been interested in the law and was now a magistrate in the county town of Dorchester (the model for Casterbridge), where he had built himself a house. From this point onward, the Wessex novels show a greater interest in legal matters. It is worth noting that the respectability of the author-magistrate did not necessarily shape similar qualities in his fictional characters. Indeed the eponymous principal of *The Mayor of Casterbridge*, written at the time of Hardy's appointment to the bench, has an exceedingly murky history—namely the selling of his wife at a country fair.

Candor remained, for Hardy, essential to his commitment as an artist even while it continued to infuriate his editors, who called it a flagrant violation of decorum. So committed was Hardy to freedom of speech in literature and the artist's responsibility in upholding this freedom that, in 1890, he published an essay in the *New Review* titled "Candour in English Fiction." This essay examines the effect of prudishness within and upon the novel. Among other things, the essay advocates conscientiousness on the part of writers, who should also abjure the "regulation finish" of everyone marrying and living happily ever after. Hardy considered this a pernicious convention that not only misrepresented the world beyond the novel but also fostered illusions in overprotective attitudes toward young readers. Romantic, idyllic endings were, he held, misleading, and they distorted youthful expectations about matrimony. Overall, the essay was constructive. It offered three solutions to the current dilemma not only of serialization and its circumscribed entry into the Victorian home but also of the hegemony—the monopoly and total control—exercised by Mudie's Lending Library. Mudie's effectively dictated what could and should be made available to the reading public.[3]

First, Hardy recommended that the popular practice of borrowing from libraries should be augmented by the less popular activity of purchasing books. To this end he was to order his publisher, Macmillan, to sell his own books at rock-bottom prices that everyone, however poor, could afford. Macmillan concurred. His next recommendation was that certain serial publications should be made available exclusively to adults. And, finally, that the French feuilleton might be adopted by magazine publishers (*feuilleton* was the name given to the popular practice in France of inserting a cautionary note of criticism at the foot of French newspapers, similar in principle to the PG rating in the movie industry). This allowed readers to gauge the style and content of adult material.

Evidently, Hardy had picked up the groundswell of a more liberal public opinion in publication politics—possibly he himself had generated it. He told the prominent feminist and suffragist Millicent Garrett Fawcett that issues of sexuality should be treated with "no mincing of matters," but then he added, "This, I fear, the British public would not stand just now; though, to be sure, we are educating it by degrees" (*Letters*, V1.264). And yes, to be sure, the stranglehold of the censorious Mudie's lending library did begin to decline during the 1890s. If the time was not yet fully ripe for Hardy's frontal attack on certain Victorian mores as launched by *Tess* in 1891, it was close. Storms of outrage were matched by thunders of praise. Suffice it to say that *Tess* would not have made it into the literary periodicals at all 20 years earlier.

But there had still been the customary tricky voyage into the Victorian drawing room. *Tess* was refused by two publishers before being accepted by the *Graphic*. Worse, Hardy was forced to bowdlerize the novel himself to render it palatable for family readership. Because physical contact between the sexes was "indecent," Angel Clare was obliged to carry the excited girls across the flooded lane not in his arms but in a wheelbarrow. And the scene where Tess acts the minister and baptizes her illegitimate baby was considered equally indecent, but for reasons of sacrilege. It too, had to go.

Once the book was out, though, critics gave it a mixed reception. Later, coming across the comments of his friends Henry James and Robert Louis Stevenson, who had privately commiserated that *Tess* was "vile" and that the explicit language of the narration was an "abomination," Hardy was able to jest: "How indecent of those two virtuous females to expose their mental nakedness in such a manner." But at the time of publication he was far more vulnerable. So, *Tess* was "coarse," "clumsy," and "sordid"? "Well," says Hardy, "if this sort of thing continues no more novel-writing for me. A man must be a fool to deliberately stand up to be shot at" (*LW*, 259).

It is evident from a chapter title in his pseudonymous autobiography (*LW*), "Another Novel Finished, Mutilated, and Restored," that Hardy was ready to abandon novel writing long before the ashes of *Jude the Obscure* (1895) smoldered in the bishop's fireplace. Hardy barely waited for reviewers to run their course.

Praise or blame, contemporary critics had come to the end of a chapter: they had had their sport with Hardy the novelist.

Part 2: The Short Stories

The short story, which has a far more venerable history than the novel, would have been familiar to Hardy as a child from the oral traditions of country folk and from his wonderful storytelling grandmother in particular. The short-story genre has its roots in balladic tales as much as in the brief narrative format of fable and anecdote—notably the ancient tales of Homer, Chaucer, Boccaccio, and Aesop. The precocious Hardy eagerly devoured a little storybook of words and pictures called *Cries of London* by the time he was three. And at nine he was annotating the Bible stories in his *Companion to the Bible*. This literary interest and activity are later reflected in the commonplace notebooks he kept throughout his career, which abound in local anecdotes and oral stories handed down from individuals, families, and communities. He also scoured newspapers for tidbits, unusual stories, bizarre occurrences, or scandalous court cases and scribbled these down in his Notebooks alongside comments on philosophers such as Comte or John Stuart Mill.

Despite this abundance and his own keen interest in maintaining a record of what he once called "the vanishing past," Hardy felt frustrated by the public lack of interest in short stories; that publishers were "as a rule, shy of them." He may, of course, have based this impression on his own difficulty with editors. His own short stories—many completed, others simply sketched early in his career—remained, like his verse, uncollected until much later on in his career. A good example of the progression from a tiny oral anecdote to the enlarged story in its literary form is "The Melancholy Hussar of the German Legion." As early as July 1877 Hardy had recorded:

> July 27. James Bushrod of Broadmayne saw the two German soldiers [of the York Hussars] shot [for desertion] on Bincombe Down in 1801. It was in the path across the down, or near it. James Selby of the same village thinks there is a mark. (*LW*, 119)

"The Melancholy Hussar" (based on this anecdote) was not published in provincial papers until 1890 and not collected in volume form until 1894 in *Life's Little Ironies*. Given the real-life provenance (place of origin) of the story, one of life's little ironies could well be George Cottrell's review in the *Academy*, which claimed that the story had a "great deal of unreality."

Wessex Tales: Strange, Lively and Commonplace, the first of Hardy's short-story collections to be published (and the first "Wessex" to appear in a title), came out in 1888. It presented a regionalist face to a world already familiar with Casterbridge and Hardy's unique dream-place settings. Macmillan published *Wessex Tales* in two fine volumes, and the collection received positive reviews. Surely Hardy's misgivings about a "shy" market must have been dispelled by these, especially with critics admiring not only his local coloring but also those touches of the uncanny, macabre, and surreal so dear to his own heart. Hardy never lost his fascination for the rare and extraordinary, psychic phenomenon, and the supernatural. Especially eerie is his folkloric tale of "turning the blood" by touching the corpse of a hanged man (a latter-day form of aversion therapy) in "The Withered Arm." Likewise his psychic drama of premonition: a tall clock crashes to the floor—a portent of a violent death in the family—and some decades later a skeleton is discovered, still buried beneath weeds in a nearby stream, dating from the day the clock went down ("The Waiting Supper").

Adept at genre crossing (mixing melodrama, say, with passages of psychological realism), Hardy could now experiment with melodramatic modes—including elements of fantasy, psychic phenomenon, and other nonrational modes (he called himself an irrationalist)—without jeopardizing the integrity of the structure and the rhythms of the genre. The longer, more formal, and more complex spatiotemporal narrative structure of the novel, as opposed to the one-act effect of the short story or poem, is frequently strained by the extravaganza of melodrama: genre crossing is put severely to the test when the plausible, psychologically realistic drama is suddenly arrested by the intervention of totally implausible melodrama.

Hardy risks this strain in the denouement of *Far From the Madding Crowd* when Troy comes bursting in on a Christmas party disguised as a hoodlum and acting like a pantomime villain. He is then slain by a deranged Boldwood and cradled in Bathsheba's mourning arms in a scene that is suddenly no longer melodrama but pure tragedy. The "hoodlum" moment of melodrama is perhaps saved by Troy's own tendency to self-dramatization—a saving-grace effect that also remedies the denouement of *Tess* where the theatrical Alec is slaughtered by the carving knife. But narratorial authority can be jeopardized by the dislocating effect of melodrama at these points even if readers *have* shared with the narrator the tensions and struggles of closure—having to bring the curtain down on a complicated plot without putting everyone under a truck! For reasons that are self-evident, closure (or racing to the finish) is far less of a hazard with the done-in-a-flash manner of the short story.

There are few genuine shocks in melodrama. But there are plenty of pseudo (play acting) shocks where events are overly predictable or ill prepared. The brevity of the short story and its distillation of ideas and dreamlike dearth of background or developmental detail make it relatively amenable to absorbing the artifice of melodrama relying as it does on immediacy of impact on the sensations for its effect. Hardy seems to have excelled in this medium. He published more than 30 short stories in just over 20 years—collected under the titles *Wessex Tales* (1888), *A Group of Noble Dames* (1891), *Life's Little Ironies* (1894), and *A Changed Man and Other Tales* (1913). He also wrote a story for boys called *Our Exploits at West Poley* (1892–93) and a collaborative tale with Florence Henniker, "The Spectre of the Real" (1894).

The only Grundyan controversy arising over Hardy's short stories concerned *A Group of Noble Dames*—a cycle of tales, romances, and fantasies based loosely on John Hutchins's *History and Antiquities of the County of Dorset*. Critics had never taken kindly to implications, in fiction, of sexual activity among upper-class English women; as far back as *Desperate Remedies*, reviewers had been incredulous, not that Hardy had depicted the amorous affections of two women in bed, but that the lady of the manor had had an illegitimate child. The notion was clearly preposterous and Hardy was "not to be trusted."

Twenty years later, real live women had managed to claim a sexual life for themselves, albeit at some cost to courage and daring. Just as the First Lady does not customarily present herself publicly as a sexual object (unlike some film and rock stars), so too the Victorian lady. Decorum was the byword. But Hardy was less interested in decorum than in hypocrisy. If noble dames in real life were having illegitimate babies and taking lovers but were safeguarded from scandal by cover-up codes of privilege and media whitewashing, in his fiction they would not be so safeguarded. Accordingly, they elope with their lovers by night ("Barbara of the House of Grebe"), conduct clandestine affairs ("The Marchioness of Stonehenge"), and even foist their illegitimate babies on unsuspecting husbands, as does Vivette in *Two on a Tower* with her newly acquired spouse—the Bishop of Melchester.

In order to assist their entry into the Victorian middle-class drawing room, Hardy employs specific narrative techniques. First, he establishes historical distance: the internal dating of the *Noble Dames* stories is mainly set back to the seventeenth and eighteenth centuries, thus both character and situation would be perceived as noncontemporary. This lends an air of remoteness and a lack of immediacy and relevance. Second, he adopts a narrative technique known as intradiegetical discourse, which deploys an alternative, internal narrator to the task of telling the tale—the Local Historian, the Old Surgeon, the Churchwarden, and other notable worthies (in true Chaucerian tradition).

Hardy is past master at this mode of discourse and employs it, less obtrusively, in the novels. In the case of his longer works, intradiegetical discourse helps, with the aid of the alternative narrator, to deflect attention away from the omniscient (all-seeing) narrator. It creates a nuanced point of view from a different angle. This alternative perspective is often needed at strategic moments to inject a tone of judiciousness into the text.

I have chosen to call this the bystander narrator. This idea was first given full critical analysis in Rosemarie Morgan, *Women and Sexuality in the Novels of Thomas Hardy* (London: Routledge, 1988). Here the agent of Hardy's intradiegetical discourse, his deployment of an alternative narrator, is regarded as operating independently of the omniscient narrator. In line with Chaucer's appointed narrators who lend their personal tone and moral values to the account, so too with Hardy's bystander narrators. Customarily, they are censorious. This assisted the novel into the Victorian household. But just as often they are time and space presences injecting the notion that there are perceptions and events that pass beyond even the omniscient narrator's vision. These last take the form of an alternative speaker, whether it be an intrusive commentator or an anonymous observer or even a conditional point of view, as when a passer-by "might have said" or "would have seen" this, that, or the other. The omniscient narrator does not necessarily abdicate authority at these points but is sidestepped. For example, when Elfride (*A Pair of Blue Eyes*) asserts herself with Henry Knight (a dangerously unfeminine thing to do), and the intrusive voice intervenes to put her down ("women are thus"), injecting a condescending, judgmental tone, the omniscient narrator will follow up, like a defense lawyer, with an incident showing her intense vulnerability. Thus the Victorian reader is reassured that there is a moral proprietor taking care of the parson's daughter, so to speak, while being drawn back into sympathy with the winning, but alarmingly unconventional, girl.

However, in the case of Hardy's short stories, this method did not always convince his harsher Victorian critics. In response to a vitriolic attack on *Noble Dames* by the *Pall Mall Gazette*, Hardy explained that the function of his narrative technique would

> guard against the infliction of a "hideous and hateful fantasy" as you call it, the action ... thrown back into a second plane or middle distance, being described by a character to characters, and not point-blank by author to reader. (*Pall Mall Gazette*, 10 July 1891)

Perhaps Hardy regarded his whole enterprise in the short stories as a rather unsuccessful experiment in terms of circumnavigating Mrs. Grundy, for he reverted in his subsequent short fiction to his customary contemporary settings and omniscient mode of narration. Moreover, he left several of his stories uncollected. It was not until 1992 that the following titles were brought together in a single volume: "Destiny and a Blue Cloak," "The Thieves Who Couldn't Help Sneezing," "How I Built Myself a House," "An Indiscretion in the Life of an Heiress," "Our Exploits at West Poley," "Old Mrs Chundle," "The Doctor's Legend," "The Spectre of the Real" (with Florence Henniker), "Blue Jimmy: The Horse Stealer," and "The Unconquerable" (with Florence Dugdale).

Part 3: The Poetry and *The Dynasts*

Hardy had always been, first and foremost, a poet. The popular belief that he ended his career as a novelist over the furor of *Jude* and, at that point, started on his career as a poet does not accurately represent the situation. It is true that his experience as a novelist confirmed his growing conviction that he could express

> more fully in verse ideas and emotions which run counter to the inert crystallized opinion—hard as rock—which the vast body of men have vested interests in supporting. To cry out in a passionate poem that (for instance) the Supreme Mover or Movers, the Prime Force or Forces, must be either limited in power, unknowing, or cruel ... will cause them merely a shake of the head.... If Galileo had said in verse that the world moved, the Inquisition might have left him alone. (*LW*, 302)

In his first (failed) novel, *The Poor Man and the Lady*, Hardy had quite earnestly tried to stir the inertia of crystallized opinion. Time and experience had discouraged but not hardened him, and as he abandoned novel writing at 50 years old, the intensity of his passionate cries remained undiminished.

He had always been a poet but had been unable to publish, let alone make a living at it. He had been writing poetry since a young lad of 17—"Domicilium" was his first poem (see "Childhood and Family" in chapter 1)—and by the time he was 20, he was composing sonnets, notably the "She, to Him" sequence, "part of a much larger number which perished" (*LW*, 55). This sequence features a woman speaking to her beloved about her feelings of jealousy and insecurity in love. Some biographers have identified the woman as Tryphena, Hardy's adored cousin. At this point it is as well to be reminded that the speaker in a poem, as in an act of ventriloquism, is wholly distinct from a real person and is defined solely in relation to the speech in that poem. A poet reinvents and transcends the world but does not, unless otherwise stated, provide a biographical account of it. As DeSales Harrison puts it, the speaker of a poem is "what a person would be if persons *were made of speech*—what a person would be if speech were the only ground in which identity could be established."[4] Northrop Frye would add that the only intention of the poet is to abolish intention, which means, among other things, that the poem's speaker is not necessarily the poet's mouthpiece.

Biographical readings are, quite properly, entertaining, but they address life, not art. We have no problem whatsoever in perceiving a stream to be a stream. It is a thing in itself. A stream is not intended to be and doesn't mean to be about clear water or flowing currents or aquatic habitat. Indeed, it might dry up or cease to flow or decline as a sustainable habitat, but it would still be a stream—well, until it reached a certain point where it would be *once a stream*. So too with poems. They are an entity. Thus Hardy's "She, to Him" verses (in common with his other verse) are things in themselves and not "about" his cousin Tryphena.

Among Hardy's poems of the early period (1860–74) are numerous ballads. One of the more famous, "The Ruined Maid," portrays a pert, vivacious woman from the city who visits her old haunts on the farm and flaunts her sexual freedom and affluence to her friends. Her situation and attitudes fly in the face of all social dictates that deem an unmarried, sexually active woman to be ruined. Notwithstanding the fact that Hardy is the poet who claimed that tragedy always underlies comedy if you only scratch it deeply enough, this poem is comic and the title is ironic. The ruined maid is supposed to have lost reputation and all prospects of a good life, but the opposite is the case, and we share her glee.

In the real world, to be "ruined" (or "fallen") ensured that no "good man" would want to marry and no decent employer would want to employ such a disreputable female. This stigma on the woman helped to sustain the prevailing moral (patriarchal) code and its emphasis on female virginity. Hardy's poem purposefully undermines the stigma (the "fall") cast upon sexually active women in a world where men, engaging in the same activity, are not so stigmatized.

Hardy was also writing lyrical ballads and songs at this time and modeled his finest lyric poem of this period, "Neutral Tones," upon Sapphic form—a quatrain utilizing a meter derived from the Greek poet Sappho.

We stood by a pond that winter day,
And the sun was white, as though chidden of God,
And a few leaves lay on the starving sod;
    They had fallen from an ash, and were gray.

Notice how the last line "falls" away from the one above: it is a winter's day and the leaves have fallen—lying (like the last line) down below. Hardy's modernism lies as much in form as in content.

Gathering some of his early verse together in the 1890s, together with compositions that had been lying around in drawers for many years, Hardy published the collection in *Wessex Poems* in 1898. Although he liked to say that he felt some critics deplored his having "taken the liberty to adopt another vehicle of expression than prose-fiction without consulting them" (*LW*, 319), *Wessex Poems* was well received.

The poems of the novel-writing years (1878–1901) and beyond include a cluster of "Wessex" poems and what Hardy calls, in his Preface, "much that is dramatic or impersonative."[5] These were collected in *Poems of the Past and the Present* (1901). In his Preface to the edition, Hardy claims that these poems were not intended to be a cohesive collection (rather typically) and that "unadjusted impressions have their value, and the road to a true philosophy of life seems to lie in humbly recording diverse readings of its phenomena as they are forced upon us by chance and change." The "diverse readings" encompass a sequence of war poems reflecting Hardy's lifelong interest in the Napoleonic Wars—in this instance transferred to an interest in the Boer War. Hardy regarded war with an ambivalent respect for the codes of honor and courage demonstrated by young men and officers engaged in hand-to-hand combat. As a humanitarian he abhorred the whole business of war; as a man he admired the bravery of the common soldier on the battlefield; as a cultural historian he was intrigued by military strategy; and as an epic dramatist he was drawn to the action and color of intrigue and heroism.

A small dash of color of a different kind, which might have caused Hardy a wry smile, is that his poem "Embarcation," written in 1899 at the outset of the Boer War, is transcribed in full on the starboard interior of the greatest ship on the high seas at this time. The new Cunard liner launched in 2004, the *Queen Mary II*, has Thomas Hardy's writing on the wall. "Now," as in 1899, "deckward tramp the bands."

The sequence that follows Hardy's war poems in *Poems of the Past and the Present* is titled "Poems of Pilgrimage," which are mostly pilgrimages to Rome. This section is succeeded by "Miscellaneous Poems," which includes one of Hardy's most famous verses, "The Darkling Thrush." Chosen by U.S. poet laureate Robert Pinski to celebrate the millennium year, "The Darkling Thrush" was read by Pinski on public radio as the twentieth century drew to a close and, indeed, as "the Century's corpse outleant."

Poems of the Past and the Present concludes with the section "Retrospect"—the last poem in the volume aptly titled "To an Unknown God." This is apt because the title retrospectively glances back hundreds and hundreds of years to an address to the Unknown God of Acts 17:23. Hardy's poem, in contrast to the biblical text, brings the ancient iconic deity into the modern world and addresses an *unknowing* God who is blind and cruel.

Hardy's experimentation with forms and themes, his innovative style and subject matter has occasionally been mistaken for ignorance and ineptitude. Like Jude, he was born ahead of his time, and the price to be paid for that is to be misunderstood. Even some of his secular critics found his death-of-God poems crude and sacrilegious. Beyond the death-of-God poems, certain ballads of his also met with scorn. In 1909 *Time's Laughingstocks and Other Verses* came out, and with it Hardy's all-time-favorite ballad, "A Trampwoman's Tragedy." Some years earlier, in 1903, he had offered this poem with open enthusiasm (quite unlike Hardy) to the *Cornhill* editor: "I send you up a rendering in ballad form of a West Country tragedy of the last century which seems to me to have a lurid picturesqueness suitable for such treatment, & to be sufficiently striking" (*Letters*, V5.58–59). But the editor, Reginald Smith, wasn't interested and declined publication. The poem, he claimed, was too outspoken for *Cornhill* readers.

This little episode succinctly illustrates the great divide that can open up between the poet's view of his work and that of his publisher: the censor these days is the editor, Hardy once said. He later countered Reginald Smith's objections by noting that if the subject matter of his poems might prove too outspoken for family reading, what then of the lurid details any family member might encounter when reading the daily newspaper? He pointed out that the subject matter of his ballad could be read aloud in "any family circle with modern details in a newspaper" (*Letters*, V3.278).

Well, of course, Hardy is trying to have it both ways. If he is correct, as he claims, that "if Galileo had said in verse that the world moved, the Inquisition might have left him alone," then Reginald Smith would seem to be incorrect in thinking that where newspapers are harmless, similar accounts evoked by poetry would make the world move—so to speak. But, if the truth be told, Hardy would have been the last person on earth to have seriously argued that what is "outspoken" in a newspaper carries the same weight as what is "outspoken" in a poem. The one entertains, the other illuminates.

With regard to "A Trampwoman's Tragedy," the poet David A. Munro, editor of the *North American Review*, did share Hardy's enthusiasm for the poem. Munro published it in November of the same year as "*The* Trampwoman's Tragedy" (Hardy preferred the more specific title). Sometimes it takes a poet to know a poet. In fact, in his own day, greatest acclaim for Hardy's verse came mainly from fellow poets who regarded him as the master of the modern. Edmund Gosse was one other fellow writer to heap praise on "The

Trampwoman's Tragedy" and, in the sister arts, where Harry Pouncy considered putting it into song, the American graphic artist Rockwell Kent posted it on a "Hardy List" of possible works to illustrate. In the end Kent chose Hardy's poem "An Ancient to Ancients," which appeared with his artwork in *Century Magazine*, May 1922.

Time's Laughingstocks encompasses a large miscellany of poems including "A Set of Country Songs" and the heavily censored poem "A Sunday Morning Tragedy"—censored presumably for treating with the use of abortifacients. These were so-called country medicines used to abort a fetus and were sold by traveling tinkers under the name of "female remedies," but in "A Sunday Morning Tragedy," a veterinary abortifacient meant for horses is purchased. The ballad tells of a mother's desperate attempt to help her pregnant daughter and of the tragic outcome.

Satires of Circumstance followed in 1914, featuring verses that Lytton Strachey regarded as the most modern of the modern. A particularly beautiful poem in this volume, "The Abbey Mason," celebrates the Gothic Revival, for which Hardy the architect never lost his fascination—a fascination that inspired his own aesthetic principle: "The seer should watch that pattern among general things which his idiosyncrasy moves him to observe."

Emma had died in 1912. The period following her death reflects some of Hardy's greatest achievements as a poet, notably the sequence titled "Poems of 1912–13," which will be discussed in detail later in the book. This sequence follows "Lyrics and Reveries" (*Satires of Circumstance*), a miscellany of early and contemporary verses reflecting on a variety of themes—philosophical, amorous, elegiac, and the world of nature.

The largest collection Hardy ever published was *Moments of Vision and Miscellaneous Verses* (1917). Nine of the poems had been collected in *Selected Poems of Thomas Hardy*, 1916—Hardy had always wanted to be published in Macmillan's "Golden Treasury" series, and this was it! *Moments of Vision* contained mainly contemporary verses that Hardy found "rather commonplace"—speaking of them to Edmund Gosse as "these late notes of a worn-out lyre." Gosse, on the other hand, hailed them enthusiastically:

> There is absolutely no observation too minute, no flutter of reminiscence too faint, for Mr Hardy to adopt as the subject of a metaphysical lyric. (Edmund Gosse, "Mr Hardy's Lyrical Poems," *Edinburgh Review*, 1918)

Citing "Copying Architecture in an Old Minster," the most notable of modern critics of Hardy's poetry, Dennis Taylor, observes that Hardy makes us see "the process which turns fresh insights into archaic formulas, tentative expressions into rigid expressions, spontaneous rhythms into repetitive patterns."[6]

Spontaneous rhythms certainly inform "During Wind and Rain" (MV), one of Hardy's most memorable poems that follows the theme of the inevitability of change and the mutability of all things. The interruptive nature of the poem's structure shapes, in stanzaic form, the breaking up of lives and circumstances. Hardy felt this to be among the best of his poems.

As Hardy's life drew to a close, he continued to produce exceptionally versatile collections. The next in line was *Late Lyrics and Earlier with Many Other Verses* (1922). In the preface he tells us that

> about half the verses that follow were written quite lately. The rest are older, having been held over in MS when past volumes were published, on considering that these would contain a sufficient number of pages to offer readers at one time, more especially during the distractions of the war.

Certainly, it would have been difficult, not to say tactless, to confront a war-torn nation (1914–1918) with "And There Was a Great Calm":

The Sinister Spirit sneered: 'It had to be!'
And again the Spirit of Pity whispered, 'Why?'

"And There Was a Great Calm" had originally been written on the signing of the Armistice, November 11, 1918. The whispered "Why" begins and ends the poem, and remains painfully unanswered and unanswerable.

Apocalypse also features in "Going and Staying" and "The Wanderer" and in surreal fashion in "Voices From Things Growing in a Churchyard" and "He Follows Himself." These are dark and disturbing poems. This darkness is not new in Hardy. It is addressed far earlier in "In Tenebris II" in *Poems of the Past and the Present* where the speaker opens up the question of evolutionary meliorism and the need to come face to face with harsh reality: "If a way to the Better there be, it exacts a full look at the Worst." The use of capitals for "better" and "worst" indicates that the concept should indeed be *capitalized*—in the sense of coming to a reckoning.

Meantime, the great Napoleonic epic drama, *The Dynasts*, had come out in three parts, in 1904, 1906, and 1908. This was Hardy's magnum opus. He had started work on it as a young lad in London some 40 years before when his dearest friend, Horace Moule, was at his side—spiritually if not always physically. Moule would feed Hardy press news from the front, while the young poet, in turn, interviewed war veterans at Chelsea and studiously researched the Napoleonic Wars in the London libraries. Later, he dreamed *The Dynasts* while writing fiction and poems all those years and had sublimated part of his dream, midcareer, in the historical novel *The Trumpet-Major* of 1880. And now, in his old age when the Wessex novels were done and the poems were in full production, he completed the great dramatic work, mostly set in blank verse, and even lived to see it produced on stage at Oxford University. In literary terms, *The Dynasts* had been his life.

Three years before he died in 1928 at the age of 87, Hardy brought out his last collection, *Human Shows, Far Phantasies, Songs and Trifles*, on November 20, 1925. Within five days almost the entire first printing of 5,000 copies had sold out, and a second impression, followed by a third impression (bearing some revisions) in December, led to the sale of 7,000 copies by the New Year. Hardy was too busy to notice. A production of *Tess* was in performance during those months at the Barnes

Theatre in Dorchester, at his home at Max Gate, and later at the Garrick Theatre in London's West End. Despite the fact that his adored Gertrude Bugler (playing Tess) had been forced out of the production by (second wife) Florence Hardy's jealous machinations, Hardy was still deeply involved in the dramatization and gave it, and the leading lady, more attention than his benighted wife would have wished.

There were also many visitors to Max Gate at this time—Virginia Woolf, Siegfried Sassoon, and James Barrie were among the many. Gustav Holst was also a welcome guest and would walk with Hardy across the heath while composing his magnificent symphony *Egdon Heath*, inspired by the opening passages of *The Return of the Native*. Of the numerous settings to Hardy's poems, the most notable are Ralph Vaughan Williams's "Soldier's Song" and Gerald Finzi's "Where the Picnic Was," "It Never Looks Like Summer," "The Oxen," and "Regret Not Me."

Hardy's last volume of verse, *Winter Words* (1928), was published posthumously. Tired of accusations of pessimism, he had decided that even in his most flippant mood, he could not escape the label, so why not mediate the point? "No harmonious philosophy," he says in the preface, "is attempted in these pages." And no harmonious philosophy is to be found. What is found is variety, diversity, complexity, and an unexpected calmness—notably in the pastoral poems "Lying Awake" and "Childhood among the Ferns."

This poet of more than a thousand verses whose period of activity spanned 70 years, encompassing the Victorian and Edwardian eras, had produced work over the longest period of *any* English poet. But even so, the period was not quite long enough. Hardy's *Winter Words*, like Holst's premiere performance of *Egdon Heath*, appeared beyond his life span. The *Winter Words* collection had been intended for his 90th birthday: "So far as I am aware," he writes in the preface, "I happen to be the only English poet who has brought out a new volume of his verse on his ... birthday." He left the space before "birthday" blank. He did not live to fill it in.

NOTES

1. Hardy was translated into Japanese in his lifetime. In 1926, Tokuboku Hirata translated *Tess: Tesu* (Tokyo: Kokuminbunko Kankokai), and in 1927, Yutaro Ito translated *Jude: Judo:ningen'ai no shukumei higeki* (Tokyo: Daidoken Shoten). Other novels, the short stories, and the poems were translated after Hardy's death in 1928.

2. All other censored words and passages have been restored to the manuscript edition of *Far From the Madding Crowd*, edited by Rosemarie Morgan (London: Penguin World Classics, 2000).

3. For further details, see Guinevere L. Griest, *Mudie's Circulating Library and the Victorian Novel* (Bloomington and London: Indiana University Press, 1970).

4. DeSales Harrison, *The End of Mind: The Edge of the Intelligible in Hardy, Stevens, Larkin, Plath, and Glück* (London: Routledge, 2005), 6.

5. *Thomas Hardy: The Complete Poems*, ed. James Gibson (London: Macmillan, 1976), 84.

6. Dennis Taylor, "Poetry," in *Oxford Readers Companion to Hardy*, ed. Norman Page (Oxford: Oxford University Press, 2000), 330.

3

Far From the Madding Crowd (1874)

Far From the Madding Crowd was Hardy's first major success. It was also the first of his novels to bear his name. However, while the story was being composed and serialized, month by month from January to December 1874, it remained anonymous. But not for long. So remarkable was its popularity that reviewers began to speculate on who the author might be. One critic suggested George Eliot, and many others followed suit. They agreed that the well-informed descriptions of the natural world and the accurate detailing of constellations in the night skies were characteristic of Eliot. There must have been some surprised faces when the first-volume edition came out in November of the same year with a new name emblazoned on the cover—Thomas Hardy.

Meanwhile, back in Dorset, Hardy had been brooding over these reviews. It was not only that he had been mistaken for George Eliot, but also that for many other critics, *Far From the Madding Crowd* had seemed to be imitating her work—and if it was not Eliot, it was Charles Reade. George Eliot's greatest novel, *Middlemarch*, had appeared in 1871, three years before *Far From the Madding Crowd*, and also treats with provincial life and mismatches: Dorothea and Casaubon, Rosamond and Lydgate. Charles Reade had published *A Simpleton: A Story of the Day* in 1873. Reade was noted for his dramatization of character and incident with a liking for factual details (an admirer of Emile Zola), but his attitude toward women was brutal. There is no indication that Hardy would have appreciated the comparison to Reade, although he was a great admirer of Eliot. This kind of speculation is enough to make any author uncomfortable, and Hardy was notoriously sensitive to misunderstandings. And whereas he thought very highly indeed of Eliot, he was not convinced that she had ever "touched the life of the fields"—her country people, in his opinion, were more like townsfolk. All in all, the whole business irked him deeply. Thus, when he embarked on his next novel, *The Hand of Ethelberta* (1876), he set it in the city, although the reason he gave was that he did not intend to confine himself to sheep and cows.

The manuscript of *Far From the Madding Crowd* has an intriguing history. Sometime back in the early 1870s, Leslie Stephen, editor of the highly prestigious *Cornhill Magazine,* had read Hardy's rural idyll, *Under the Greenwood Tree* (1872), and had started searching for the anonymous author. He knew nothing of Hardy's experimental, if somewhat graceless, attack on class privilege in *The Poor Man and the Lady, A Story with no plot: containing some original verses* (1868, rejected by Macmillan). Nor did he know of the melodramatic, plot-driven *Desperate Remedies* (1871), a hoped-for potboiler Hardy had written (and funded) on the advice of sympathetic Macmillan editors, notably George Meredith, who had detected signs of literary promise in *The Poor Man and the Lady*. Discovering *Under the Greenwood Tree*, Stephen had been utterly delighted and started searching for the anonymous author. He then wrote to Hardy to say he had been filled with great pleasure by the book's admirable descriptions of country life and surely "such writing would please the readers of the *Cornhill Magazine* as much as it had pleased him?" (*LW*, 97).

Hardy was, at that time, putting the finishing touches to *A Pair of Blue Eyes* (1873), his third published novel. He was still an anonymous author and still working as an architect, struggling financially and also emotionally: he badly wanted to become a poet, a writer. Naturally, he responded promptly to Stephen's invitation. The *Cornhill* was, after all, the most prestigious literary journal of the day. He would certainly submit a story for serial publication, but he wondered to himself, what would it be? At this stage he was uncertain, but he didn't want to seem unwilling so he sketched an outline, a "pastoral tale" comprising "a young woman-farmer, a shepherd, and a sergeant of cavalry" (*LW*, 97). He had not yet conceived of a third suitor, the gentlemanly Boldwood, or of the subplot featuring Fanny Robin, or, indeed, of the full plot that was later to cause so much trouble with its themes of seduction, illegitimacy, and homicide. Thus it was that, with nothing more than a sketchy outline followed up by a few chapters for the first few installments, editor Leslie Stephen commissioned *Far From the Madding Crowd* virtually sight unseen.

The next episode in the manuscript's history was equally haphazard. Customarily, publishers did not trouble to return manuscripts to such obscure authors as the anonymous creator of *Far From the Madding Crowd* of 1874. Consequently, when serialization was about to conclude and Hardy started revising for volume publication (the usual procedure with successful serials), he wanted to restore the passages Stephen had censored but had no original manuscript to refer back to.

It did not strike him as odd in those early years that the manuscript had never been returned, but he was surprised to be told, some 40 years later, that it had been found, almost perfectly intact, in the basement of the London offices of his former *Cornhill* publishers, Smith, Elder & Co. On receiving this news he instantly took up his pen: "How surprising that you should have found the MS," he wrote to Mrs. Reginald Smith, "I thought it 'pulped' ages ago." Smith had written asking permission to put the manuscript up for auction, the proceeds to be donated to the Red Cross for the war effort (World War I) and Hardy had responded with characteristic modesty: "What a good thought of yours, to send it to the Red Cross, if anybody will buy it" (*Letters*, V5.243). This must be the ultimate oddity, that he should be so exceedingly modest and evidently unaware that by 1918 his first editions were fetching very high prices at Sothebys.

Hardy was not told how much the manuscript fetched at auction, but this was the first time in his life he had ever seen it in its entirety. One leaf had gone missing, so he copied it afresh from the published version and inserted it with the others, before the leaves went off to be bound—the only portion of the manuscript that is not an original. He was obviously moved to see, as he said rather wistfully, that this was the work of a much younger man. He never saw the manuscript again.

Following is a brief history of the text (incidentally, this account approximates the textual evolution of *all* the Wessex novels—12 out of a total of 14—that first appeared in serialized form). Returning in time to the summer of 1874, Hardy is now completing his last *Far From the Madding Crowd* chapters. When the final installment is about to appear in the bookstores in December, his publishers will collect up all 12 periodical numbers and Hardy will revise them for volume publication, as speedily as he can. In November the first edition will come out—timed to coincide with the last serial installment. Some segments from the manuscript (as far as Hardy could recollect them), together with words and phrases previously censored by the editor, are restored. The first edition will provide the copy-text for all subsequent editions, albeit modified by various editors over the course of time.

Several decades and many editorial versions later, Hardy makes more revisions, some prompted by outside criticism, some by hindsight evaluation. He then prepares for the 1912 so-called definitive Wessex edition. Occasional editorial interventions (variants and errors) have also crept in along the way. This is why the manuscript edition or, next in line, the first edition, finds favor with scholars desiring the most authentic text untouched by the historical process.

As for the postserialization revisions to *Far From the Madding Crowd*, Hardy restored as much of the original as he could recollect. The *Cornhill* version had, after all, been severely compromised. Those censored passages that had stung him to protest, such as the coffin scene with Fanny's stillborn babe, must have remained deeply imprinted on his memory, for he was able to reproduce them almost verbatim. But the truth was that although he had learned much about publication politics from his editor Leslie Stephen, in the month-by-month process of editorial criticism and censorship, he never lost his fierce contempt for all forms of "tampering with natural truth," as he put it some 14 years later in "The Profitable Reading of Fiction."

PLOT AND STRUCTURE

The narrator of *Far From the Madding Crowd* is omniscient—having infinite and extensive knowledge of all people and all events—with the occasional intervention of a bystander narrator (see "Part 2: The Short Stories" in chapter 2). Because *Far From the Madding Crowd* was originally composed in 12 installments for the *Cornhill Magazine*, with each installment comprising four to five chapters, the structure is geometric. That is to say, the major events and crises occur in a relative arrangement of parts. Thus, in the July installment, containing chapters 29–32, the crisis point is Bathsheba's elopement and the events that surround it. In the August installment, chapters 33–38, the crisis point is the storm and all that devolves upon it.

When Hardy first sent editor Leslie Stephen his plot sketch of a "pastoral tale" comprising "a young woman-farmer, a shepherd, and a sergeant of cavalry" (*LW*, 97) he had not fully conceived *Far From the Madding Crowd*. Thus the first few chapters embark on a tale fundamentally in line with the plot sketch and certainly conforming to Stephen's notion of another *Under the Greenwood Tree*–type story—a rural idyll. We meet shepherd Gabriel Oak covertly peeping at the beautiful Bathsheba Everdene on her way through country lanes to stay with her aunt, where she will fulfill the classic romantic role of milkmaid. The scenes that follow trace a variety of rural incidents, including Oak's precipitate, premature proposal of marriage to Bathsheba. By the time chapter 5, "A Pastoral Tragedy," arrives, the first crisis has occurred, but the predominant picture of harmonious country life remains intact.

At this point the plot starts to abandon this schema. Good shepherds courting beautiful milkmaids vanish, and the intriguing Mr. Boldwood (not in Hardy's outline) arrives on the scene. Complications arise from a scandal involving a housemaid and a soldier billeted at the nearby garrison at Casterbridge; the plot thickens as the seductive soldier intervenes in Bathsheba's busy life—now an estate manager and farmer—and a host of complex issues now begin to occur, changing the course of the plot so that it no longer conforms to its original outline.

Ultimately, the plot (as opposed to the story), which is indivisible from the structure, patterns the play of fate and fortune, incident and action upon Bathsheba's young life. The conflicts of love, decision making, and character development devolve upon the interplay of one inexperienced young woman and her three suitors: she is headstrong, innocent, impetuous, and untried; Oak is dogged, patient, staid, and judgmental; Boldwood is superior (in class, money, and age), commanding, repressed, and obsessive; Troy is dashing, adventurous, irresponsible, and seductively charming.

Just as the seasons play out their days and nights of fluctuating weather, mapping development and change in the natural world, so too with the characters: their fortunes are unpredictable, their plans frustrated, their intentions unfulfilled, their needs ebb and flow, and their desires are destabilizing. To this end of mirroring the inner world of his characters in external forms in nature, Hardy composed each installment according to the seasons of the real world. Thus, when his readers began the first installment in January with bright coal fires burning in their living rooms, the frosty hillsides of Dorset were resounding with the bleating of ewes lambing down in the snow (while Oak nearly suffocates in his lambing hut, forgetting to open the ventilator). Likewise, in the stifling temperatures of August, when Londoners might be dreaming of "those cool sequestered vales," Bathsheba's neglected grain stacks unprotected and exposed, are neither cool nor sequestered but assaulted by late summer storms while her husband drinks until dawn with revelers in the barn.

And at a broader, symbolic level, Hardy also places his Wessex construct at the center of a purposeful anomaly or misfit—a form of antipastoralism. This becomes evident when the verdant pastures where sheep may safely graze transform into grotesque death traps. In effect, the deadly temptation to which nature's creatures are susceptible provides a close correspondence to the conflicting passions in human affairs.

CHARACTERS

Bathsheba

Far From the Madding Crowd is, in many respects, the precursor of *Tess of the d'Urbervilles* (1891), with the role of Tess split between the trusting homespun girl (Fanny Robin) seduced by the sweet-talking charmer (Sergeant Troy), and the courageous, self-determined young woman struggling to make her way in a world made by men for men (Bathsheba). Unlike Tess, however, Bathsheba is by birth middle class, by education accomplished, by inclination daring and adventurous, and, on the reverse side, vulnerable, unguarded, and rash. Both principals share, however, an important attribute—not necessarily a creditable attribute, in the eyes of Victorians—and this is a luxurious sense of their own sexuality. This is an attribute that many sexologists in the Victorian world beyond the novel claimed "nice women" did not possess.

The boss-woman aspect of Bathsheba's career brings its own unique problems because there is not a single man in her world who believes she has a right to it. Management is for men. Bailiff tasks are for men. Issuing pay packets is for men. This view is held (initially) by all the characters from Gabriel Oak down to the most menial laborer. The only man who does not hold this view belongs in the past. He has known her since she was a child. He is her uncle. Impressed by her capacities and fully trusting in her abilities—albeit against the advice of trustees who felt she was too young and too beautiful—Uncle Everdene leaves his estate and its management to his niece, thus showing a complete disregard for prevailing sexually discriminating codes and practices (is it from her uncle that Bathsheba inherits not only an estate but also a rebellious will?). Hardy thereby provides an alternative male model (who never appears on the scene) by which his central characters can be understood.

The problems arising from these prevailing codes and practices are many. Bathsheba is repeatedly subjected to male spying and the judgmental views of her menfolk—thus, feeling undermined and exposed against her will, she becomes defensive. Struggling to maintain her dignity, she ends up haughty and disdainful. Losing confidence, she is arrogant. In her complexity, her youthful contradictory impulses, her self-protective hauteur born of fear and insecurity, and her sexually challenging excitement and self-unseeing recklessness, she is rarely free of male censure and pays a very high price for this. She has no female models, after all. With no mother, sisters, or aunts, she has only the trusty companionship of her maid, Liddy—not the best of advisers for a spirited young mistress suddenly faced with a freedom and a sexuality she barely understands.

Gabriel Oak

Of the three men who court Bathsheba, Gabriel Oak has a very clear idea of what a "good woman" should be and tries hard to mold Bathsheba accordingly. In creating this characterization, Hardy had problems: How to give this stolid, conventional patriarchal figure some charisma? How to sustain his role as part of the novel's center of interest? If it is in character for Oak to plod on and on, how to restore him to the action as "hero"? The difficulty is resolved by constructing certain scenes that will throw Oak into a strong light, displaying his courage and selfless devotion—hence, the fire and storm episodes. Both threaten Bathsheba's ricks, but the hero enters to save the day. Likewise in the scene of the blighted ewes, the hero again enters to save the day.

However, in the event of having the hero step in to save Farmer Boldwood's neglected crops, Hardy (who easily tires of the good-shepherd stereotype) exposes another side to Oak's nature. Capable and controlling, Oak is also ambitious and acquisitive. Over the months he has worked his way up from shepherd to bailiff on Bathsheba's estate and has earned every penny of it. But when poor crazed Boldwood loses his reason and Oak steps in to save his day, it is not as a shepherd or bailiff but as a business partner. From this point on, Oak will take a high proportion of Boldwood's farming profits, revealing the hard-nosed, materialistic side of his nature. There is an uncomfortable sense that Boldwood, in his unstable mental state, may not be acting in his own best interests by giving Oak such a large cut. The more serious charge is: should a person of integrity such as Oak take advantage of a sick man's mental illness?

In this respect, Hardy's characterization of Oak has markedly departed from the original good-shepherd archetype. This is not to be regretted as far as his own artistic endeavor is concerned. As his characterizations develop over his novel-writing career, he enhances their complexity (as in Oak), introducing elements of universal human weakness, inconsistencies in behavior, confused egotistical emotions, and contradictoriness of behavior intent or action long since condensed into psychiatry manuals. These human attributes defy simple psychological analysis. Hence, the artist forfends in his readers the kind of categorization or stereotyping that reduces a character to a formula and subsequently to a diminished force within the novel's center of interest.

Boldwood

Farmer Boldwood, on the other hand—who is not a working farmer but a gentleman farmer (one who owns but does not labor)—is engrossing from first to last. As noticed earlier, he was not a planned character in the original scheme of things, but as soon as Hardy conceived him, he took on a vivid life. He tries to woo Bathsheba, spurred to obsessive fantasies by her lighthearted gesture of sending him a valentine. This instantly challenges his preferred monastic life, and he becomes besotted by the idea of possessing her. His is a classic case of Eros. The arrow is aimed at his heart and he sickens not with love of Bathsheba but with love of possession.

In terms of plot, Boldwood's role is to thwart and frustrate, thence to be thwarted and frustrated. Accordingly, he is incompetent at courting. He becomes clumsy and insensitive—insensitive to her nature and needs, less insensitive to his own. He hunts her down—tracking her, watching her, trapping her in corners—a sexual predator.

Gabriel Oak, who is himself given to spying and thinks nothing of his own harassment activities, tries to convince Bathsheba that because she has enchanted Boldwood, she is duty bound to give herself to him. After all, she has cost him. Bathsheba is outraged and indicates to Oak that this is nothing short of prostitution (note: this is couched, narratorially speaking, in figurative terms—even Bathsheba would balk at speaking of prostitution explicitly). At the same time she is stricken—she feels oppressed and guilty. The outcome of this situation is dark and tragic.

Sergeant Troy

By contrast, Hardy's "wicked soldier hero" (as Hardy liked to call him) does not disturb the reader—only Bathsheba. He is a flatterer, good-humoredly aware of his own charm, and callous in his philandering. Hardy's close engagement with this character (as manifest in the manuscript) may have something to do with the fact that initially, long before he has to shape him as the villain of the piece, Frank Troy is the outsider and underdog. He is uprooted, something of a lost soul who was well born but stigmatized by his illegitimate birth. Possibly, too, his fine command of literary matters catches at his author's heart (characters can do odd things to their authors). However, when Troy appears to be implicated in the disappearance of the young servant girl—Fanny Robin—Hardy does expose him for what he is, revealing his callous nature as when, back in the barrack room, he mocks the loving girl and later jilts her (it is with some sleuthing that the reader can deduce that Fanny knows she is pregnant at the time of being jilted—nothing is made explicit).

Now, what Bathsheba sees is a dashing soldier with a ready wit and a willing tongue. He has glamour—a far cry from the homely Oak and the gentlemanly Boldwood. Troy teases her, makes her laugh (always a seductive thing), beguiles her, and arouses her sexually (neither Oak nor Boldwood has this power over her). Bathsheba is captivated, although she does hear rumors. Being infatuated, she does not allow herself to believe them (when the reader knows what Bathsheba does not know, that Troy is a philanderer, this is called dramatic or situational irony).

A close examination of the original manuscript reveals a reluctance on Hardy's part to thoroughly blacken Troy's character. But, again, the plot needs a denouement, and the story has to come to closure, so blackened he is—albeit with touches of melodrama that indicate a certain lack of authorial engagement in the act. In like vein, Oak tends to become eclipsed (he virtually disappears at the center of the story) and is subsequently restored, accompanied by one or two unfortunate errors in revision, which also vouch for a lack of authorial engagement. And lastly, Bathsheba's characterization emerges rather less wild and rather more ladylike under Stephen's pen than under Hardy's.

He had a great fondness for spirited, independent-minded, devil-may-care women. But then he grew up with one and loved her dearly. She was his sister Mary.

ROLE OF MINOR CHARACTERS

Literary and dramatic tradition engages secondary and minor characters to fulfill several important functions in the furtherance of plot, enhancement of the story line, and character portrayal. These functions are often performed by the secondary and minor characters within the subplot. The subplot acts as a reinforcement to the main plot (plot is the narrative organization), where minor characters enact parallel situations often in some mirroring capacity to the plot proper.

In Aristotelian terms, the plot has to be constructed so that no incident can be displaced or omitted without impairing the unity and coherence of the whole. The same goes for the subplot. Thus, when minor character Fanny Robin, in *Far From the Madding Crowd*, trudges through the snow by night to the Casterbridge barracks to search for her husband-to-be, Troy, and encounters only lies and deceit, or when she calls on him for financial help and he fails her, or when she dies and he mourns her and loves her all the more once she's dead, Bathsheba's own experiences with Troy are mirrored to a nicety. A mirror will reverse the image, of course, and that too may be apparent in subplot techniques.

For example, Bathsheba pursues Troy to Bath (on horse, not on foot), where, humiliated and deceived, she marries him (as Fanny tries to do). Later, when she implores Troy to help with her estate or when she begs him to stop gambling all her money away, he fails her (this is an economic crisis for Bathsheba, whereas for Fanny it is a matter of life and death). And when Bathsheba, presuming Troy dead, is about to marry another, he reappears on the scene, believing he has lost her he tries to claim her all over again (Fanny is already dead when Troy reclaims her as his true love).

A pattern is now emerging. The subplot, in which the secondary characters play the most important part, intensifies and highlights the incidents and situations of the plot proper and, in turn, adds tension to the story (readers may be only subliminally aware of the patterning; full awareness would increase their enjoyment). The only minor adjustment to the mirror action in terms of *Far From the Madding Crowd*'s plot and structure is that all the secondary events, all the "Fanny" incidents, take place in the *rising action* of the novel before the *crisis* point has been reached, whereas in Bathsheba's case, the incidents tend to cluster around the crisis point before the *denouement* is reached. But there is no law to say that the subplot must pace the plot proper, in terms of temporal structure—the mirror can be picked up and turned on the central action at any point, or vice versa.

Perhaps one of the more subtle ironies of Hardy's tale is that Bathsheba, whose life is so deeply affected by Fanny's, never meets her face to face. Their only encounter is in the coffin scene. Here she gazes down on the golden-haired young girl and recognizes, with misery and anguish, the origin of the lock of hair in Troy's watchcase.

There are no male secondary characters in *Far From the Madding Crowd*, but Bathsheba's maid, Liddy, could be described as secondary rather than minor because she plays a substantial role as Bathsheba's helpmeet and confidante. Without Liddy's aid and encouragement, Bathsheba might not have sent Boldwood the valentine that sparked his obsession with her. Liddy also conveys some of the servants' gossip and thus allows Bathsheba (and the reader) to see behind the scenes, so to speak. Then, it is with Liddy's help and support that Bathsheba is able to rebound, albeit with considerable emotional pain, from the tragic events surrounding Fanny's demise and Troy's desertion.

Moving from plot to characterization, Liddy's loyalty and devotion not only provide the reader with an obvious contrast to Oak's in that her love is unconditional (she never spies or plays the part of moral watchdog or tries to change Bathsheba), but also, by virtue of that same loyalty and devotion, Bathsheba's lovability is highlighted—she quite clearly earns the affection and respect of her maidservant. This in turn rouses the reader's compassion for the impetuous, sometimes arrogant, and often misguided heroine. Liddy, sweet natured and sensitive, isn't particularly smart, but she commands the reader's respect at all times: she provides a reliable and trustworthy witness to character and event.

The minor characters, on the other hand, are mostly male. And this is where Hardy's rustics come in. As in Shakespeare, the rustics have a very special role to play. They offer sideline commentary on the action as well as lending light comic relief at various moments of tension and drama. Again, as in Shakespeare, they function as the rustic chorus not because they speak in unison but because they speak in concert albeit in parts, and those parts are set in counterpoint to the main theme, the main action.

Hardy tends to individualize his rustics. This is not traditional as far as their choric role is concerned. One thing he strongly opposed was the stereotyping of the rural laborer and the reduction of all individual traits and characteristics to the type of country bumpkin known generically as "Hodge"—a popular caricature of the straw-sucking, brain-addled farmworker. Inadvertently, Hardy falls back on the Hodge stereotype from time to time, but he also stresses the fact that there are as many varieties of character and temperament among rural laborers as there are among urban workers. Hence, the Malthouse gang in *Far From the Madding Crowd* is composed of characters (not stereotypes), from the happy tippler, Joseph Poorgrass, with his "multiplying eye," his stuttering fear of women, and his literary pretensions; to the all-knowing pontificator, Mark Clark; to Laban Tall, who is constantly belittled by his nagging wife; to the ancient maltster, who is so proud of his age that, to help it along, he counts a working season as a working year and thus comes up with the mathematical calculation that he must be well over a hundred years old.

What the rustics do have in common is not that they speak in unison but that they are unified in their voice. Their superstitions and articulated assumptions about women, about the church, and about their community of shared values follow the common herd, the kind of mainstream assumptions to be found in daily newspapers. A good case could be made, in fact, for their mirror role to the principal male, Gabriel Oak. They watch and gossip (especially over women), where Oak spies. They hold the unconventional Bathsheba in superstitious awe, where Oak judges and corrects her, measuring her against "all women" (a good woman is thus). However, the main point here is that, in general, their views and observations on situations and events are unified by a common, conventional outlook, and hence they are dubbed, by critics and scholars, the rustic chorus.

Going back as far as Greek theater, the role of the chorus varied in performance style from dancers and singers who sang and chanted, to commentators or participants in the action. In Elizabethan theater the choric line was often reduced to a single speaker. In Hardy, the rustics fulfill the last of these roles, commenting on the action and imbuing much of it with a sense of the absurd as well as participating in the action and offering comic relief.

Unfortunately, much of the comic dialogue is lost on the modern reader who may not only have difficulty with the rustic dialect but might also find the allusions, especially the sacrilegious talk (which requires biblical knowledge), hard to follow. Even Leslie Stephen, Hardy's editor of *Far From the Madding Crowd*, put his pencil through much of the rustic dialogue, indicating to Hardy that it was too prolix. But then he disliked revealing that he was a prude, so if he was actually watching out for blasphemy (and there is plenty of that among Hardy's rustics), he might well have chosen to explain his censorship in other terms.

Here is a sample of one of the rustic dialogues excised by Stephen.[1]

Joseph Poorgrass is on his way back to Weatherbury from the Casterbridge Workhouse[2] with Fanny's coffin in his cart (chapter 41). At Bathsheba's request, Parson Thirdly is waiting at Weatherbury church to conduct a burial service, but Poorgrass decides he needs a drink on the way home and breaks his journey at the old woodland inn called Buck's Head. He finds his drinking buddies inside.

> "I hope Providence won't be in a way with me for my doings," said Joseph again sitting down. "I've been troubled with weak moments lately. Yes, I've been drinky once this month already, and I didn't go to church a-Sunday, and

I dropped a curse or two yesterday, so I don't want to go too far for my safety. Your next world is your next world, and not to be squandered lightly." (248–249)

A rather "drinky" debate follows on the relative merits of Protestantism and its various factions called Dissenters, Chapel, and the Church of England.[3] As Jan Coggan puts it

"a man can belong to the church and bide in his cheerful old inn, and never worry his mind about doctrines at all. But to be a dissenter you must go to chapel in all winds and weathers, and make yerself as frantic as a skit. Not but that chapel-members be clever chaps enough in their way. They can lift up beautiful prayers out of their own heads, all about their families and shipwracks in the newspaper."

"They can—they can," said Mark Clark, with corroborative feeling; "but we churchmen, you see, must have it all printed aforehand, or, dang it all, we should no more know what to say to a great person like Providence than to the man in the moon." (249)

Coggan then debates the odds of getting into heaven and finally concludes that he will

"stick to my side, and if we be in the wrong, so be it. I'll fall with the fallen."

"The same here," said Mark. "If anything can beat the old martyrs who used to smoke for their principles here upon earth 'tis being willing to smoke for 'em hereafter." (249)

This—with martyrdom smoking equated with burning in hell—was all too much for Leslie Stephen and his "parson's daughter" yardstick of propriety. It may be one thing to ally yourself with the Church of England because doctrines don't matter and you can still spend time in the pub getting "drinky," but to compare the Christian God (Providence) with the man in the moon is quite another. The prevailing image of the man in the moon was of a grinning, lecherous old voyeur (who spies on romantic couples by night) or, simply, a leering idiot. Leslie Stephen put his pencil through the entire passage telling Hardy that it added nothing of value and should be cut.

When Victorian society demanded that the novel be edifying to young readers, it was not including iconoclasm (attacks upon cherished beliefs). If the rustics succeed in getting the reader to chuckle with them at their notion that Christian belief is the source of all absurdities, then at least the narrator should offer some kind of rebuke, or a stronger indication of their own absurdity. But Hardy does not.

THEMES

Reflecting the broader philosophical sphere of society as it exists in the background of Hardy's Weatherbury world, within and beyond the novel, the rustics—who manifest the laboring hub of his partly real, partly dream country—express, in their opinions, beliefs, and superstitions, the irrationality of the human condition. Hardy found a kindred philosophy in the work of Arthur Schopenhauer (1788–1860). He had already immersed himself in the work of the early socialist thinker Charles Fourier (1772–1837), who inspired much of his revolutionary zeal, particularly on the class war. It is significant that the proletarian hero, male and female, was a relatively new arrival in Hardy's day and that his working-class principals and class-based themes were unmatched among novelists of his period. Even Dickens's principals are fundamentally middle class. Hardy never deviated from this: he began and ended his novel-writing career with a class polemic featuring a working-class protagonist: *The Poor Man and the Lady* (1868) and *Jude the Obscure* (1895).[4]

On the other hand, and at a less overt level, the metaphysical theme of an irrational, absurdist universe that will feature centrally in Hardy's later work develops gradually over the course of his novel-writing career. According to the philosopher Schopenhauer, the world is an irrational, blind force, godless and without guidance, in which human desire and human instinct, if unguardedly acted on, only create misery and desolation. If humanity purged itself of desire, instinct, and even of will, it would reach a state of nirvana, in which frustration and hatred (from thwarted desire), aggression and possession (from drives based on instinct), and misguided controls such as dictatorships or the misrule of governments (will) would not threaten humanity's wellbeing. On the positive side, the ultimate moral action for Schopenhauer is compassion and loving kindness.

In Hardy, this philosophy reveals itself in a variety of contexts in his poetry and more diffusely in his fiction. One notable example of the irrational or, in this instance, of an irrational institution is the Victorian institution of matrimony—hence the many mismatches and matrimonial incongruences portrayed in Hardy's denouements. This theme begins right here, with *Far From the Madding Crowd*.

Whereas on the one hand the rustics banter and joke about misalliances and broken Commandments, and whereas on the other Hardy has pledged at this early stage of his career to provide a "getting married and living happily ever after" ending, the denouement is, in fact, kept purposefully ambiguous. At surface level, Hardy fulfills his contract, but all is not well. To be sure, the beautiful lines paraphrased from the *Song of Solomon* about the "only love which is strong as death—that love which many waters cannot quench, nor the floods drown" convey precisely that close, companionable love that augurs well for a happy union. The problem (as Hardy knew) is these particular biblical lines are those of a woman besotted with lust for her lover. It may take an educated reader to pick up on this, and no doubt the average Victorian skipped contentedly on toward the seeming happy ending—but Henry James, for one, wasn't at all convinced.

If readers didn't stop to figure out these anomalous biblical lines, they surely wouldn't have had their romantic expectations frustrated by Hardy's "last words," either. Or, to be accurate, the last words are Joseph Poorgrass's. With characteristic pomposity he delivers the newlyweds a little speech: "'Ephraim is joined to idols: let him alone'. But since 'tis as 'tis, why it might have been worse, and I feel my thanks accordingly" (353). Poorgrass has recalled the lines (possibly from some Sunday sermon) from the book of Hosea in which "Ephraim is joined to idols." But he does not appear to know the context. It is in possessing the "spirit of whoredom" that Ephraim will be "oppressed and broken." Fortunately, this ap-palling curse, coming as it does from Poorgrass, probably falls on mostly deaf ears within and beyond the novel.

But Poorgrass's words are a sign of things to come, thematically speaking. In Hardy's next major novel, *The Return of the Native*, the "oppressed and the broken" are so barely eclipsed by Hardy's alternative "happy ending" that many readers tend to forget that there ever was an alternative ending. And by the time of *Tess* and *Jude* the "oppressed and the broken" are most emphatically those who marry and do not live happily ever after. This critique is intensified in *Jude* by the fact that the Victorian institution of marriage comes under unmitigated attack from the principal, Sue Bridehead, as well as from the narrator.

Thus it is that in *Far From the Madding Crowd* the rustics add philosophical texture to the thematic fabric of the novel. By extension, in the more formal un-derstanding of the word *absurdism*,[5] they bridge the incoherence and indetermi-nacy of the natural world and its collision with the meaninglessness of existence by attempting to create meaning and order where there is none. They draw on belief systems from the outside world, as much to give significance to all that is incomprehensible as to give a semblance of order to all that is disorderly. They spout biblical sayings with a comic piety and all the wrongness of a Mrs. Mala-prop, and then, in the very same breath, they invoke pagan beliefs without car-ing about the difference. Thus local superstitions, traditional omens, and ancient portents intersect with Ecclesiastes and Job, providing a delightfully incongruous series of signs pointing the way, quite arbitrarily, toward Destiny or Providence or God—or, at any rate, some kind of controlling power to which humanity can attribute all wrongs.

However, the most obvious theme of *Far From the Madding Crowd*—aside from the evocation of England's "green and pleasant land" (for the more nostalgic read-er)—is that most popular of Victorian themes, a young girl's coming of age. In common with a whole host of predecessors, from Jane Eyre to Maggie Tulliver and beyond, Bathsheba Everdene's story centers on her growth to womanhood. Why was this so predominant a theme in Victorian times? The explanation possibly lies as much in social science as in literature, but the most obvious is the rise of women and the inordinate struggle of that rise. If Hardy is representative, the position of women (called by Victorians, The Condition of Women) in the 1870s was that of an oppressed class gaining social equality and economic opportunities in painfully slow degrees. Women still had a long way to go toward liberation.

It is plain from the first few manuscript chapters that Hardy thought he was going to make Gabriel Oak the center of interest. But a creative writer frequently has to take the cue from his or her characters, and no sooner did Bathsheba appear on the scene than the story became hers. Coping with her growth to womanhood in a world "made for men by men," as she puts it, Bathsheba is bitterly conscious of her disadvantageous position—a theme Hardy pursues in a variety of ways in his later novels. In contrast to Oak, who is offered bank loans so he can acquire property (sheep and real estate), Bathsheba's role of estate manager is threatened by the distrust of her uncle's trustees on the grounds of her sex. And later, upon marriage to Troy, she is faced with the loss of all legal rights to ownership of her property. In the real world, the Victorian husband became the legal owner of the wife's property upon marriage, although he was no longer entitled to appropriate his wife's earnings. This was so new a development under the law, that many a husband continued to keep his wife's income under lock and key, and there was little she could do about it. Likewise, a husband was legally entitled to put his *wife* under lock and key, if he was so inclined. The Married Woman's Property Bill of 1870 gave a married woman the same rights as her unmarried sister. In this respect, many of the issues in *Far From the Madding Crowd* are of current interest to Victorian readers. A wife could now legally own her earnings. However, few women had either the financial resources or the backing of the legal profession to sue their own husbands in the case of matrimonial violations of any kind.

On top of her legal status as her husband's property, Bathsheba also has to face the suspicion and criticism of the predominantly male world in which she lives and works. She is aware of being constantly watched and monitored. Inevitably this puts her on the defensive in almost everything she does. Where Oak suffers no criticism for poor husbandry when he carelessly feeds a dead lamb to his sheep-dog, which, heated with blood lust, overdrives the flock to its death, Bathsheba is blamed for just about every mishap that occurs under her management. Even when she succeeds in catching Baily Pennyways (the bailiff) for thieving, and, dismissing him, takes over the role of bailiff herself, her workfolk are appalled. This, they are convinced, will lead to everyone's ruin.

In common with her compeers in Hardy's other novels, Bathsheba is very young: she has yet to be tried and tested—the very essence of the coming-of-age ritual. Many societies have specific rituals for initiating youth into adulthood, and most of these put the individual through severe tests of character and endurance (also called rites of passage). This is Bathsheba's experience, too, although she is subjected to emotional and psychological, not physical, trials. As the last image in the novel shows, the initiation has been severe indeed: the lovely girl who once embraced life with spontaneous gaiety "never laughed readily now" (353).

SYMBOLS, ALLUSIONS, AND FIGURATIVE LANGUAGE

Hardy was first and foremost a poet. The devices of rhythmical, figurative, and metaphorical language, together with the strategies of symbolic action, all came naturally to him. Equally, his usages were innovative. For example, in *Far From the Madding Crowd* he coins words such as "emotional," "feminality," and "phenomenal"—words that didn't exist in common parlance at the time. Newly invented words are called neologisms, and over the period of his writing career, Hardy created hundreds of these. Editor Stephen might (and did) score his pencil right through them, but subsequently most became common usage. The *Oxford English Dictionary* (OED) numbers nigh on a thousand Hardy neologisms, most of them in use today. These include some revived archaisms and less popular dialect words such as "baint" (be not) and "chiel" (child). Hardy was an enthusiastic philologist—a lover of language and learning—and he was keen to preserve the everyday language of men and women, which, in the Wessex region has its roots in ancient Anglo-Saxon linguistic formations. Fortunately, the OED shared his enthusiasm and words such as "emotional" are now part of our everyday language.

But then there was the reverse situation. Hardy would use ordinary, everyday words that turned out to be unmentionable in polite society. He obviously had no idea that he couldn't use the word "buttocks" (even though these buttocks belonged to horses). Nor was he aware that "wantonness" was taboo (in modern parlance, female sexual playfulness). But his worst transgression was his poignantly tender rendering (in the manuscript) of Fanny's last sleep with her stillborn babe in her arms. "No!" said Leslie Stephen, "No babies!" The whole subject of babies and a woman's procreative body was pornographic. Indeed, the image of Fanny Robin as pregnant (the word itself was unmentionable) is entirely eclipsed by the *Cornhill* illustrator, Helen Paterson. Instead, we have a young woman with a 19-inch waist on the day she gives birth. A comparable mode of censorship these days would be the blotting out of secondary sexual characteristics (buttocks and breasts) on television.

Apart from ordinary, everyday language where buttocks and birthing were blotted out for their connotative power, for what they might evoke in the mind of the reader, Hardy also offers an abundant array of literary, classical, and biblical allusions. These were considered high intellectual treats in his day. They are invariably thought provoking, frequently ironized (rendered ironic), and often delightfully picturesque. It was not necessarily the aptness of the allusion or the brilliance of the literary analogy that excited the interest and pleasure of readers. Sometimes their charm, like insider jokes or the family anecdote, arose simply from their familiarity as part of a shared cultural heritage.

As a rule, the smarter, more ironic the allusion, the more intense the reader's bright moment of recognition would be. Even the unschooled were, in Hardy's day, familiar with Bible stories and classical mythology. Therefore, at one level of familiarity, when Cainy Ball's "pore mother"—being neither a "Scripture-read woman" nor a churchgoer—mistakenly christens her infant son Cain because she had thought "t'was Abel killed Cain" (from Genesis 4:1–15), we might smile. Humor depends very largely on an audience's sense of its own prior knowledge.

In the real world, and by extension within the novel, biblical phrases and names would have been picked up—even by unlettered folk—from Sunday sermons and church worship or possibly from the current popular Bible readings that took place in private homes. Within the Weatherbury world, the rustics use these assimilated phrases playfully, indifferent to their meaning or relevance. Like Cainy Ball's mother, they recall only a smattering of the biblical text but enjoy the sense of their own learnedness just as readers in turn enjoy their malapropisms.

Allusions, in Hardy, work on several levels. For example, at a more complex level of mythmaking, he is making the point (with the Cain story) that belief systems have their origins as much in folk culture as in sacred writings. Just as Cainy's story becomes a part of local oral history in *Far From the Madding Crowd*, so it also becomes a paradigm of the storytelling process. Myths begin with stories, and stories generate beliefs, eventually to become embedded within the culture.

A more knowing participant in the allusions business is Levi Everdene. This is Bathsheba's father—an educated man (back in the history of the book) who knows his Ten Commandments. To titilate sexual desire, he would, as a young married man, pretend he was having illicit sex with his own wife and would invoke the Seventh Commandment—Thou shalt not commit adultery (modern readers might consider this kinky or even rather silly, given the vast choice of sexual playthings on the market. Victorians, by contrast, had it censored and cut from the serial altogether).

Still on the subject of sexuality, Hardy also uses allusions to indicate (covertly) a state of arousal in his characters. To state this explicitly would be impossible, especially where women are concerned, so Hardy alludes where he cannot be candid. There is the fine example, in Bathsheba's case, of Exodus 17:6. In the original story the Lord commands Moses to strike a rock on Mount Horeb, which then unleashes a spring of water. Hardy modifies the idea to fit the situation. As Troy dips his mouth to kiss Bathsheba for the very first time, it brings "upon her a stroke resulting, as did that of Moses in Horeb, in a liquid stream—here a stream of tears" (163). Intense desire overwhelms her sense of shame—the body tells its own erotic story. But as far as contemporary readers were concerned, there is nothing to censure. Indeed the passage could be read aloud (a common practice) in the Victorian drawing room with impunity.

At another level of signification, it frequently occurs that the sheer absurdity of the allusion (mock-heroic), or the comparison to be drawn from it, draws the reader into a complicit relationship with the narrator. This, in turn, may arouse sympathy for the character in view. When, for instance, the new and rather nervous young mistress of the Everdene estate begins her payroll activities for the very first time, and when "the remarkable coolness of her manner" takes on the "proportionate increase of arrogance and reserve" shown by "Jove and his family" when they moved from "their cramped quarters on the peak of Olympus into the wide sky above it" (72), so the light mockery of the allusion invites the reader's indulgent smile. The comparison is plainly absurd. Here is our young woman farmer struggling to be authoritative, and here is the mighty Jove ascending to the stars. Unlike the purposefully obscure relation set between Moses on Mount Horeb and Bathsheba's liquescent bliss, the Jovian allusion exaggerates the situation to the point of ridicule, and the reader's response is shaped accordingly.

Allusions and symbols should not be confused. Some of Hardy's allusions may be mistaken for symbols at first sight but may well be, instead, a pictorial enhancer designed specifically to address the interest of the educated reader. When, for example, in the shears-grinding scene Gabriel Oak is said to stand "somewhat as Eros is represented when in the act of sharpening his arrows" (114), we are not invited to regard this as a symbol of Gabriel Oak's erotic (Eros) stature. Rather the contrary. Notice that the allusion refers to a representation of Eros and not that Oak is some kind of manifestation of Eros (in that case Eros *would* signify as a symbol).

The Eros story is as follows. The boy god of love (otherwise known as Cupid) the young son of Venus is traditionally depicted with bow and arrow; he is said to whet with blood the grindstone on which he sharpens his arrows. This is the image depicted in a host of art works. And one of the most popular of these in Hardy's time was Raphael's suite of 32 pictures illustrating the adventures of Psyche, the beautiful maiden loved by the boy Eros but visited by him only at night. Forbidden to seek out his identity, Psyche one night steals a look at him while he sleeps; he awakens and flees; she is then enslaved by Venus and treated most cruelly; when these trials end, the lovers are wed. So it is that from Shakespeare's *Midsummer Night's Dream* ("Cupid's strongest bow") to Rafael Mengs's painting *Cupid Sharpening His Arrows*, to the statue of Cupid stringing his bow (at the Louvre), or sleeping (Rome), or mounted on a tiger (Negroni), to the array of Cupids in literature (Horace, Ovid, Apuleius, Moliere), and to the designer saturation of cupids on Victorian mantelpieces, drapes, and even tableware that, pictorially speaking, Hardy was drawing on a shared cultural heritage of unquestionable familiarity to his Victorian contemporaries. In sum, the allusion is designed to excite images of other images, not of Cupid (Eros) per se. And that image is of Eros's *manner* of handling his weapon, whetting it with blood.

Now, at another level of discourse (which ties in with this particular allusion), weapons are indeed symbolic. Gabriel Oak seems, to all intents, a good shepherd, a strong man, and a devoted and faithful lover. He is all these things, but there is more. And Hardy's weaponry symbolism helps us to discover and understand the "more." In tracing the symbolic function of weapons in *Far From the Madding Crowd*, a pattern emerges that links the tools and blades of all the male characters in highly significant ways. From the knife that slips in Oak's hand in the shearing scene (wounding the she-creature in his care) to the sword so flamboyantly displayed by Sergeant Troy to Boldwood's shotgun (an intimidating weapon for an overbearing man), the kind of weapon each man wields and the way in which he wields it tell us a good deal about the undercurrent of male violence in this novel.

Tracing the symbolic function (or extended metaphor) of tools, blades, and weapons leads to other forms of symbolism. Most fundamental of all in this novel is the landscape itself. Wessex provides a dual correspondence not only to the myth and magic of a golden-age world but also to the strife that is absented from Hardy's title but re-presented in the story proper (see "Setting" in this chapter). Hardy's re-presentation of strife shapes his Wessex construct in several ways.

For instance, the degree to which the human dilemma of, say, relational discord makes its impact on the reader depends in part on its manifestation in nonhuman forms. What do we infer from a scene that is moonlit as opposed to a scene that is stormy? A woman appears in both scenes, but our expectations of mood and event are shaped (differently) by the setting—the moon, the storm. Hardy's Wessex functions in a similar way, symbolizing in the external world much that is unseen and unseeable in the inner world of mind and heart.

In *Far From the Madding Crowd*, certain dissonant forms in the natural world remain, at first sight, relatively hidden—the lambing season arrives late and the bee swarming (for honey making) is irregular and unruly. Their ultimate emergency lays bare the close relationship between the disorder among men and women and the aberration in nature. In the event, the least hidden, most palpably felt of these emergencies coincides with the most public of strife manifestations in Bathsheba's personal life: as late summer storms in the outside world wreak havoc on her crops, so is there chaos on the inside as her husband wreaks havoc with her workforce, driving them drunk and insensible.

Sometimes spoken of as an external correlative, when the external world is shaped to mirror the internal world of the character(s) in view, the symbolic function of the landscape is best interpreted in terms of its consistency within the metaphorical structure of the novel overall. Just as the various tools, blades, and weapons are shown to have a dual function—at once literal and figurative, at once a shearing aid *and* a manhandling of the female—so, also, many nature symbols are structured to perform both as literal images and as figurative signifiers. The storm is just one part of the pattern. Springtime is another—signifying (literally) a climatic change of sweeter, warmer days and the end of darkness, *and* (figuratively) as renewal and regeneration of human hopes and desires. Similarly, harvesttime is not just a month in the year for gathering in the crops but may also signify a maturation process in human nature (notice this is the season of marriage, or rather mismatch, in *Far From the Madding Crowd*).

Alternatively, when Gabriel Oak battles the rick fires and saves Bathsheba's haystacks from burning to a cinder, this accords well with his psychological state of mind at this time, battling his own fires of unrequited love. Likewise, when the excited Bathsheba secretly meets with Troy to watch his sword display, the external correlative, the symbolic setting here is denoted by Hardy's chapter title "The Hollow Amid the Ferns." This, in topographical terms, describes a hidden dell on the hillside concealed by tall, feathery fronds of spring ferns. In symbolic terms, the connotation is sexual, suggestive of the female, physical body. Later, when Bathsheba runs distracted and crazed from her house at night, she ends up in the very same spot. But it is now later in the season. The hollow has been flooded with rains from the summer storms and is now filled with stagnant water, rank with oozing decay. It no longer signifies a suggestive setting for seduction and erotomania (Hardy's word), but aptly shapes a scene as close to Bathsheba's sense of horror as might be imagined. Now reading setting alone, we read desolation and a ghastly corruption of a former state of affairs. In sum, interpretation of Hardy's symbolism requires scrupulous tracing of the extended metaphors and imagery interwoven in the web of a larger, more complex symbolic construct.

SETTING

As we have seen, the setting of *Far From the Madding Crowd* is Hardy's Wessex— a part-real, part-dream country based on his homeland in Dorset—situated in the southwest coastal region of England. Here, in the village of Weatherbury (modeled on Puddletown, close to his Bockhampton birthplace), Bathsheba Everdene inherits her uncle's house and farming lands and, at 19 years old, sets about management of the estate. The setting is rural England at its loveliest. It is sheep-farming country flanking the southwestern coastland, which, topographically speaking, is characterized by undulating hills (as opposed to flat acres of cornfields), gorse-filled heathlands, deciduous woodlands, verging onto barley and hay fields leading down to the sea cliffs of the English Channel—the kind of cliffs where Gabriel Oak's benighted flock meets its fate. The climate in this region is moderate; short winters (in some areas roses bloom throughout the winter), mean that lambing can occur as early as January. The local brew is barley based but it is cider (fermented from pommery—apple mulch), which is made freely available to the laborers. Among Hardy's rustics, Joseph Poorgrass is most renowned for his tippling and resulting "multiplying eye" (as he calls it).

The village centers around the ancient Saxon church; the county town is Casterbridge (modeled on Dorchester), where Fanny Robin makes her way to the workhouse; and the nearest city[6] is the Roman watering place of Bath—to which Bathsheba Everdene rides by night on horseback to meet with Sergeant Troy. The village of Weatherbury boasts a huge medieval barn, a malthouse for the preparation of barley malt for beer, and such rural necessities as a sheep-dipping pool in the meadows and lambing huts on the hillsides. The malthouse, with its presiding ancient maltster, provides the communal meeting house for the rustic community in this novel. This is where Bathsheba's laborers convene before and after work for a good tipple and where they gossip about the trials and tribulations of their new mistress.

At the mythic level, Hardy's rural representation is of England's golden age—so called for its preindustrial state of carefree happiness and harmonious interaction of man and nature. Victorian nostalgia for the lost ancestral village expressed itself in many forms, from genre paintings depicting healthy, happy laborers relaxing wearily but contentedly on their scythes in the evening sun, to stories of water babies frolicking in the rivers and streams, to the poetry of rural idylls where nymphs and fairies evoke the magic of perpetual youth, to the elaborate construction of follies, which were simulated Gothic ruins and ancient, atmospheric temple gardens built to adorn the grounds of the wealthier classes.

Hardy takes his title from one such rural idyll: Thomas Gray's "Elegy Written in a Country Churchyard."

Far from the madding crowd's ignoble strife,
Their sober wishes never learn'd to stray;
Along the cool sequester'd vale of life
They kept the noiseless tenor of their way.

In common with Gray, Hardy has been celebrated for championing oppressed humanity. However, his use of Gray's phrase for the title of his novel is purposefully ironic. Whereas "Elegy Written in a Country Churchyard" lauds the freedom from care, social conflict, and violence that Gray's country dweller enjoys, *Far From the Madding Crowd* extols no such thing. On the contrary, what Hardy's microcosmic universe reveals, beneath its veneer of mythic "idyll," is "ignoble strife" at every turn. Nevertheless, his natural world does provide a backcloth of "sequestered vales"—"even to the leanest pasture, being all health and colour. Every green was young, every pore was open, and every stalk swollen with crowding currents of juice" (125). The world is health giving, fertile, and filled with enchantment—but ever subject to challenge and change. It is nature, after all.

ALTERNATIVE READING: RECIDIVIST FEMINISM AND MATERIALIST CRITICISM

Scholars adopting a particular school of theory, such as feminist, Marxist, materialist, gender, historicist, and so on, frequently claim a new approach to reading Hardy. Such claims are well founded where fresh insights are attained, but frequently the "new" has been explored before in a different guise, on different cultural territory. What, then, validates the "new"? In many cases it is less the theory than the cultural territory. For example, a recent theorist in gender studies (offshoot of feminism) analyzed Hardy's use of mythic allusions in relation to Bathsheba and argues that by aligning her with the goddesses Venus and Diana, Hardy is positing "a universal and permanent aspect of female nature."[7] This critical approach to Bathsheba's characterization arises from the new cultural territory of the twentieth century, but the theory itself is not new. It shaped, for example, the interpretive approach of many a Victorian reviewer who presupposed, in line with the prevailing cultural ideology, that all women did, in fact, partake of a universal nature—it took only a short leap to fit allusions to Venus or Diana into that concept. Indeed, current debates raged during Hardy's lifetime on whether woman was a product of nature or of culture—the perennial question being "under which universal law does woman actually come?" Fitting Hardy's allusions into preconceived concepts, reading them not as extratextual pointers to a more complex reading but as the "somatic anxiety" of the author or as Victorians claimed, as authorial misrepresentations of womankind, presupposes that the author, in both cases, projects his personal problems, cognitive or otherwise, on to his fictional text. This aligns the modern critic, in this instance, with the Victorian in a single stroke.

For Hardy, who is in one breath a feminist, in another a literary naturalist, and in another a social Darwinist—in other words an artist adhering to no universal law of any kind (even his agnosticism was pretty lawless)—the challenge was to defy prevailing ideologies, especially those that diminished individualism and that consigned individuals (notably the working classes and women) to second-class status, to a single universal category. So in his view, his allusions to Diana or Venus would have augmented rather than defined identity. That being said, critics and readers often approach a text subjectively—indeed there is a school of criticism that advocates this: textual interpretation can never be entirely free of ideology. Hardy acknowledges this when he states in his postscript to the 1912 edition of *Jude* that there can be more in a book than the author consciously puts there.

Reinforcing what I would call the neo-Victorian approach to *Far From the Madding Crowd*, our "universalist" scholar goes on to say that Bathsheba must grow out of her Diana phase and must recognize her need for Oak. Leaving aside the fact that Hardy's allusions do not function in this temporal way within the narrative (they do not initiate or conclude phases), the point here is, yet again, that Victorian critics also opined in this vein: Bathsheba must in some way change and must become more deserving of the good man (Oak). This manner of dictating what the woman must or must not do is essentially a Victorian style of criticism (within and beyond the novel) and in Hardy's day was called moral criticism. It followed the cultural prescription that novels would and should present a moral standpoint.

So what is new? Our scholar's historical and social context—the cultural territory—is new, certainly. It is only the critical approach that is not new. And in terms of cultural territory, the "new" in this instance is characterized by the currency of the discourse: it utters itself in terms of the erotic, the phallic, and the emasculated. This Freudian dimension (Freud invested in types—stereotypes, archetypes) was not a feature of Victorian critical discourse.

Materialist criticism follows a similar trajectory. Exploring the historical, social, aesthetic, and ideological context of the novel, the materialist critic examines the process of production with a view to repoliticizing the text in view. Readers familiar with the principles of Marxist criticism will recognize the signs. Just as gender criticism borrows much from feminist scholarship, so too the materialist critic derives much from Marxist theory.

Initially, a materialist view of history, as expressed by Marx, held that the mode of production in material life determines the social, political, and spiritual processes of everyday matters, systems, and beliefs. It isn't the consciousness of individuals that shapes their existence but rather the material conditions of their lives that shape their consciousness. Thus, the argument might go that Gabriel Oak is given to spying on Bathsheba not because he possesses a strong streak of voyeurism and an insatiable desire to possess Bathsheba by stealing her privacy and self-possession, but because he is a shepherd. Shepherds watch.

There is an element of determinism in materialism. In the social production that individuals enter into, they engage with definite relations that are indispensable and beyond their will. Oak as shepherd, as bailiff, and as financial investor participates in an agrarian economy that, in its totality, constitutes the structure of society. The fact that there is no call for shepherds at the market Oak attends after losing his flock, where he plays his flute to gain attention, shapes his destiny as well as providing an indicator of his economic value to the community as a whole. A materialist critic might point out that this slump in the market where Oak could not get a job as shepherd makes the loss of an entire flock all the more significant in terms of Oak's role within the structure of society.

Very shortly, Oak will compensate for this economic disaster by saving Bathsheba's ricks from burning, and what Hardy incorporates into *Far From the Madding Crowd,* but which Oak would not have at the forefront of his mind, is that the economic structure of society is definitely shaping his consciousness (and also Bathsheba's). This sequence of loss and profit has to be balanced in the end, by subordinating the former to the latter. This forms the basis of a capitalist society of which Oak and Bathsheba are a part. In line with this and his newly shaped capitalist consciousness, Oak aspires to gain profits from Boldwood's estate; in turn, Bathsheba consciously invites Oak throughout the story and finally in the denouement, to stand by her to lend his labor. What if her economy had failed? In this event, Oak might well have sought work elsewhere, or emigrated, as he plans on doing at one point—his material life being determined by the character of the social conditions in which he has been engaged.

Historical materialism views the historical process as a struggle. The materialist critic would no doubt emphasize Oak's perpetual state of insecurity, as a unit of labor in the Weatherbury economy—likewise, Bathsheba's perpetual state of insecurity in her lone struggle against sexual prejudice.

The next step for the materialist scholar is to explore Hardy's writing as a process of cultural/ideological production: writing is labor, and whereas writers produce a text, they do not produce the linguistic and ideological tools of their trade. In like vein, readers are products of the historical process. Every reader brings his or her own ideological, experiential tools to the text. This does not in any way change that text. On the contrary, it fulfills the potential of the text—given, as Hardy says, that there can be more in a book than the author consciously puts there. "Writing" and "ideology" are key words in materialist criticism. There is nothing enchanted—as poet Maya Angelou describes the writing process—about creating a novel or a poem. There is nothing transcendent about the creative writing process. Writing is labor and ideology the tools that determine the writer's writing. Consequently, the state of the art—whether it be pulp fiction or literature—is determined via the discourse of criticism.

This is the weakest link in materialist theory. That Hardy purposefully placed fragments of his poetry in his fiction to such a degree that the popular poet Coventry Patmore spoke of *A Pair of Blue Eyes* as being a poetic text—the poetry infused in the prose—does not mean that he created a poetic text (in the view of materialist critics). Writing and literature are separated in the production process, and the literary text, or poetic text, is determined at the historical moment of production, at the moment of consumption—that is, via the reader (consumer) and (to repeat) the discourse of criticism. The problem that arises here derives from a dualism in materialist theory. Whereas the act of writing is labor and the tools that the writer has accessible are the prevailing ideologies of the day, which necessarily makes the writer a cipher of sorts, the notion of authorial intention is not altogether dismissed. Indeed, it becomes implicit in many instances. For example, a materialist critic might argue that the world of Wessex is not a reflection of the real world nor a fictionalized version of that world (Hardy says part-dream, part-real). It is, instead, a product of the contradiction between certain conflicting ideological formations and the aesthetic project. Problems arise here with this supposition because the aesthetic project lies within the domain of the author's ideas and imagination. So, already, a large part of the author's determination is at work indicating that writing involves more than labor. To begin with, there is the idea of aesthetics—whose, if not the author's? Then there is the project—this implies planning, organization, outcome, and so on—whose, if not the author's? And finally, the concept of "conflicting ideological formations": if conflicting, who is determining the conflict if not the author? One might argue, for example, that Marxism conflicts with socialism (which it does at several points), but another could just as readily argue no conflict. In other words, "conflicting" implies a point of view—whose, if not the author's? This, then, presupposes some kind of authorial intention. Yet who would or could know this? The presupposition is unfounded because no one can know what an author intends (unless this is purposefully articulated).

Addressing *Far From the Madding Crowd* more specifically, the materialist critic, reading contemporary ideologies into the text, perceives Gabriel Oak to be a typical Hodge regardless of the fact that Hardy's contemporary critics (to whom Hodge was rather more familiar) did not share this perception. The approach is interesting and thought provoking, for what the critic is doing here is to project a prevailing class ideology onto the text that prevailing views did not share. It is thought provoking because it is a perfectly legitimate projection and certainly offers new insight into Hardy's text. It is, in a sense, ideology speaking to ideology: the modern materialist critic's class ideology addresses that of the contemporary class ideology said to inform Hardy's text.

Hypothesis gone mad? Maybe—but provocatively so. On the other hand, there is no doubt that Wessex is an ideological landscape. Hardy himself claimed as much. A Homeric universe—that is to say, a microcosm—right down to the Pillars of Hercules on its southernmost boundaries. Nor is there much doubt that he creates a working community in which alcohol plays a significant part and that there is no narratorial moral condemnation of it—although the materialist critic provides it. Siding with Gabriel Oak—who storms at the tipplers at Buck's Head, "Upon my soul, I'm ashamed of you; 'tis disgraceful, Joseph, disgraceful" (250)—the materialist critic claims moral condemnation. Curiously, there was no such outcry by Victorian critics. Hence, yet again, modern ideology confronts the ideology said by materialist critics to inform the background of Hardy's novel. This is where cultural territory enters the scene. The moral condemnation is Oak's, not the narrator's, and, more importantly for our purposes, it is the moral condemnation of the modern critic who not only calls such episodes shocking but attempts to substantiate the claim by avowing that it is with Oak that the reader identifies (note: *this* particular reader does not so identify).

Ten years after *Far From the Madding Crowd* came out, Hardy published "The Dorsetshire Labourer" (*Longman's Magazine*, 1883) in an attempt to address some of the issues raised by his critics on the condition of rural labor. The essay is significant in this context of materialist criticism for its acute consciousness of the prevailing ideology, for its attack on stereotypes (the countryman as "Hodge"), and for its defense of dialect and concern with the displacement of rural labor and home ownership. Hardy's focus is on social attitudes, the attitudes that shape ideologies. Materialist criticism, in Hardy's case, claims that his class of origin (the rural artisanal class) forms the ideological basis of his thinking. This tends to marginalize his education and wide reading, but it provides insight into what might be called the social construct that is Thomas Hardy.

NOTES

1. This is now restored to the text for the first time in more than 100 years in the manuscript version of *Far From the Madding Crowd*, edited by Rosemarie Morgan (London: Penguin Classics, 2000).

2. *Workhouse:* public institution and/or correctional facility for paupers in the parish (or union of parishes). Protocols and practices varied from parish to parish, but most required that inmates provide labor in return for shelter and food.

3. *Dissenters:* name given to Protestants who opposed state interference in religious matters and founded their own communities over the sixteenth- to the eighteenth-century period. *Chapel:* loosely refers to the Wesleyan or Methodist factions of Protestantism and includes Dissenters. *Church of England* is also called the Anglican Church—the established church in England technically governed by the reigning monarch.

4. *Hero:* In classical mythology the hero represented a character of superhuman qualities favored by the gods and was chiefly male. In Homer, the hero exists for the sake of the literary action. More recently the word "protagonist" has replaced the word "hero" to include, as in *Jane Eyre*, the hero as female. In addition, the hero or protagonist no longer possesses superhuman qualities but, at a more realistic level, is cut down to size.

5. Readers may be more familiar with the concept of absurdism in drama, such as in the plays of Samuel Beckett and Harold Pinter. The emphasis is on the grotesque and ludicrous, and the underlying belief is that there is a tension between man's determination to discover purpose, meaning, and order in a world where no evidence can be found for a design of this kind. The existentialist Camus held that courage and stoicism grow from man's belief that he is an exile in a meaningless world.

6. A city is distinguished from a town by virtue of having a cathedral.

7. See Marjorie Garson, *Hardy's Fables of Integrity: Woman, Body, Text* (Oxford: Clarendon Press, 1991), 35.

4

The Return of the Native (1878)

The Return of the Native—Hardy's fifth published novel—was first issued in 12 monthly installments (January–December 1878) in the magazine *Belgravia*, a sensationalist periodical. "Of all places, *Belgravia!*" protested one of his devoted literary friends, Mrs. Proctor—in shock at such a comedown. Hardy was, at this time, gaining a reputation for flouting the conventions, for erring on the side of what he called candor but what his more puritanical critics called impropriety. Editor Leslie Stephen had already rejected the first few chapters of *The Return of the Native* because he "feared that the relations between Eustacia, Wildeve, and Thomasin might develop into something too 'dangerous' for a family magazine."[1] Hardy, seeking to make a living by writing, was anxious to be published, so he then submitted his manuscript to *Blackwood's Magazine* and subsequently to *Temple Bar*. Both turned it down.

It is worth noting at this juncture that literary magazines filled the cultural place for Victorians that television fills today. At varying levels of intellectual discourse, highbrow to lowbrow, periodicals featured articles on the arts, sciences, social concerns, political activities, and so forth, and most sought to commission works by the great authors of the day, including poets. Leslie Stephen's *Cornhill* was rated highbrow, *Belgravia*, lowbrow. And just as today television programs are widely discussed and provide an index to the culture, so too with Victorian periodicals. Not only were they a major focus of attention in drawing rooms, where they would be read aloud, as also in clubs and public reading rooms, but they also supplied topical matter for dinner parties, letters to editors, and all the usual outlets modern societies reserve for current affairs, art, literature, opinion, and gossip.

This was Hardy's audience for *The Return of the Native*. And after many false starts and bowdlerizations, he eventually produced a story that would sell, albeit to *Belgravia*. He would, as with all his novels following *Far From the Madding Crowd*, restore many of the serial cuts and bowdlerized passages to the volume edition, which would ensue as a matter of course when the serial went into its final installment. Books, unlike serial publications, were available to a restricted adult readership via libraries such as Mudies (which did in fact exercise its own form of censorship, by selection) and, of course, commercial booksellers.

The Return of the Native was published in a three-volume edition by Smith, Elder on November 4, 1878, and met with a mixed reception. The *Evening Standard* (May 1878) praised plot and description but deplored Hardy's "tedious love of tiresome commonplace characters." One suspects the reviewer hadn't actually read the novel, because the outcry generally was that Eustacia was far too voluptuous, far too "Bovarian" (as in *Madame Bovary*) and sensual and not in the least commonplace. Vigilant of prevailing codes of decorum, Hardy wrote to his illustrator, Arthur Hopkins (February 1878), "I think you have chosen well for the May illustration—certainly the incident after the mumming, with the mummers looking on, will be better than the mumming performance itself. Eustacia in boy's clothes, though pleasant enough to the imagination, would perhaps be unsafe as a picture" (*Letters*, V1.54). Eustacia was, according to one critic, a "thoroughly selfish, cruel, unprincipled, and despicable woman" (*Eclectic*, 1879). Most reviewers, however, reluctantly conceded that Hardy's powers of description were exceptional and that here was a truly fine novelist in the making.

PLOT AND STRUCTURE

The plot of this "Novel of Character and Environment" is structured around the geometrics of Egdon Heath—its divergent and convergent courses and the random human activities therein. Eustacia first encounters Clym in half glimpses of sight and sound (initially, his disembodied voice, simply) before she takes the initiative and engages herself as one of the mummers performing, in disguise, at his Christmas festivities. On his part, Clym first catches sight of Eustacia on his return from Paris as he is walking across the heath—and, enchanted, *he* then seeks a way of meeting up with *her*. Their most tender moments occur when they meet by pure chance.

As the hierarchy of characters moves down in scale of importance, so the characters are more inclined to meet by design—albeit a design that is often flawed. Wildeve and Thomasin have been courting before the action starts, but when they do arrange to meet for the first time in the novel, it is at church for their marriage ceremony, which doesn't take place. Then, when they reschedule the wedding—a fugitive, miserable affair—they remain incompatible thereafter. Conversely, Thomasin's random meetings with Venn ultimately yield a relatively stable connection.

By the same token of design and disruption, Wildeve arranges to meet Eustacia by means of her bonfire signals, but the courses taken by this pair are tracked by Diggory Venn (by his spying activities), and the lovers' spell is thus rendered vulnerable and is eventually broken. Significantly, Eustacia's impromptu trip to join the dance, where she encounters Wildeve quite by chance, results in one of the most ecstatically joyous moments in their relationship.

Then there is Mrs. Yeobright's carefully planned visit to her son for a reconciliation. The course she takes is hazardous and the outcome unexpectedly tragic. And finally, that plotter of all plotters, Diggory Venn, who spies on other people's activities and plays havoc with fortune (notably Mrs. Yeobright's legacy), succeeds in steering others off course while he remains on track. He is never far off when someone is losing his or her way. Venn ultimately plays a central part in the tragic destruction of lives, but, as the archetypal schemer, he escapes calumny altogether. In common with the very best of devils, he appears benign and harmless while juggling with everyone's fate at will.

Ambiguity of intention, action, and event mark this novel. Hardy made several revisions to that end, rendering more complex the motivation and behavior of his characters. Perhaps the most ambiguous scene of all is that of Eustacia's death. The debate continues to this day as to whether it is suicide or misadventure. Likewise, mismatches, mistaken courses, and crossed communications puncture the narrative structure. This convolution is, in a sense, writ across the earth. The ancient Via Ikeniana, which traverses the heath "from one horizon to the other," is almost obliterated by disuse and the overlaying of a newer highway. As dusk falls, its white surface gleams in the gloom, but this great Western road of the Romans no longer goes anywhere.

As the section "Setting" illustrates, the Egdon paradigm itself is the plot and structure of the novel. Whereas Egdon watches and waits, sustaining turbulent weather and seasonal fluctuations, seemingly poised and ready for the next moment of flux, the principals don't possess the same endurance, yet they are the central players in that flux. Eustacia yearns for life in the great arteries of the world—not a particularly unrealistic dream were it not for the fact that few middle-class women possessed means of their own—higher education, careers, and a steady income (unless marrying into money) remained a dream for most women of Eustacia's class and background. Hence her passion for life and learning and love outside the bounds of matrimony will, of necessity, be frustrated—but she watches and waits just the same, only to discover that not even matrimony can relieve the enervating emptiness of her days. Clym, in turn, has his courses blocked: he dreams of personal eminence and philanthropy but is hopelessly vague in his aims and poorly prepared in his method. At the extreme end of unpreparedness, Wildeve—rootless, restless, and purposeless—relying solely on Eustacia for stimulus, sustains nothing and no one. He is directionless at every turn. Possibly he comes closest to embodying existential nihilism than any other character in Hardy, with the exception of Jude. Lastly, Mrs. Yeobright, the archetypal controlling mother—not as myopic as her son but with ambitions complicated by class prejudice, sorely hindering Egdon's social relationships—she too would take alternative courses, or would have her son take them, if only she could have her way.

CHARACTERS

Eustacia

In the process of revision for *The Return of the Native* prior to publication, Eustacia's characterization underwent significant modification. Like Bathsheba before her, she had emerged from Hardy's pen in the first flush of writing a spirited "bad girl" of some considerable power prone to fits of temperament, mood swings, and witching-hour passions. With Bathsheba, *Cornhill* editor Leslie Stephen had enforced specific revisions—among them, anger modification. Anger was out (nice women didn't show anger), and vexation was in (vexation was feminine—being aggrieved by petty annoyances).

Eustacia's case is more extreme, however: she is considerably more nonconforming than her predecessor. Bathsheba may protest the patriarchal world she finds herself struggling in, but Eustacia goes further and rebels against practically every social convention imaginable, especially prescriptions of feminine behavior and the conventions of marriage—as Sue Bridehead will do even more vociferously in the more liberal climate of the fin de siècle (the century's end) some 20 years on.

At the manuscript stage of composition, Eustacia is decidedly more wild, more excitable, and less intellectual than the (first edition) young woman who is "learned in print, and always thinking about high doctrine," as the rustic, Humphrey, puts it (II.i). One critic illustrates the very real threat she presents, even a century after publication. He is John Paterson, author of *The Making of The Return of the Native* (1960). Paterson, avowedly patriarchal in his views, claims that in the holograph manuscript (urtext), Eustacia is not just a "bad girl" but seriously evil: her "hot words of passion," he writes, are "demonic," and her anger is not anger but "satanic pride" (Paterson,18, 19). In passing, this association between female anger and witchery not only throws light on Leslie Stephen's anxiety about according anger (as opposed to vexation) to Bathsheba, but also exposes the sexual double standard: male anger is not thus interpreted.

The common understanding in patriarchy is that the beautiful, desirable nonconformist woman is the cause of man's downfall. It is not that he is to be blamed for his excesses and his uncontrolled behaviors, but that she is to be blamed for provoking them. Evidently, Eustacia's nonconformity is severely threatening insofar as she is not controllable, not receptive to the dictates of men (her grandfather doesn't even try), and thus Paterson attempts to dehumanize her. He argues that when the lonely girl "laughs at herself,… sighs between her laughs, and [gives] sudden listenings between her sighs" (19), she is plainly evil. She is not just talking to herself (as we might think and as Hardy conveys), soliloquizing, or simply imagining things as does, say, Shakespeare's Hamlet. She is a witch. Paterson calls it "diabolism."

It is one thing for the superstitious Egdon folk to fear that Eustacia might possess supernatural powers, but it is rather disturbing when modern critics adopt the same view, particularly given the history of the victimization of "witches," of which the educated reader would surely be apprised. Victorian asylum mentality, when women were institutionalized for emotional outbursts and uncontrolled passions, appears to be the mind-set here.

Certainly, Eustacia has a reputation on Egdon of witchcraft. Quite apart from anything else, the power of her beauty over young men leads heathfolk—Susan Nunsuch, for one—to fear that their sons will be placed under some kind of spell. The demonic Venn jealously perceives Eustacia to be something of a rival, something between a witch and a devil, and thus he stalks her in attempts to bring her down. The stalker has considerable power over the victim—spying is a form of theft, after all—but Venn rationalizes his Peeping Tom habits as pure vigilance undertaken in Thomasin's interests. This has, in the past, persuaded critics (of Paterson inclination) that the stalker is, in this case, benign. Few legal minds would share this view. Venn's claim of protecting Thomasin's interests would avail him nothing in a modern court of law all too familiar with the stalker's "protection" excuse.

Back in the world of Egdon, Eustacia's powers of enchantment are such that the superstitious rural community seeks to demonize her: men lust after her while fearing her spellbinding power, and men and women alike blame her for men's desires. It was with prudent foresight, then, that Hardy, perceiving a potential problem with Eustacia's nonconformity and witchery associations, revised the manuscript and not only modified the latter but also raised her class status to that of granddaughter to the gentlemanly Captain Drew (later Vye). This helps to narrow the gap between the wayward heroine and the middle-class drawing room she has to enter, as it were. Similarly with anger modification. If an educated critic of the 1960s can demonize Eustacia—in effect, adopting the attitudes of simpleminded heathfolk for whom anything unfamiliar is to be feared and maligned, for whom the inexplicable remains perforce, supernatural—then what hope would there be of gaining the common reader's understanding of this beautiful but emotionally turbulent young woman?[2]

While he was writing *The Return of the Native* in the mid to late 1870s, Hardy would have had just such issues in mind, for he was reading the work of a liberated but socially persecuted woman he admired greatly, George Sand. Openly rebellious and unconventional, Sand was to Hardy one of the immortals of literature. As he read her novel *Mauprat,* he took notes, carefully observing the following:

> Men imagine that a woman has no individual existence, and that she ought always to be absorbed in them; and yet they love no woman deeply, unless she elevates herself, by her character, above the weakness and inertia of her sex.[3]

Leaving the pages of *Mauprat* for his own novel, Hardy turns to Eustacia, and to a husband who ignores her "individual existence" and, instead, "follows out his own ideas" (249).

In mindless self-absorption, Clym regales Eustacia with tales of "Parisian life and character" and, to her torment, sings songs of Paris (where she longs to be) as he works on the heath. He is seemingly oblivious to her "sick despair, of the blasting effect upon her own life of that mood and condition in him" (IV.ii.248).

It is part of Hardy's method in *The Return of the Native* to expose the anger and frustration experienced by the intelligent woman confined, mind and body, to an inutile (nothing to do), unvarying, and isolated existence. This condition spoke to countless middle-class Victorian women confined to house and home with no opportunity whatsoever for expanding their horizons (short of reading novels). Thomasin's domestic world, with all its conventional trappings, throws Eustacia's into relief by contrast; the estranged solitary woman belongs to no circumscribed world, least of all Thomasin's, in the sense of settling in it, becoming habituated to it, or wishing to remain in it. Where Thomasin fulfills reader expectations of the submissive, forbearing, and dutiful wife, Eustacia does not.

At 19, wild and sexually hungry, she dreams not of domesticity but "To be loved to madness—such was her great desire. Love was to her the one cordial which could drive away the eating loneliness of her days. And she seemed to long for the abstraction called passionate love more than for any particular lover" (III.vii.71).

What a discreet way of putting it. In the world of men, the phrase "sowing his wild oats" renders free sexual activity respectable. There is no equivalent phrase for women.

Eustacia also battles with hypochondriasis.[4] This psychological condition is closely detailed throughout the text and appears to be a chronic "depression of spirits." She finds a partial relief in walking (still recommended today for depression), but her mood swings, despondency, and "languid calmness, artificially maintained" intensify the "eating loneliness" of her days.[5] Like most chronically depressed people, she feels that "nothing is worthwhile"—a feeling that ultimately overwhelms her when, struggling with the unbearable upheaval of her marriage and the churning "chaos of her mind" (345), she completely breaks down. Alone, unaided, and crazed in her mind, she crouches down in a "rocking movement," as in a catatonic state—"the wings of her soul were broken" (346).

Eustacia's personal battle, then, is not only with her suffocating confinement, her sexual hunger, and the monotony of her lonely, isolated days in a community that alienates her at every point (Clym protestingly asks his mother *why* Eustacia was excluded from his homecoming party), but also with clinical depression. She longs for remission, for stimulus. To Wildeve she tries to explain:

> I should hate it all to be smooth. Indeed I think I like you to desert me a little once now and then. Love is the dismallest thing where the lover is quite honest. O, it is a shame to say so; but it is true! ... my spirits begin at the very idea. Don't you offer me tame love, or away you go! (I.ix)

Wildeve bores her. But she tactfully expresses this in terms of needing more challenging company. That she craves sensation and stimulation is made palpable at several textual thresholds where her "spirits *begin*" with the "Ah!" "Ah!" of her articulations with Wildeve and the "O!" "O!" "O!" of those with Clym. She craves sensation and predictably cannot conceive of adequate objects for her desire. How could she imagine adequacy? She has been starved of "life"—the "life ... and all the beating and pulsing that are going on in the great arteries of the world" (276).

Eustacia is not "romantical nonsensical," as her grandfather would have it. She is empowered with a deep imagination—"Seeing nothing of human life now, she imagined all the more of what she had seen" (I.ix). Showing quite a startling maturity for one so young she tells the passive, romantically inclined Clym that "nothing can ensure the continuance of love":

> You have seen more than I, and have been into cities and among people that I have only heard of, and have lived more years than I; but yet I am older at this than you. I loved another man once, and now I love you. (III.iv)

Her candor is engaging (Tess, later, is unable to speak of these things with the same ease). And her fundamental acceptance of serial monogamy—there was one, now there is another—coupled with her ideas of nonexclusive love, places her well ahead of her contemporaries (aside, perhaps, from George Sand).

The narrative stresses her alienation still further: Her "celestial imperiousness, love, wrath and fervour" are "somewhat thrown away on netherward Egdon," whereas on Olympus "she would have done well with a little preparation. She had the passions and instincts which make a model goddess, that is, those which make not quite the model woman" (I.vii).

The model woman in this instance is, of course, the "good" little Thomasin—submissive not imperious, docile not fervent, amiable not angry, demure not outspoken and passionate. Evidently, the model goddess belongs in a different world:

> Has it been possible for the earth and mankind to be entirely in her grasp for a while—few in the world would have noticed a change in the government. There would have been the same inequality of lot, the same heaping up of favours here, and contumely there, the same generosity before justice, the same perpetual dilemmas, the same captious alternation of caresses and blows that we endure now. (I.vii)

Is this an observation on the world and humanity or on Eustacia? Given the weight of the paragraph it would appear to be the former. And, of course, the world is not Olympus: it is not polytheistic or filled with joyous Hellenism, let alone sexually emancipated men and women.

Clym

Moving on to the principal male character in *The Return of the Native,* Clym Yeobright, Hardy's revisions mainly intend to gentrify him—again, possibly to maximize all chances of reader identification.[6] For example, Clym's place of employment from whence he returns to Egdon was originally Budmouth (based on the small, cosmopolitan port town and spa of Weymouth in Dorset). Hardy altered this venue to "revolutionary" Paris, where Clym is at the same time "promoted" (by Hardy) from assistant jeweler to manager to a diamond merchant.

In common with so many of Hardy's central male characters, Clym is idealistic to a fault. He claims to his mother that he wants to make a permanent home on Egdon and will inaugurate a school there—to educate the Egdon eremites out of their superstitious, backward ways and bring them into the modern world—but he has no resources and provides no practical schemes. Even if he did succeed in gaining financial support, that a handful of heath workers already strongly set in their rustic ways might not make such a school viable doesn't appear to occur to him.

Aligned at first with John the Baptist (who prepared the way for the Redeemer), who "took ennoblement rather than repentance for his text" (III.ii), Clym, we are told somewhat contradictorily (in the next breath), does not have a "well-proportioned mind." And despite the narrator's efforts to reclaim him from mediocrity, mediocrity is where he ends up. Demonstrating no special rural skills, he is ultimately reduced to manual labor—cutting the furze used for animal fodder and fossil fuel.

Clym is gentle and dreamy but shortsighted, physically and mentally. He at one point suggests to Eustacia that she might become the matron of his proposed school (Eustacia a *matron?*). The narrator makes it clear that these young people are, in fact, in love with an *idea* of each other, not the real person. Eustacia, who has invested Clym with a glamour based solely on his having lived in Paris and a romantic propensity based solely on the gossip of the rustics, persuades herself that he will eventually take her to Paris, despite his unwavering denials. Clym, on his part, who invests Eustacia with mystery and romance but also the malleability, dependency, and obedience he expects of a woman, persuades himself that the restless girl will settle down to become a contented wife. That she has an educated, if overimaginative, mind, a philosophical thoughtfulness he doesn't appear to possess, and a fervent—sometimes obsessive—desire to "be in the world" is entirely ignored.

The narrator is initially optimistic about Clym. But this dissipates (as does Clym's centrality as the title bearer of the novel). Readers are led to expect rather more of this hero than he yields, in terms of his sensitivity to the condition of fellow humans, his capacity to love, and his philosophical depth. Hardy creates in Clym a precursor to Jude in humanitarian outlook on life and futuristic thinking. But none of this develops with any force.

Frequently, characters begin to take over and shape their author's thinking—a hazard of serial writing. This appears to be the case here. Eustacia tends to eclipse Clym, who remains distanced from the reader in a way that she does not. An added complication is that Eustacia has already occupied center stage by the time Clym arrives on the scene. The narrator makes every effort to build up reader interest in Clym's advent, but he remains a pale figure in contrast to the two strong women at his side, Eustacia and his own mother, Mrs. Yeobright.

With his mother, Clym is in total affinity, we are told. The two enjoy a rare and wonderful understanding, complete empathy. Again, the narrator makes every effort to emphasize this, but where is the evidence? Where does it show? The scenes with Eustacia and Clym have a powerful impact—the crossed tracks, the deep attraction, intellectual exploration, mutual respect, intense disagreements, light banter, and the sexual desire. But between mother and son, affinity is nowhere.

Mrs. Yeobright

Mrs. Yeobright features importantly in *The Return of the Native*. She looms larger than a minor character. Representing the stereotypical matriarch of the Victorian overworld of the novel—maternally possessive, efficient in her household management, ambitious for her son, manipulative in her protectiveness, and actively class conscious—she functions as the primary agency of class division in *The Return of the Native*. This is fully in character. As a young woman she married "down"—to a farmer—and is never quite reconciled to the fact that Eustacia is now marrying "down" to her son.

These power relations inevitably add a strong undertow to the conflicting courses in the Egdon world (class difference, in Hardy, provides a strong surge of energy, a charge to power relations, and also clads the "other" with the allure of unattainability). Indeed, Mrs. Yeobright's actions fuel much of the social instability in which the fluctuations of sexual desire are an inherent part. Pivotal in her niece's, Thomasin's, fortunes, she first forbids her marriage banns in a most public and humiliating manner and then alienates Wildeve to the point where Thomasin arranges to marry him in a clandestine manner—unsupported, alone, and unhappy.

In the meantime, Mrs. Yeobright has been encouraging Venn's attentions to her niece, regardless of the fact that Thomasin has eyes only for Wildeve. No doubt the older woman is wise to the mismatch between Wildeve and Thomasin, and, of course, Venn did once have respectable origins. She is also wise to the rumors about Eustacia and Wildeve and appalled by Thomasin's failed church wedding—a dreadful blight to her reputation. The villagers, too, are mortified that Wildeve and Thomasin's celebration on their purported wedding night went wrong. Then, finally, there is the tittle-tattle about the church wedding excursion itself. Will Thomasin now *have* to marry Wildeve?

At the same time, Mrs. Yeobright's wisdom doesn't appear to extend to psychological insights into the young people in her care. Opposition rarely cools the hot passion of youth. Likewise, in her attempts to obstruct Clym's involvement with Eustacia, Mrs. Yeobright simply inflames his love for the younger woman.

Ultimately it is she, the mother, in her unannounced arrival (ironically to make peace) at her son's matrimonial home at Alderworth who triggers the breakup of his marriage. Indeed, this woman has a good deal of power. Interestingly, though, she does not have the last word.

That Clym is the only major character to survive and is given the last word, so to speak, as itinerant preacher, seems to resolve the Hebraic-Hellenist opposition that serves as a major motif throughout the novel. So, does Christianity triumph over Greek joyousness? In 1912, Hardy, famously, added a Note to Book 6, "After courses," as follows:

> the writer may state here that the original conception of the story did not design a marriage between Thomasin and Venn. He was to have retained his isolated and weird character to the last, and to have disappeared mysteriously from the heath, nobody knowing whither—Thomasin remaining a widow. But certain circumstances of serial publication led to a change of intent. Readers can therefore choose between the endings, and those with an austere artistic code can assume the more consistent conclusion to be the true one.

Was there, then, editorial interference enforcing a happy-marriage ending and a converted Clym? Was this alternative ending also intended to mute the series of tragedies, perhaps? There is, in fact, a good case to be made for redeeming Clym but in a purely factitious ending ("falsified" would be rather too strong). This (factitiousness) was Hardy's forte, after all. Very few of his earlier endings are what they appear to be: it may be an inapt allusion (end of *Far From the Madding Crowd*) or the subversive move, in *A Laodicean*, of revealing Charlotte's love letter to Paula in the selfsame moment of her marriage to Somerset. Or it may be the last words given to Grace (*The Woodlanders*) or to Elizabeth-Jane (*The Mayor of Casterbridge*)—whatever the method or the device, readers are invited to question the convincingness of the seeming happy ending. Indeed, even as early as *Under the Greenwood Tree*, avowedly the "happiest" of his novels, Hardy subverts the thrust of denouement by revealing at the very last moment that there are secrets Fancy Day will not tell.

Whatever Hardy's "original conception of the story" in *The Return of the Native*, its outcome didn't initially appear to his publishers to be felicitous. A triumph of Christianity together with a proselyte preacher in the denouement would have encouraged many a publisher, but no publisher was encouraged. Had Hardy, even in desperation, given his publishers the news that there would be a "getting married and living happily ever after" ending with "Thomasin … the good heroine … ultimately marry[ing] the reddleman, & live[ing] happily" (*Letters*, VI.52–53), there would surely have been considerably more editorial interest in this novel.

When Hardy wrote those words to his illustrator in February 1878 it was evidently too late for Leslie Stephen and his ilk. They had already rejected the novel, which presumably had only the original "artistic" ending in view. By February

1878 Hardy had made substantial inroads into the story, which was probably completed the following month, in March 1878.[7] Clearly, he had now abandoned his original conception of the story and had sealed Clym's fate as tragic-hero-turned-preacher, but when he actually made that decision is not known.

Publication politics no doubt played a significant part in Clym's transformation. Quite apart from the fact that it remains colorless and unconvincing, there are two sound aesthetic reasons to support the idea that transformation was not Hardy's preference. The first to consider is that preachers in Hardy are very much an enfeebled class and are in the main, drawn unsympathetically. Second, there may be agnostics in plenty among Hardy's major characters, but the self-professed believers tend to belong to the laboring classes or to charlatans such as Alec d'Uberville.[8] Clym fits nowhere in this aesthetic scheme of things.

ROLE OF MINOR CHARACTERS

In his early narratology Hardy offers his readers an array of Grundyan censors; these implied censors diminish with time as his growing reputation empowers him to speak with a greater degree of candor. The device of the implied censor, omnipresent in most Victorian extratextual sources (newspapers, magazines), was almost invariably directed at women—presumably as a means of social control in keeping with the proliferation of behavior manuals. In Hardy, the censor device helps to redeem many an authorial indiscretion (notably, his omitting to stand in judgment of the wayward heroine).

In *The Return of the Native*, a relatively early work, Diggory Venn takes on this role: in his creeping and crawling spying activities, he is the very embodiment of the Victorian censor. Typically, he acts and speaks with that judgmental voice customarily directed by Hardy's Grundyan bystander narrators at the nonconforming heroine.

Venn is also invoked as a punitive figure in a wider sense—the Egdon community uses him to scare misbehaving children: "The Reddleman will come for you!" He is itinerant, and in common with most road traders such as tinkers and gypsies, he is an easy target for suspicion and blame (albeit that his family came from the Egdon region). He is, of course, creepy to look at, being stained with the red clay (ferrous oxide) of the reddling compound he trades. (Reddle is used to mark, as in color-coding, the ram on his underbelly, ultimately to stain the pregnant female.) Venn, in turn, preys on the sexually-active woman—Eustacia, tormented as she is with sexual hunger. Is he the latter-day equivalent of the sexual predator?

Stripped of all this mystique, Venn is flat, characterless, and dull, as perhaps befits an allegorical character. Perhaps his most interesting act in the entire novel is to conceal himself with turves so he can crawl unnoticed to spy on the unsuspecting lovers, Eustacia and Wildeve, or, on another occasion, to take a potshot at Wildeve with his gun. His symbolic, allegorical role (expressing thoughts and ideas) remains opaque, however, subordinated to his watchdog role monitoring

Eustacia. Perhaps the most transparent of signifiers is that Venn bears a demonic guise—in terms of allegory, this brings him closely into line with Gide's devil (or Shakespeare's Iago), who operates in guises of plausibility.

Venn's transformation at the end of the novel is, however, less than plausible. Rather, it adds to the factitiousness of Hardy's alternative ending. Suddenly shocked to see this "ordinary Christian countenance" standing before her, Thomasin gives a little scream and cries out, "Oh, how you frightened me…. I thought you were the ghost of yourself" (VI.i). Hardy must have silently chuckled at the concealed irony of this statement, given his original ending to the novel, in which Venn disappears, never to return. In the authorial imagination at least, this is most aptly the "ghost" of the reddleman.

Thomasin, next in importance among the secondary characters, was originally intended to be Clym's sister. She is now Clym's cousin, Mrs. Yeobright's niece, and lives at Bloom's End. Vestiges of the "sister" still remain, however, in the text. A good example is Thomasin's deep concern about bringing shame to the family home when her marriage plans are overturned, matched by Clym's anxiety about the scandal this might create—although to his credit he is more upset about Thomasin's feelings of humiliation. He is remarkably ardent about this issue, quite the man of action, even opposing his mother's wishes. This is less the reaction of a cousin than of a closely protective brother. Incidentally, at the composition stage of the novel, Thomasin spends a week away with her assumed husband (Wildeve) before discovering that the marriage license is invalid. Hardy cut this "dangerous" passage, but the "scandal" lingers on in the minds of the characters just the same.

Thomasin's function, in terms of plot, is to complement Eustacia; she is everything Eustacia is not. She has a pragmatic approach to marriage, whereas Eustacia would do without marriage altogether; she is quietly domesticated (and becomes a mother by the end of the story), docile, and obedient, where Eustacia hotly rebels against her enforced seclusion. And where Eustacia passionately seeks to be a "splendid woman," Thomasin stores apples in the loft.

Wildeve, once an engineer, is now an innkeeper. Mrs. Yeobright abhors his class and trade rather than the man himself. Torn between his intense attraction to Eustacia and his affection for Thomasin, Wildeve never really settles for either. He is the foil to Clym, who has less passion and more intellectual zest (some contemporary critics felt that *The Return of the Native* appealed too much to the intellect and not enough to the emotions).

Among the minor characters who provide commentary on the action, the most significant are the "watchers"—Susan Nunsuch and her little son Johnny. Nunsuch is the only true witch on Egdon, with her incantations, wax images stuck with pins, and her attempts to physically injure Eustacia, whom she fears. Johnny, at risk of becoming spellbound by Eustacia, according to his mother, *is* mesmerized by her, acting as her go-between and servant, but he is not exactly her slave—she pays him for his labor. Johnny, as the keeper of the fire, is unwittingly implicated in Eustacia's clandestine meetings with Wildeve. He is also the witness to Mrs. Yeobright's demise. He plays the part of the innocent abroad and offers a rare glimpse, in Hardy, of a child's view of a rather baffling adult world.

Young Charley, who is employed as Captain Drew's (Vye's) factotum, serves a similar function of naïf, highlighting Eustacia's allure and lovability: he doesn't simply hang upon her every word but also watches over her with gentle devotion. Captain Drew (Vye), on the other hand, leaves her to her own devices, genially amused by her exploits, especially her participation in the mummers' play as "one of the bucks," as he calls it.

The rustics in *The Return of the Native* sustain a backcloth of timeworn traditions and simple honest values. They speak candidly (albeit superstitiously) about people and events without censure or class divisiveness, and if they were criticized by the occasional contemporary as being unrealistically cultivated, they cannot be accused of prudishness. Their banter includes some teasing of Christian Cantle's homosexuality—"maphrotight" being a colloquial way of referring to his hermaphrodite nature and bisexual orientation.

THEMES

A central motif in this novel is the opposition between the inner Victorian world of the novel and the Hellenic spirit embodied in both Eustacia and the Egdon paradigm.[9] This is known among scholars as the Hellenic-Hebraic opposition. The disjunction is powerfully evoked by the personification that is Egdon juxtaposed with the life of its inhabitants. Egdon's highest elevation, Rainbarrow, is shaped from an imaginative amalgam of three barrows unified and centralized within the landscape (in actuality the barrows are spatially separated and peripheral to the heath). Why is this particular construct significant? Because geographical heights lend themselves to ideological emblems: temples in Greece, castles in Europe, and flags of glory universally. Such elevations are patterned in architectural forms—the spires of churches, the domes of court houses, and the towers of cathedrals.

The ideological clash between Hellenistic polytheism, Greek joyousness, and the pursuit of happiness on the one hand, and Christian monotheism, self-redemption, and the pursuit of godliness on the other is emblematized by the dramatic entity that is the Atlantean brow of Rainbarrow in the first instance and the Hades of netherward Egdon in the second. Where Eustacia crowns the former as the "perfect finish" to its "architectural" mass, Venn, the Mephistophelian devil, emerges from the latter.

Hardy returns to the motif of Greek versus Hebraic human values in *Jude the Obscure*—the oppression of the human spirit is a universal theme for Hardy. The force of oppression usually has its origin in social codes and practices, but latterly, especially in his poetry, the agency of human suffering, misery, and oppression is the Christian God—Hardy's "Immanent Will," or Prime Mover—who fails, in a lack of consciousness, to address the human condition.

An embellishment of this theme in *The Return of the Native* is the overthrow of the status quo. Again, this is a theme pursued by Hardy in many of his novels. Clym fails, just as Angel and Jude fail, to bring enlightenment into the community. More overtly, the oppression of women struggling in a man-made world for free self-expression, autonomy, equal opportunity, and personal liberty remains unresolved. As *The Return of the Native* makes clear, the world is not yet ready for change. Hardy never abandons this theme.

The Egdon paradigm embodies several of these aims. But whereas the human struggle is frequently precipitate or mismanaged or quite simply mistimed, Egdon solemnly watches and waits. Where Clym fails to achieve his mission and where Wildeve and Eustacia fail to find fulfillment, Egdon awaits the right moment. "Almost crystallised to natural products by long continuance," the peak of the natural world soars "above its natural level" and while the world sleeps

> the heath appeared slowly to wake and listen. Every night its Titanic form seemed to await something; but it had waited thus, unmoved, during so many centuries, through the crises of so many things, that it could only be imagined to await one more crisis—the final overthrow. (I.i)

Within the community, at a gossipy level, "overthrow" is the talk of the natives. The temporal setting is midcentury—the time of social revolution in Europe. Eustacia's Paris is in the throes of political turbulence; Grandfer Cantle recalls the Napoleonic Wars; other locals discuss the matrimonial upheavals of Wildeve and Thomasin. All is on the brink.

The main theme, then, is, in a complex way, ideology—its elements of myth and its driving cultural forces. To what extent are these characters driven by ideology? For those who subscribe to a Christian ideology—represented by Mrs. Yeobright—the world is divided on a self-salvation basis between the deserving and the undeserving, between one class and another. For those who are attracted to a pagan ideology—Eustacia, for example—the world is an arena for anarchy: the defiant will protest freedom to the bitter end, or die for it, as she is willing to do. For Clym, returning from Paris and evidently touched by that city's socialist activities, and for Thomasin, who adheres to traditional ways notably the ideals of conventional marriage, there is no meeting point whatsoever. These two cousins barely have a single conversation throughout the entire novel.

In line with the idealism of social or matrimonial relations, there is also the perennial theme of romance. In Hardy's earlier novels the hero takes on some of the allure of the natural world in which he works. Oak, in *Far From the Madding Crowd*, is the classic example. In *The Return of the Native* there is no parallel: Clym, the "native" and therefore the most eligible contender, swears to a love of Egdon, but there is nothing to show for this. Unlike Oak, he does not earn his bread by husbandry and displays no affinity with the world of nature. Clym is an intellectual hero. His match with the highly imaginative Eustacia is therefore mentally energetic. Elements of antiromanticism creep in, as ever in Hardy, when

prosaic reality displaces the dream. This antiromanticism is thematically reinforced by the one (doomed) marriage that survives long enough to have issue,
that of Thomasin and Wildeve.

Hardy, as is commonly known, was irritated by romantic plots with happy
endings: the conventional Victorian denouement—getting married and living
happily ever after—imposed a perniciously false coloration on life, within the
novel and beyond in the ideology of the culture. Predictably, given the rejection
of editors when he submitted *The Return of the Native* for serial publication, he
feigned an appearance of decorum: he would provide a conventional marriage for
Thomasin, but Eustacia the wild would flee her ties and remain unclaimed at the
last. Evidently, Thomasin, the conventionally "good" heroine, was dispensable
in terms of sacrificing her to market needs and those prevailing ideologies that
dictated what was "good" for women and what "good" women did.

Generally, a pervasive theme for Hardy is that of the clash between town and
country, or between native and alien intruder. There are aspects of this clash in
The Return of the Native with Clym's rejection of life in one of the "great arteries of the world," Paris, and Eustacia's longing to leave Egdon for that very city.
The clash is embodied, in effect, in the conflicts between these two. Conflicts
are complicated, as here, where he who rejects the city still dreams of it, and
she who rejects the country is deeply attached to it. For Eustacia is no intruder,
despite the efforts of the heath community to make her one. In her loathing of
her starkly lonely environment, she remains the only character to roam the terrain constantly. Equally, she is the only one directly engaged with the elemental
forces of the heath, drawing water from wells and building fires. And finally, it
is she, not Clym, who is spiritually reabsorbed into Egdon "as if she were drawn
into the Barrow by a hand from beneath" (V.vii)—ultimately to drown in its
waters.

Theoretically, given Hardy's predilection for this theme of outsider-insider opposition, there should be a greater clash between the intruder, Venn, and the "insider"
natives. True, he attempts to displace Eustacia, the native girl (in the original urtext, the holograph manuscript, she is born on Egdon), but there is no parallel clash
between Venn and the other natives, aside from his crucial part in the misappro-
priation of Mrs. Yeobright's money. In sum, this particular opposition is shadowy,
vestigial only, in *The Return of the Native*.

However, the title of *The Return of the Native* is interesting in this context. It raises the question as to who or what the "native" might be. At one level, the nativity,
the genesis of Hardy's Wessex, is, for the first time in his novels, manifest. Once an
ancient kingdom during the Heptarchy, Wessex now "returns," but as an imaginative
construct. And in a curiously elemental way, this native land (Hardy's natal land)
"returns" its most notable denizens to its own body, so to speak. Clym, once engaged
in commercial work in Paris, ends his days as a solitary preacher within its confines;
Eustacia and Wildeve are drowned by its waters; and Mrs. Yeobright is poisoned by
a creature indigenous to Wessex—the adder. The question then arises, how is the
"native" determined? Simplistically by the return of Clym, more complexly by the

return of Wessex, or thematically by the return of some of Egdon's denizens to its own earth? Possibly the answer lies in an amalgam of all three.

SYMBOLS, ALLUSIONS, AND FIGURATIVE LANGUAGE

The Return of the Native was composed during Hardy's happiest time—with hindsight he spoke of this brief period in his first marriage as "the Sturminster idyll." Idyllic *The Return of the Native* is not, although it is harmonious in terms of its form and structure. The symbolic qualities of Egdon Heath are, in particular, most finely balanced. The manner in which this microcosmic universe personifies the condition of mankind—its wars and upheavals, its capacity to struggle and endure, and its periods of stress and moments of sublimity—extends to natural-world personifications of the principals.

There is, to take one important example, the aspect of reciprocity in the Egdon construct, most apparent when the heath appears "a near relation of night, and when night showed itself an apparent tendency to gravitate together"—"the sombre stretch of mounds and hollows seem[ing] to rise and meet the evening gloom in pure sympathy" (I.i.10). This aspect of reciprocity operates at several levels in the novel, not just in terms of atmospherics. First, there is the beautifully balanced ecosystem. This consists primarily of heathcroppers—ponies—that are sustained by the furze (fodder) that is sustained, in turn, by the sandy soil that is, in turn, the habitat of efts, snakes, and the multitude of teeming insects, some of which feed off the droppings of the ponies, and so on.

Second, there is the biodiversity of the heath, the interdependence of man and nature going back beyond the Bronze Age. Third, there is the reciprocity of human beings engaged in sexual relationships. This, of course, Hardy could not openly delineate for reasons of censorship. Taboos are culturally specific. Sexuality was a taboo subject, and most problematic of all was female sexuality. For most of his contemporaries, prior to the emergence of the science of sexology during the late nineteenth century, female sexuality remained a legitimate mode of discourse *only* within the medical context of disease[10]—mental or physical dysfunction. Candid as he wished to be, Hardy had to school himself in judiciousness during his early career as a novelist. Male characters, yes! Typically, as in *Far From the Madding Crowd,* the unmarried young male such as Troy can be portrayed as sexually active with impunity. He is a rascal and he is wild, but he is not an unmentionable object. Nor is he silenced, rendered mute, or without a voice, as is his sexual partner, Fanny Robin, of whom any passing mention was heavily censored by editor Leslie Stephen.

Thus any suggestion, even the smallest hint, of female desire had to be embedded in metaphorical or symbolic mode, much as it is in poetic discourse. Accordingly, in customary style, Hardy turns to the natural-object metaphor (figurations of Egdon) in order to evoke the sexual nature of his heroine. A fine example is to be found in the hermaphroditic image of the mollusk (snail) that "couples" the lovers Eustacia and Wildeve as they meet to make love in the twilight of the heath:

> Their black figures sank and disappeared from against the sky. They were as two horns which the sluggish heath had put forth from its crown, like a mollusk, and had now again drawn in. (I.ix)

"Horny" is very much a modern, twentieth-century term, but there is no doubt that Hardy is conjuring an image here that points to the mutual sexual arousal of both the male and the female. The metonym "horns" serves aptly to convey twinned erectile protuberances and therefore heightened sexual appetites in *both* his lovers.

This concept of mutuality goes further still. Imaginatively reinforcing the latent "force" of Eustacia's nature by rendering her combative and sturdy, her mouth "cut as the point of a spear" (69), Hardy, in turn, complements her latent warrior quality by endowing Clym with attributes that are passive and soft. For Clym, "the beauty here visible" is meditative, not quite "thoughtworn" and born of "placid pupilage" (II.vi). By contrast, this woman of "Tartarean dignity," this "Artemis," "Athena," this "Hera" (I.vii) is constantly restless, perpetually on the move, and endlessly roaming. Her confined and confining world so maddeningly deprives her of sensory experience that she is driven to pull the thick skeins of her hair through the gorse, the prickly tufts of "Ulex Europeaeus," just to gain the sensation of torn roots and stimulating entanglement (I.vii).

Still employing the natural-world symbolism of Egdon, but this time to stress the meddlesome nature of the reddleman, Hardy turns again to the heath's fauna. However, in this instance the figuration is that of a blind tunneling animal—the mole. Already aligned with the devil (in earlier episodes), Venn, caught up in his Peeping Tom habits, now covers his body with pieces of sod, and as he creeps along "the turves upon his back crept with him … approaching thus, it was as though he burrowed underground" (I.ix). Legend has it that the devil burrows underground, and, aptly enough, in the human political arena, a spy is nicknamed a mole.

In Clym's case, the unvarying, unchanging character of Egdon aptly mirrors his inability to effect any changes in the static social community into which he was born. Where Eustacia embodies the wild beauty as encountered in the sighting of the rare bird, "the courser," on Egdon, who was killed by a trophy hunter, Clym embodies the wasteland that is Egdon's other face. He returns from Paris to the rural community with just a tang of foreign, alluring, exciting modernity. But the social conditions he seeks to reshape on Egdon, that "bucolic placidity" of a superstitious rural society, ultimately shape him instead. His vision and his intellectual modernity are as myopic as his physical vision. Despite avowing that he can "rebel, in high Promethean fashion, against the gods and fate" (250), Clym is as mentally fettered as Prometheus—the Greek mythological hero bound, in perpetuity, by chains, as a punishment for giving fire to mortals.

It is worth noting, at this point, that the most significant of punitive symbols attached to a man-made structure on Egdon is the inn sign of the Quiet Woman Inn. The figure portrayed is headless. The resonance of this sign, a woman decapitated and rendered forever mute, permeates this novel where it punctuates the narrative at least 19 times.

Allusions to pagan deities in *The Return of the Native* are mainly reserved for Eustacia and range across a wide spectrum, indicating something of her infinite variety. She is aligned with Artemis, the hunting goddess, who is also the goddess of war and chastity; with Athena, a warrior who additionally personifies wisdom and fertility while abhorring marriage (apt for Eustacia); and with Hera, the chief goddess of sexuality. The imperious Eustacia possesses "the raw material of a divinity" rather than the qualities of a "model woman." Predictably, her reading material and role models are also warriors—unconventional in an age when young women were reputed to be romancing their minds by reading novels. Indeed, so unconventional did she appear to Hardy's illustrator, Arthur Hopkins, that he depicted her in an early installment as masculine. A dreadfully disappointed Hardy asked, as tactfully as he could, if she could be represented in the future, "more youthful in face, supple in figure, & in general with a little more roundness & softness" (*Letters*, VI.52).

At a wider level of signification, Hardy's pagan symbolism serves to distinguish and separate the Hellenic Eustacia from the Hebraic community of Yeobrights and reddlemen in which Clym will eventually settle to become a preacher. For Victorians the Hebraic-Hellenic opposition was of pervasive cultural interest;[11] for Hardy it becomes a paradigm of conflicting social relations. *The Return of the Native* explores this paradigm in greater detail than do any of the other Wessex novels, with the possible exception of *Jude the Obscure*.

Egdon itself is alluded to in Greek mythological terms as bearing a Titanic form that, again, carries pluralistic meanings. The Titans were not only earth giants but also children of the sky, and after they overthrew Uranus, they were consigned as outcasts to the Underworld. To complement the "Greek," Hardy provides a biblical allusion, speaking of Egdon as an "Ishmaelitish thing"—an outcast of a different order. (After the birth of Isaac, Ishmael—a name also given to a follower of a branch of Shia, Islam—was banished by his father into the wilderness [Genesis 25:15].) In like vein, where the narrator, in one breath, alludes to the Mænades (priestesses of Dionysus), in another—a few paragraphs later—come the Philistines (1 Samuel 17:6). By the same token, juxtaposing the Hebraic and the Hellenic, the question of truth is given first to the Greek truth-sayer, Socrates, and then, in an about-turn, to the biblical interrogator, Pontius Pilate—"What is truth?" (John 18:38). The implication is that by virtue of context, a potential dialogue is *possible* within the orbit of ideological opposition.

Hardy is liberal with his allusions. And in *The Return of the Native*, as in all the Wessex novels, there is a fair sprinkling of references to painters and writers both ancient and modern[12] as also to other notables such as medical experts, prime ministers, and even (in a signal warning about Venn) to "Farmer Lynch," popularly known as the instigator of irregular acts of summary justice during the American War of Independence. These allusions and analogues, as extratextual forays, perform a variety of functions. They add depth and complexity to the text proper and to those in the know to the educated, they afford a bright moment of recognition: author, narrator, and reader are in collusion—good neighbors all, greeting each other in the byways of paragraphs and sentences.

Perhaps, though, one of the least discussed aspects of this kind of extratextuality is the manner in which it breaks boundaries. Socrates and Pontius Pilate may have been separated by time and clime and, of course, by text, but for one extraordinary moment they are aligned in the same discourse. This suggests that the narrator seeks to shape the reader's reading, to pursue not just entertainment but also knowledge and understanding. By virtue of an association of ideas, allusions and symbols purposefully complicate any given narrative moment, scene, or characterization. Taking Venn as a prime example, do we wish to be convinced by the surface text— by the seeming congeniality of the figure? Or do we wish to explore the allusions and analogues much as do pioneers on the open trail who pick up clues to a new destination, to a better understanding of the unfamiliar and strange?

SETTING

Of all Hardy's novels, the one to generate the most topographical interest was *The Return of the Native*. This—Hardy's sixth published novel—is the quintessential Wessex novel; its internal setting, Egdon Heath, encapsulates the very spirit and foundation of Hardy's microcosmic universe, as Wessex ultimately came to be understood. And it was in 1878, with the publication of *The Return of the Native*, that Hardy created his first Wessex map. On October 1, 1878, he wrote the following letter to Smith, Elder & Co., the publishers of the first volume edition:

Dear Sirs,

I enclose for your inspection a Sketch of the supposed scene in which the "Return of the Native" is laid—copied from the one I used in writing the story—& my suggestion is that we place an engraving of it as frontispiece to the first volume. Unity of place is so seldom preserved in novels that a map of the scene of action is as a rule impracticable: but since the present story affords an opportunity of doing so I am of opinion that it would be a desirable novelty, likely to increase a reader's interest. I may add that a critic once remarked to me that nothing could give such reality to a tale as a map of this sort: & I myself have often felt the same thing.

The expense of the engraving would not, I imagine, be very great. In the drawing for the book it would be desirable to shade the hills more fully than I have done in the sketch.

Hoping that you will be disposed to give the suggestion a trial, I am, Dear Sirs.

Yours faithfully

Thomas Hardy
(*Letters*, V1.61)

This letter to his publishers was the first of many to come on the subject of maps. And indeed, Smith, Elder & Co. did print Hardy's delightfully nonspecific but curiously corporeal[13] map of Egdon as frontispiece to the first edition. However, Macmillan's Wessex Novels edition of 1895 replaced Hardy's map with another, titled "The Wessex of The Novels" (first published in *The Bookman*). This appears to be a simplified copy of Hardy's own exquisite drawing of "The Wessex of the Novels & Poems" but lacks the character and finesse of Hardy's own map. He was not at all pleased with it and asked one of his colleagues, John Lane, not to reprint it. Unfortunately it was reprinted, and by some strange anomaly, it features today as the frontispiece to the Penguin first edition.

"Unity of place" was then of paramount importance to Hardy (and was enhanced in later revision). From prehistoric Bronze Age burial mounds[14] to ancient Roman roads to the politicization of the land—notably the early-warning system formed by hilltop beacons—Egdon unites,[15] in a combination and rearrangement of these features, the entire region within its compass.

To elaborate a little, the age-old beacon fires (possibly dating back to prehistoric times) would be ignited on coastal lookout points. The barrow vigilantes would pick up the alarm, ignite their own fires, and transmit the invasion signal hilltop to hilltop, to regions of the capital (London) many miles away, where it would mobilize the British Admiralty. Legend has it that on a good day the beacon alert would travel from the South Dorset coast to London within the hour. Be that as it may, although these beacons are not deployed in *The Return of the Native*, they do form part of the cultural and historical backcloth to the novel, thus stretching the reader's consciousness deep into time and space.

By the time of the midcentury (the internal dating of the novel) the Napoleonic Wars would have been over, but invasion fears still exist in the living memory of some of the Egdon worthies, such as Grandfer Cantle. The point here is that time, historical time, is very much united with present time not only in the Egdon construct but also in the minds of Hardy's characters.

This aspect of temporal unity, or rather, continuity, is made manifest in various other ways. The setting of hilltop fires, for example, has been appropriated over time by a slightly different counteraction tradition—the locals (in common with their compatriots universally) now celebrate the annual effigy burning on November 5 of Guy Fawkes (leader of an abortive terrorist attempt to blow up the Houses of Parliament in 1605). In sum, the bonfire motif in *The Return of the Native* encompasses a conglomeration of traditions and political activities, spanning time and space in both a literal and a figurative way. These activities also incorporate ancient pagan solstice rites; hence with the elders of the community resurrecting past threats of Napoleonic invasion with a sure sense of their ongoing relevance and the more superstitious folk raising ghosts, demons, and witch lore at every opportunity, the Egdon world is clearly united in its sense of its own past.

In terms of unity of place, with the return of the native, Clym Yeobright, the community is complete and entire unto itself. The remains of the Via Ikeniana, the Roman Road, which runs from heath end to heath end, mysteriously carries no traffic. According to Hardy's map, it comes from the east and leads out to the west. Only the reddleman enters or exits by the Roman Road.

As we have seen, Egdon embodies the pagan spirit of pre-Roman times, thus expanding the compass of the internal setting to greater (universal) proportions. That Hardy links his female principal, Eustacia Vye, with ancient Hellenic deities, as if she were imbued with the pagan spirit of primeval Egdon, intensifies the sense that she who dreams of warriors and revolution and who resists bondage in marriage will and must remain estranged from the "Victorian" overworld in which she finds herself trapped.[16]

Then, too, there is the aspect of Egdon's predominance. Of all the Wessex novels, there is none to compare with *The Return of the Native* for sheer atmospheric, elemental supremacy. The very center and apex of the Wessex world, Egdon is anthropomorphized—human characteristics are projected onto it—to embody a whole complex of human values and traits, from endurance to inconstancy, reciprocity to caprice, lightness of being to darkness of spirit, and a good deal more. Indeed, these moods and characteristics shape, in turn, the thoughts and actions of the heathfolk in profound ways. There is death, of course, at the hands of Egdon, just as there is life and continuity in the form of a little girl born of the union of Thomasin and Wildeve and named after Eustacia. There are occupational hazards (Clym's blindness, exacerbated by the close cropping of furze), and there are tragedies caused by isolation, by the distances that have to be crossed in attempts at communication ("crossed" communications in the case of mother and son, husband and wife), not to mention a whole series of mishaps arising from turbulence, both social and atmospheric.

There is an absence of agricultural or architectural interest to draw the eye away from a landscape in which man and nature interact as one—a rare absence in Hardy. The only architectural construct of any significance is, in fact, part nature, part man made. This is Rainbarrow (or Blackbarrow in the first edition)—a majestic tumulus, Bronze Age burial ground, constructed on Egdon's highest elevation. In the opening scenes, Eustacia is seen silhouetted against the dark night sky as the perfect and "necessary finish" to the "architectural" brow of Rainbarrow. At closure she is drawn down from this regal position, back into the bowels of the heath, to drown in the rushing waters of the weir.

The close detailing of Egdon's atmospherics remains one of Hardy's greatest literary achievements. Two contemporary critics, the Folletts, while noticing, in general, the "half-inaudible discord" of Hardy's endings—that they leave a "taste" that is "bitter-sweet, like that of life"—considered his greatest literary quality to be his scientific detachment. In this, they regarded *The Return of the Native* as exemplary. The internal setting of the novel, they wrote, manifests in quite a unique way a "microcosm of personality," which in turn sets the stage and the mood "for the interplay of almost cosmic forces."[17]

Egdon itself is a mood. Noted for its function as central character to the novel, it personifies the mood of immanence (of things inherent—about to come into being). Musician and composer Gustav Holst (of *The Planets* fame), captivated by *The Return of the Native*, walked the Dorset heathlands just before Hardy died, to soak up yet more atmosphere for his symphony. Capturing Egdon's mood and sense of immanence in his musical composition "Egdon Heath," Holst moves with power and subtlety from the adagio of the quiet emergency of the novel's opening scenes through the poco allegro of nether regions alternately light and dark, restless and sudden, gloomy and glad, to an andante maestoso that aptly conveys that sensation so palpably felt in *The Return of the Native* of threshold, of all things verging on the brink. The brink of somewhere or something unknowable—forever poised.

Egdon Heath, created for *The Return of the Native*, will go on to feature later in other works by Hardy, notably his epic poem, *The Dynasts*; his second-to-last novel, *Tess of the d'Urbervilles*; his short story "The Fiddler of the Reels"; and also in assorted poems:

The Roman Road runs straight and bare
As the pale parting-line in hair
Across the heath.[18]

ALTERNATIVE READING: PSYCHOANALYTIC CRITICISM

The Oedipal conflict between mother and son, Mrs. Yeobright and Clym, has been well aired in psychoanalytic readings of *The Return of the Native*. In the 1878 edition this motif was more opaque (enhanced in later editions). Hardy knew his Sophocles, of course, and may have had the incestuous aspects of the Sophoclean drama in mind, but this is pure speculation. Certainly there are resonances. Clym's father is absent (although Clym didn't kill him), and his mother has a deep hold over him. Even though he defies her in marrying Eustacia, her death destroys him: "Whatever she was in other people's memories, in his she was the sublime saint whose radiance even his tenderness for Eustacia could not obscure" (VI.iv).

One psychoanalytic explanation for this "sublime" incarnation would be bereavement theory. Guilt at the death of a loved one can take the form of idolizing the object in death where they are not so idolized in life. Idolatry effects a psychological process of separation, of distancing. To idolize, to place another human on a pedestal, is to displace them from equal standing with the self. Equal standing implies closer identification, empathy, and a more in-depth, sincere understanding of the other. In contrast, an idol is rarefied, out of range. In certain religious practices idolatry is discouraged: it distances the object of worship from the sinning mortal who needs models, not idols.

Clym's idolization (and idealization) of his mother in death remains inconsistent with his actual relationship with her in life. Guilt is a form of self-compensation. The guilty self seeks punishment (again, back to religious practice—confession is intended to absolve the soul from guilt; atonement for the act is made by a token self-flagellation through prayer). Punishment can take the form of berating the self (as with Clym) or blaming the self (as with Clym).He appears not to mourn her loss. His focus is solely on her sublime saintliness and his own culpability. Yet, in life, she was to him no sublime saint. He first opposes her by refusing to return to Paris and second by making Eustacia his wife.

Nevertheless, the mother-son bond is strong, and in psychoanalytic criticism, the fact of Clym's loss of sight leads to renewed parallels with the Sophoclean drama. When Oedipus learns the truth, that he has been married to his own (unknowing) mother, Jocasta, he seeks her out only to find her dead. She has hanged herself. At this point he blinds himself. He takes the shoulder pins from her dress and pierces his eyes.

In Hardy, Clym—married to Eustacia and no longer living with his mother—is already going blind (not helped by reading books by candlelight), what Hardy calls "opthalmia" (245). The symbolism of the son's blindness in connection with a close (incestuous) maternal bond is associated with self-castration in psychoanalytic theory. The idea is that optical blinding has sexual ramifications—usually impotency or castration. There is even a medical condition related to all this—an ailment called "eye floaters" or poor vision associated with excessive sexual activity, specifically with overejaculation.

Freud picked up on these ideas and formulated the Oedipus complex, which argues, in part, that separation from a domineering mother can cause anxiety sufficient to render the son impotent. Hardy gives no indication that this is Clym's dilemma—and although Eustacia does say, in a moment of heated dispute with him about his "social failure," that "I fear we are cooling.... And how madly we loved two months ago" (IV.ii), this does not appear to be anything more than a sad acknowledgment that their "in love" phase has waned.

Recent psychoanalytical critical attention has given little attention to the other characters in this novel. *Literature, Science, Psychoanalysis, 1830–1970* makes a brief foray into the subject with a glance at egoism and a query as to why Eustacia's story does not offer "a model for thinking ... about how one acquires a vision of community, or about individual moral agency" (Small, 79), but the anomalous nature of this query bears little fruit.[19] Eustacia is, after all, wholly hermetic, and the last thing on her mind (or on her author's) is the "vision of community." This is Clym's concern, and as the narrator shows, his vision is defective. There is clearly room for a psychoanalytical study of Eustacia, especially in light of Hardy's revisions to the urtext (the holographic manuscript), which have, to date, received no substantial feminist or psychoanalytical critical analyses.

NOTES

1. Thomas Hardy, *The Return of the Native*, ed. Tony Slade (London: Penguin World Classics, 1999), xxxix–xl.

2. On the young, alluring woman subjected to accusations of witchcraft, see Nancy van Vuuren, *The Subversion of Women as Practiced by Churches, Witch-Hunters, and Other Sexists* (Philadelphia: Westminster Press, 1973). Certain critics claim Hardy's revisions to Eustacia's characterization expose autobiographical ambivalence rooted in attempts to conceal his obsession with a young woman in his past. The biographical fallacy says more about the critic than about Hardy. Both Eustacia's characterization and the Egdon paradigm (the Quiet Woman is quiet because headless) speak directly to the much-maligned French feminist George Sand, whom Hardy was reading at the time.

3. See Gothenburg Studies in English, 29, *The Literary Notebooks of Thomas Hardy*, 2 vols., edited by Lennart Björk (Göteborg, Sweden: Acta Universitatis Gothoburgensis, 1974), vol. 1, p. 272.

4. *Hypochondriasis:* a generic term for a range of neurotic psychological disorders such as mild depression, low spirits, irritability, and vague and apparently baseless dissatisfaction with one's lot. See *The Return of the Native*, edited by Tony Slade (London: Penguin Classics, 1999), note 8, p. 406.

5. See Book 1, chapters 6–7.

6. Some recent critics have tried to draw parallels with Hardy's own life, claiming that gentrifying the principals was one way of mollifying his class-conscious wife, Emma, who would have drawn similar parallels. Emma was also a writer and possibly better understood the transformations a creative writer makes from life to art. That she grasped the limits of transference from life to art and the new birth a writer creates is apparent in her words to Hardy in a letter of 1874: "Your novel seems sometimes like a child all your own & none of me." *Letters of Emma and Florence Hardy*, edited by Michael Millgate (Oxford: Clarendon Press, 1996), 3.

7. See Pamela Dalziel, *The Return of the Native, Oxford Reader's Companion to Hardy*, edited by Norman Page (Oxford: Oxford University Press, 2000), 366.

8. Gabriel Oak might be said to be emerging from the laboring class. His religiosity is, incidentally, a late development notably in revision in an attempt to aggrandize his status as hero. At the outset of *Far From the Madding Crowd* there is no mention of Oak's churchgoing or religious affiliation. Late revisions include his appointment as churchwarden.

9. See also David de Laura, "The Ache of Modernism in Hardy's Later Novels," *E.L.H.* 34 (1967): 388–89.

10. Whereas discourses on female sexuality were consigned to medical society journals and lunatic asylums, male sexuality was accommodated as a matter of course by the provision of brothels. According to one source on Victorian London, there were more brothels in each London district than places of worship. See the "sin-map" in Ronald Pearsall, *The Worm in the Bud: The World of Victorian Sexuality* (London: Sutton History Classics, 1969).

11. Prometheus, the Titan, stole fire from Zeus and gave it, with many other gifts, to mortals on earth. Enraged, Zeus consigned Prometheus to perpetual torment: Zeus's eagle would devour his liver, renewed each night, in perpetuity.

12. These include Wordsworth, Richter, Byron, Homer, Herodotus, James Thomson, Aeschylus, Balthasar Gracian, John Gay, Plato, Rousseau, Samuel Johnson, John Keats, Comte, Samuel Rogers, Virgil, John Kitto, Sheherezade, Milton, Edward Dyer, John Dryden, and the Domesday Book. Artists number Raphael, Dürer, Rembrandt, Phidias, Benjamin West, Sallaert, and Van Asloot.

13. With its hollows and swellings, clefts and projections, this map resembles a unisexual abstraction of the physical body, both male and female.

14. The colloquial name for these sepulchral mounds is "barrow"; the formal name is "tumulus."

15. To this end, Hardy takes the three peripheral hill mounds (barrows) of the Dorset heathlands and combines them into one—Rainbarrow (earlier Blackbarrow). This then forms the centerpiece to his Egdon construct.

16. The pagan Celtic mythological universe is essentially animistic and is governed by the goddess of life and fertility. The powers of the goddess over the lives of men included both light and dark manifestations; accordingly, Eustacia is both alluring and desirable, brooding and disruptive.

17. Helen Thomas Follett and Wilson Follett, *Thomas Hardy, Some Modern Novelist: Appreciations and Estimates* (New York: Holt, 1918), 127–50.

18. Thomas Hardy, "The Roman Road," *The Complete Poems of Thomas Hardy,* edited by James Gibson (London: Macmillan, 1976), 264–65.

19. See Helen Small's "Chances Are: Henry Buckle, Thomas Hardy, and the Individual at Risk," in Helen Small and Trudi Tate, editors, *Literature, Science, Psychoanalysis, 1830–1970* (Oxford: Oxford University Press, 2003), 64–85.

5

Tess of the d'Urbervilles (1891)

The publication history of *Tess* is extremely odd. It begins with not beginning. Instead of settling down to work as soon as the new novel was commissioned, Hardy brought out his first collection of short stories. Indeed, he was so pleased with *Wessex Tales* (1888), a two-volume collection, that he immediately offered copies to some of his literary friends: Robert Browning, Frederick Harrison (the positivist philosopher), and Mary Sheridan (wife of Irish playwright Algernon Thomas Brinsley Sheridan). In his enthusiasm he also tried to persuade his publishers to bring out another, less expensive edition, ever keen to have his books marketed at the lowest, most affordable price for the common reader. Then, as if this were not prevarication enough, he set about publishing the first of three significant essays on the theory of fiction, "The Profitable Reading of Fiction," in which he takes up three main positions. These are, in brief, to view reading as mental profit, to stretch intellectual knowledge to wider mental horizons,[1] and to expand aesthetic appreciation of form and structure.

Meanwhile, Hardy was not expanding *his* horizons in the direction of *Tess*. He remained unhurried by the fact that in March 1887, W. F. Tillotson & Son, acting as commissioning agents, had offered him 1,000 guineas for *Tess,* or, at any rate, for a novel of the same length as the recently published *Woodlanders* (1887). He had signed the contract, veered off course to produce *Wessex Tales* and "The Profitable Reading of Fiction," and then, to compound the hiatus, plunged back into *The Dynasts.* This was quite an extraordinary thing to do. Not only had this magnum opus, an epic drama based on the Napoleonic Wars, been started 20 years earlier (and was, therefore, an evolving work as opposed to a commissioned work), but he openly confessed that he was unable to write poetry at this time. Unlike *Tess* (when it eventually emerged), to which he never gave the same devotion, *The Dynasts* did not turn out to be the greatest long work ever to flow from his pen.

To put all this in perspective, when *Far From the Madding Crowd* was commissioned by Leslie Stephen in 1873, Hardy was still putting the finishing touches to *A Pair of Blue Eyes* (his third published novel), yet he succeeded in having his first installments on the editorial desk within the year—revised, proofed, and on bookstore shelves a month or so afterward.

So what was the problem with *Tess*? Certainly, Hardy was having severe difficulties with editors, critics, and reviewers, but this was nothing new. Did he feel that now that he was a renowned public figure, editors should curb their attempts to muzzle him and critics should put away their scourging whips? It is true that he was painfully sensitive to negative criticism, but then he did flout the conventions and surely expected at times to be flayed. And it is true that he suffered from periodic depression. "As to despondency," he wrote to his literary friend Edmund Gosse during this slack period, "I have known the very depths of it—you would be quite shocked if I were to tell you how many weeks & months in bygone years I have gone to bed wishing never to see daylight again." However, he goes on to say (perhaps to cheer his despondent friend, who was also in low spirits) that the worst is over, adding, with a gleeful touch of bathos, "One day I was saying to myself 'Why art thou so heavy, O my soul, & why art thou so disquieted within me?' I could not help answering 'Because you eat that pastry after a long walk, & would not profit by experience'" (*Letters*, V1.167).

Despite his recovery from depression, the months rolled on with no *Tess*. Winter came and went, and still he had not started. Then another year elapsed. And if by February 1889 he was almost ready to begin, he was also oppressed by the idea of being in "arrears," as he put it. However, by July he had at least thought up a title and an outline. There had been several false starts, but "The Body and Soul of Sue" it would be. A list of scenes followed some weeks later, together with yet another title, "Too Late, Beloved!" (the aptness seems rather grim—almost Freudian). Still no sign of a manuscript, aside from the short stories he continued to produce. However, when September came it brought some activity: the arrival of the first portion of the manuscript on Tillotson and Son's desk. This contained Alec's violation of Tess and the birth of her illegitimate baby and its baptism—scenes of candor that would later cause consternation among Hardy's critics. There was no consternation at Tillotson's, only what appears to have been immediate relief. For nobody stopped to examine the chapters but sent them instantly to the typesetters, and the first proofs were ready in record time.

Just as Leslie Stephen had once read Hardy's rural idyll, *Under the Greenwood Tree*, and had commissioned, sight unseen, a new novel on the basis of that reading, only to be shocked by what he received—*Far From the Madding Crowd*'s tale with its scenes of violence, insanity, illegitimacy, and homicide—so now with Tillotson. He was appalled when he finally looked at the proofs. He wrote straightaway to Hardy asking for changes, revisions, and cuts, but Hardy objected. Tillotson promptly refused to publish the novel, and the contract was canceled by mutual agreement. There were no hard feelings, and Hardy, still avoiding "Too Late, Beloved!" (*Tess*), continued to send short stories to Tillotson for some time to come. Indeed, "The Melancholy Hussar" arrived on the editorial desk within a few weeks of the canceled *Tess* contract, in October 1889.

The question arises, why would Hardy cancel a major book contract without making even the meanest effort to revise the offending sections? He was, after all, accustomed to making such revisions, and later in this strange odyssey, this is precisely what happened—changes and cuts so radical that they amounted to a brutal self-bowdlerization of his text. There is no simple answer to this question, but there are several possibilities. These include his feelings of ambivalence about writing another tragedy. Casting his mind back at this time to *The Return of the Native*, he questioned whether he should really write such sad stories, "considering how much sadness there is in the world already." Rationalizing these feelings he decided that the "cure of, or even relief from, any disease" is to understand it: "The study of tragedy in fiction may possibly here & there be the means of showing how to escape the worst forms of it" (*Letters*, V1.190).

Contingent upon this and that Tess's story, by virtue of its central theme of the "fallen woman," almost certainly will be tragic, there is the problem, for Hardy, of maintaining sufficient authorial distance in order to create an identity with which he doesn't too closely identify.[2] Or, put another way, how to avoid killing into art (as one critic puts it) a character who exists (for the author at least) as a palpably real entity? Added to these possible causes of writer's block, there was Hardy's increasing frustration with serial publication, that it demanded one set of standards, and volume publication another. Then there was also the problem of his inertia, which suggests a loss of vision, which may appear to be the very reverse of overidentification but could well be the result of it.

Earlier that year, just a few weeks before sending Tillotson the first part of his manuscript, Hardy had confessed to James Osgood, who was overseeing the American serial publication in *Harper's Bazar*, that he could give no adequate account of the story. His lack of vision is apparent at this juncture in his cursory description of Tess as a milkmaid. "Cursory" because this only describes her temporary occupation at Talbothays. She is also a substitute haggler, a poultry manager, field-worker, and, most importantly, teenage mother (though he would hardly mention her illegitimate child to Osgood). Hardy does add that she is "a lineal descendant of one of the oldest county families in the kingdom—of Norman blood and name."[3] But no sooner does he make this point than he casts it aside, stating that "this is only by the way" (*Letters*, V1.196).

For an author in the throes of composition, this is strangely vague and even capricious, given that a publisher would be seeking something substantial to offer his publicity office at this stage. It is as if Hardy is altogether lost, or that Tess is not yet found. Of course, the writer's task is almost inexplicably complex, and such a hiatus may well have been complicated by the awkwardness of Tess's "position" being based on fact, as Hardy tried to explain his dilemma. A factual base is often an impediment to vision. Psychoanalytic theories of aesthetics argue that for an artistic creation to launch from the recesses of the author's imaginative storehouse, there has to be a psychological integration of personal experience. Once integrated, there then has to be a transcendence of it, a release of the imaginative construct from the constraints of the material world, the illustrative from the literal, the significant and illuminating from the ineffable actuality of human lives. A writer of our own times, Maya Angelou, explains this "launching" process, this act of transcendence, as "enchanting" the self. Had Hardy not yet "enchanted" himself?

At any rate, the next few months following the canceled contract with Tillotson were even more distressing for Hardy. First, he wrote to the London *Graphic*, which had been mainly interested in publishing his short stories, indicating that he had a serial story that might be available in January 1891. That this date was over a year into the future points clearly to his state of stasis—he had still not made any headway with the novel. Hedging his bets, he made the same offer to *Murray's Magazine*, which expressed great eagerness to publish—that is, until they read the manuscript. They then declined on the grounds of what they called its "improper explicitness" (*LW*, 232). Hardy then offered it to *Macmillan's Magazine*, whose rejection followed a similar course (too much "succulence" said the editor). However, his offer to the *Graphic* was accepted for July 1891, which, upon consideration, Hardy decided was still too short a time and so he asked for a postponement to 1892. He was evidently still lost. This later date was declined. Worse still, the *Graphic* offered him a considerably lower fee than Tillotson's.

Hardy's health began to suffer during this difficult winter of colds, London fog, and inertia—the writing of *Tess* was a major part of what he called the "mazes" in which he felt trapped. But by the end of 1890, now three years after Tillotson's original offer, he had made some headway with one-third of the proofs in hand—although he was subsequently cautioned by his publishers that because he had delivered the manuscript "so much later than was agreed on" (*Letters*, V1.229) there might be deductions for costs (this was not enforced).

Meanwhile, he had been obliged to make radical cuts and revisions to his manuscript. He was forced to remove the (sacrilegious) baptism scene, which was published separately in *The Fortnightly Review* as "The Midnight Baptism" (May 1891), as well as the Chase episode, which was adapted as "Saturday Night in Arcady" and published in the *National Observer* (November 1891). And where Angel Clare carries the excited milkmaids in his arms across the flooded lane, a wheelbarrow had to be substituted so that the girls could be safely carted across the water without being exposed to any arousing contact with the male body. Despite the aggravation of these changes, Hardy turned mortification to gratification and declared that such a practice of removing offensive material from a novel and publishing it independently entirely out of context was completely unprecedented.

So *Tess* is now out. The first installment appeared simultaneously in England and Australia on July 4, 1891 (a few weeks later in America)—censored, revised, self-bowdlerized (as poor Tillotson had wished), and finally, after four years of demurral, proceeding with a fully engaged author at the helm. Hardy was now committed to *Tess*. Paradoxically, the arduous journey, its troughs and misdirections, and its conflictful endeavor to bring the heroine home gradually roused Hardy to a passionate devotion he felt for none other in his fiction—not Elfride Swancourt, not Bathsheba Everdene, not Eustacia Vye—none, save Tess.

Indeed, one or two critics arguing in reverse, from effect to cause, have tried to claim that the inordinate delays in composition were due to Hardy's prior attachment to Tess (or, rather, to her living model, who remains unidentified). The evidence does not support this, nor does Hardy's publication history. Of all his attachments to living models, the Emma he first met in Cornwall and whom he had sincerely hoped to love was the greatest. Yet Elfride and *A Pair of Blue Eyes*, for which Emma and St. Juliot (Cornwall) provided much of the inspiration, suffered no delays in composition: *A Pair of Blue Eyes* was written for serialization and published in less than two years following Hardy's first meeting and intense, if short-lived, infatuation with Emma, his wife-to-be.

If attachment to the fictional Tess was the outcome of a difficult birth, for Hardy, this no doubt intensified as each new crisis and each new reconstruction of her "life" met with editorial censorship. Accommodation of crisis and the psychological pain of destroying one's own art work can lead to compulsive acts of possessiveness and retentive states of obsession. The process of destruction and restoration can, in turn, result in fetishism, as the desired object is repeatedly lost and retrieved.

Thus, as he prepared the novel for volume publication when the serial was drawing to a close in December 1891, restoring passages and chapters where these had been removed for the *Graphic,* Hardy's defense of Tess came fiercely to the fore. It was around this time that he appended to the first edition the subtitle "A Pure Woman"—a banner to his own commitment and an ethically inflammatory banner at that. It was also at this time that he explained to his friend Lord George Douglas, "I ... lost my heart to her as I went on with her history" (*Letters*, V1.249). And, if bringing Tess home had forged in him an inextricable bond, in mourning her death he was broken: "I have not," he told Thomas Macquoid, "been able to put on paper all that she is, or was, to me" (*Letters*, V1.245).

PLOT AND STRUCTURE

The plot of *Tess* is structured around the seven phases (book divisions) of Tess's short life—her growth to womanhood. "Phase" is an interesting demarcation in itself. Unlike the customary "book" or "part" or "section"—each a spatial marker, none temporal—"phase" signifies a stage of change or development as well as unobtrusively linking Tess's growth to womanhood with the rhythms of the lunar cycle. "Seven" is, in turn, redolent of universal meanings: it is given as the Age of Reason, the Seven Ages of Man (Shakespeare), and the Seven Pillars of Wisdom. And, of course, the seventh day is the Christian Sabbath—the sacred day of fulfillment in the Genesis story of Creation; the day of rest from labor and of thanksgiving. In sum, unlike any other novel in the Wessex canon, *Tess* structures the life of its principal in clearly marked, universal sequences of growth and change.

The Phases are divided both thematically and cyclically. Beginning with "The Maiden," in which the 16-year-old girl faces her first crisis of guilt and responsibility (the death of Prince), and shortly after the trauma of her sexual violation (The Chase), Phase the First concludes with her chastened awareness that her innocence has gone. As in the Edenic story—the "serpent hisses where the sweet birds sing"—she knows she is now "another girl than the one she had been at home" (I.iv).

Phase the Second, "Maiden No More," begins a new cycle. She is pregnant and decides that she must leave Trantridge. She has struggled to resolve her parents' economic dilemma and has struggled even more to endure Alec's unwanted attentions, which she could, of course, now exploit to secure financial aid for herself, but she will not:

> Of all things, a lie on this thing would do the most good for me now; but I have honour enough left, little as 'tis, not to tell that lie. If I did love you I may have the best o'causes for letting you know it. But I don't. (II.xii)

Tess isn't prepared to live a lie; although, had Alec proposed marriage, she does wonder in a rush of artless self-searching whether "she might have been impelled to answer him by a crude snatching at social salvation" (II.xii).

Tess is unerringly honest, and one of the psychologically astute aspects of Hardy's treatment of her phases, of the cyclical rhythm of her days, is that no sooner has she thought one thing than a contradictory thought creeps into her mind. One moment she is resolved and the next, uncertain. Who, in all truthfulness, would not have pondered the possibility of "social salvation"? Acting on that thought would, of course, be a very different matter, but *thinking* it is a psychological truism.

Some critics have taken this variability, these mental states of flux and self-contradiction, to be a flaw in characterization rather than a flaw in character (indecisiveness being a flaw human beings are rarely without). This is to misunderstand Hardy's purpose. He insisted on portraying human imperfections in his characters. He was determined to demolish the stereotype, the "doll of English fiction"—the equivalent of the beautiful, perfect Hollywood type. Models of perfection, being unattainable, are tyrannical. Excellence can be achieved, perfection cannot. Yet, in breaking the popular stereotype, Hardy was accused by some contemporary critics of misrepresenting womankind. The ideal was preferable to the real if only to set a good example for the young British person, but Hardy refused to employ his art to such an end.

Moving on to Phase the Third, "The Rally," we encounter an apt turnaround, a renewed cycle and a different trajectory from the preceding episodes of the Chase and the crises of Tess's life. She now repudiates the past, embraces the new and unknown, and rallies. Meeting Angel Clare, she needs, in every psychological sense imaginable, to be able to summon a rebounding spirit if she is to move on from the trauma of her past and to engage in a new and trusting relationship. Her efforts, however, are often painfully difficult, and she barely understands her own emotional distress. For example, when Angel first takes her tenderly in his arms to kiss her for the very first time, she stiffens.

> Tess's eyes, fixed on distance, began to fill.
> "Why do you cry, my darling?" he said.
> "O—I don't know!" she murmured regretfully. (III.xxiv)

Angel mistakes her reaction as being caused by his precipitate action. Had he been "too quick and unreflecting"? Clearly she has a lot to tell, and this isn't the right moment, but it is far more complicated than that. She freezes at the first embrace, at the sudden sexual contact, because she has been traumatized. Instantly, instinctively, she falls into the distancing posture she is accustomed to adopting with Alec. She stares defensively right past the male gaze and fixes her eyes on the middle distance. Then, just as instantly she reacts to her own rigidity with a sense of shock at what she is doing with the man she loves. And this is when the tears come, as tears do, in reaction to acute stress. Alec's violation has left an indelible mark.

Phase the Fourth is titled "The Consequence." For Tess, the cycle continues, and her days are mixed with the rapturous joy of loving Angel and the fearful dread of having to tell him about her past. She makes several attempts but either she is sidetracked or she sidetracks herself—again, psychologically plausible self-protective behavior. And when she finally writes him an explanatory note, it accidentally slips under the carpet as she pushes it under his door. The cycle of intention undermined by accident seems unbreakable. Tess's resolve is challenged; she feels quite overwhelmed.

Meanwhile, for Angel the consequence of meeting and loving Tess presents a challenge of a different kind. His parents, at Emminster parsonage, have a nice, middle-class, pious young lady lined up for him, so he now has to deal with their resistance, their class attitudes, and, to some extent, his own repressed prejudices. Typically, being in love involves a good deal of idealization, and Angel is no different. Indeed, his idealization of Tess is partly the cause of her failure to confess. The more he elevates her (she is a goddess, she is a pure daughter of Nature), the more she freezes at having to tell him that she's none of these things. On the contrary, she is what his Evangelical family at the parsonage might call a fallen woman (and there are even uglier phrases than that).

With a cruel twist of all that is fateful, Phase the Fifth, "The Woman Pays," sees Tess moving in another new direction, but now in misery and distress. With a sense of terrible injustice, she has to pay yet again for the sexual transgression committed by Alec. Surely she has paid enough? She has been made pregnant by Alec, borne his child, nurtured it, baptized it, and buried it. Now she is confronted with Angel's sexual double standard: the woman he has been loving is, he says, not herself but another woman in her shape (V.xxxv). She tries desperately to cope with the heartbreak of this brutal rejection but, understandably, plunges into deep despair.

When Phase the Sixth reintroduces Alec into her life, as "the Convert," another new cycle begins. A "preacher" appears on the scene bearing "the same handsome unpleasantness of mien" and in whom the "former curves of sensuousness were now modulated to lines of devotional passion" (VI.xlv), and Tess is jolted by the shock. She attempts to flee. Summoning some of the old spirit of rebellion, "her energies returned." Walking "as fast as she was able," she is appalled at this turn of events, reflecting, as she races ahead, on the change "in their relative platforms. He who has wrought her undoing was now on the side of the Spirit, while she remained unregenerate" (VI.xlv). Inevitably, Alec tracks her down. The ensuing conflict results in one of the finest dialogues in the book. The feisty Tess revives, and her power over Alec, together with her unassailable honesty, initiates another new phase—daunting, battling, killing.

Finally, Phase the Seventh, "Fulfilment," sees a whole host of reversals. Alec's affectation of religious piety reverts to sexual exploitation of Tess. Angel's repudiation of her reverts to loving commitment (although he is no longer the beautiful youth brimming with dreams but a near skeleton of his former self), and Tess, in the meantime, has reverted to the Trantridge period and, for the sake of her destitute family, has returned to Alec. The phase "Fulfilment" doesn't end with this alliance, however. In accordance with the fulfillment of the seventh day of creation, Tess will now rest. Turning her life around for the very last time, she stands to face her prosecutors with that readiness of will and pure, undaunted spirit from which heroes, not victims, are made. Where Christs' words were "it is done," Tess's words are "I am ready."

CHARACTERS

Tess

Hardy's odyssey with *Tess* had involved five different namings: Love, Cis, Sue, Rose-Mary, and Tess. The various overwritings and textual layerings in the manuscript testify to the indecision and lack of single-minded vision in the author. Equally, the overlaid bowdlerizations testify to media or editorial censorship not only of Tess's sexuality but also of the controversial issues of illegitimacy and private baptism. One might well read the first edition as a palimpsest, or as a great master, for which a variety of prior sketches and subsequent overpaintings have been made, constituting assorted acts of origination. Most alterations, cuts, and reinstatements offer an alternative and more complex reading. Perhaps a better analogy lies in Darwinism: in forms of adaptation, survival, and genetic mutation, *Tess* is a prime example of textual evolution. The species remains recognizably the same, only the colors, contours, and nuances of habituation vary. At the center is Tess herself, who epitomizes that selfsame concept: she develops, textually as well as in personhood, over time and according to chance, hazard, change, ingenuity, risk taking, and happenstance—in sum, adaptation.

Her crises (the death of Prince, the Chase assault) are weathered, albeit leaving her deeply scarred, and she moves on. Only the past remains, a shadow on her young life. When she meets Angel Clare, she is at the peak of sexual maturity. Brimming with good health, good spirits, and good intentions, she finally yields to his pressure to be married, although against her better judgment. She would rather simply live and love—being, after all, courageous, independent minded, and capable of sustaining herself. By the time she reaches the end of the Talbothays period, she has proved her capability in all these things. In respect of free love, she is most decidedly a daughter of Nature. Culture alone insists on marriage just as society insists on virginity and the church insists on the subordination of the woman in matrimony.

Marriage in Hardy invariably heralds insuperable crises. As Troy rather cynically puts it, in *Far From the Madding Crowd*, "all romances end at marriage" (XL, 236). And, in *Tess*, one thing is certain: as the bridal night draws to a close Tess's innocent love is in jeopardy. It is not only Angel Clare who questions it. Critical debates are ongoing: is Tess naive in believing Angel will forgive her indiscretion as she has forgiven his? Even her own mother regards her as a fool for telling, as does the occasional modern critic. Indeed, in line with Joan Durbeyfield, one scholar recently argued that Tess is "oddly incompetent":

> Despite her obsessive fear of Angel's learning her history, Tess is unrealistically unable to predict his response when he does—improbably naïve in her jubilation that her transgression is "just the same" as his.... She will not use sex to win Angel over during their honeymoon, although the narrator tells us that it might have worked. (Marjorie Garson, *Hardy's Fables of Integrity: Woman, Body, Text* [Oxford University Press, 1991], 137)

Joan Durbeyfield would agree with every single word of this. Indeed, Garson here exemplifies what I have earlier called recidivistic feminism. The cultural context is twentieth century, the critique is mainstream Victorian.

The question arises in the context of moral philosophy: is it incompetence or incorruptibility? Or maybe even incorruptibility taken to extremes? The Garson argument of incompetence may be shared by Joan Durbeyfield and her ilk, but is it representative solely of Victorian moral criticism? Many Victorians argued that Tess should have behaved differently, but Hardy's whole point is that she abides by her own moral code, not society's. Do modern critics engage constructively in this debate? Or are we still locked into Victorian morality on this issue?

I have no answers to these questions but Hardy's revisions to the bridal night scene are illuminating in the "incompetence" context. Angel confesses to what he calls his "fall," his "dissipation with a stranger" and, after listening attentively, Tess springs up with heartfelt relief that her own fall is, after all, no more serious than his. "It can hardly be more serious, dearest," says Angel, condescendingly, smilingly.

> "It cannot—O no, it cannot!" She jumped up joyfully at the hope. "No, it cannot be more serious, certainly," she cried. "I will tell you now."
> She sat down again.

Their hands were still joined. The ashes under the grate were lit by the fire vertically, like a torrid waste. Her imagination beheld a Last Day luridness in this redcoaled glow, which fell on his face and hand, and on hers, peering into the loose hair about her brow, and firing the delicate skin underneath. (IV.xxxiv)

This is the first edition.

But, in a later revision for the 1912 Wessex Edition, Hardy augments Tess's words. After she says, "No, it cannot be more serious," he adds, "*because 'tis just the same!*" (my italics).[4] This stress on Tess's assertion that her situation is "just the same" testifies not to her incompetence or that she is "improbably naive in her jubilation" but that she is under considerably nervous tension. Underlying her momentary flash of relief there is deep anxiety. Notice how she struggles to convince herself (and Angel) that surely she "cannot," "cannot," "cannot" be condemned by him when their situation is "just the same." The repetitions are telling. They reveal her mental effort not simply to sound convincing but also to convince herself. Her "jubilation," moreover, may express a spontaneous reaction of hope, but it is frighteningly brief. No sooner has she jumped up joyfully than she sits down nervously, filled with dread. "Her imagination beheld a Last Day luridness"—that is, the fires of hell.

Close textual analysis invariably yields far more than we might expect at first glance. Hardy's continued concern over Tess's awful sense of suspense, her dreadful uncertainty about how her story will be received, is ratified by yet more revisions—most important is the alteration to the subjunctive mood (in the revised version), which has, "Imagination *might have* beheld a Last-Day luridness" (my italics).[5] The omniscient narrator, who earlier spoke of "her imagination," has handed over to the bystander narrator, who now, most revealingly, does not place "imagination" in the possessive case (as being Tess's imagination). Hence, Tess's state of mind, her imagination, is not under scrutiny. Instead it is *anyone's* imagination. This necessarily includes Angel's "hellish" imagination—as Tess, for example, would most fearfully be intuiting. And, equally revealingly, the revised passage shifts the mood to the subjunctive, to the "might have," which eradicates the previously confident assertion and replaces it with uncertainty. And it is this voice of uncertainty that (sympathetically) mirrors Tess's own.

One last point to consider before we leave this mirror scene is the manner in which the "Last-Day luridness in this red-coaled glow" *peers* into her face and *fires* her delicate skin. Lurking in the imagery here are shades of a previous horror: Alec's forced entry into her body—not so much "firing" her "delicate skin underneath" as piercing her "delicate feminine tissue" inside. If this appears to be too loose an association, it may be worth recalling that elsewhere Alec's presence is made visible by the red-coaled glow of his cigar. The implications of this associated imagery are several, but for our purposes here, the aspect of Tess's innocence (as in The Chase episode) as opposed to her naivety is to the fore. She remains, in both instances, shocked by the force of her male trackers. Both will scorch and scourge her, taking her completely unawares.

The controversial Chase scene was, incidentally, removed from the serialization of *Tess*. The American *Harper's* version featured a paraphrased account of it, as part of Tess's confession to her mother, but the *Graphic* substituted a bogus wedding ceremony in which Alec seduces Tess by tricking her into marriage. Interestingly, both the *Graphic* and *Harper's* include a protest by Tess's mother that Alec could be sued—in the *Graphic* for tricking her into marriage and in *Harper's* for rape. The difference between seduction and rape was that the former was a social offense incurring punitive damages of discreditation of reputation that could severely affect a gentleman's life, whereas rape was a legal offense that had to run its course through the law courts. Either way, this awareness of legal rights considerably sharpens Joan Durbeyfield's character albeit that family poverty could not have afforded litigation.

Another interesting aspect of Alec's trickery is that he forces Tess to gulp alcohol in the urtext (holographic manuscript), but in the 1891 version Hardy substitutes a small druggist's bottle. Given the time and clime, this could have been a narcotic, but the upshot is what we nowadays understand to be date rape, in both cases. Victorian legislation came down harder on drug rape than on non-drug rape (which is harder to prove, in terms of nonconsent).

Ultimately, Hardy's alterations, self-bowdlerizations, and postpublication revisions to the Chase episode tend to color Alec less black and Tess less naive and certainly more conscious and self-aware. If the purity issue is to stand the test of philosophical scrutiny, after all, the conscience, self-responsibility, and even susceptible nature of the subject (Tess) should not be undermined by implications of a "dumb," insensible nature or an intoxicated or drugged consciousness. Purity would count for far less if there were no sensibility involved in the moral index. It was, therefore, important for Hardy to have Tess fully sentient (not drugged) during the action in the Chase—albeit that she was exhausted and taken unawares by Alec's forcible penetration of her body.

Hence, with time and thought Hardy came around to endowing his Tess with human traits, not *idealized* attributes (that's Angel's job) but real, human attributes. Some of these are specific to Tess herself—her volatile temper, impulsiveness, rash courage, sensuality, and obstinate spirit. Others are specific to Victorian mores such as a young girl's conditioned role to please, as also to submit *docilely*. Then there is her susceptibility to the "privilege" of being singled out (the pet) of someone of a higher class (Alec). Possibly the least well understood of Tess's Victorian characteristics is her overly trusting nature together with an innocence and inexperience we might find hard to understand these days. Indeed, a superficial reading might well find it improbable that an adolescent girl brought up by Joan Durbeyfield would be as ignorant as Tess seems to be of the sexual intentions of a man such as Alec. However, Joan is not the most enlightened or reliable of mothers (there were, after all, methods of birth control available in Victorian times): she leaves her children in the evenings to go drinking at Rollivers—her "chief plan for relieving herself of her diurnal labours lay in postponing them" (I.iii); she is thoughtless in her parenting—waking her 16-year-old daughter to do the drunken father's work just a few hours after she has gone to sleep, exhausted from taking care of the little ones while her mother is at the pub. And she is singularly gullible in her social pretensions—to wit, being duped by her husband's story of pedigree and placing her faith in a fortune teller's guide. Hence, for reliable parental models, Tess would have to search elsewhere.

Thus, predictably, in The Chase episode, Tess is seen to be frighteningly vulnerable as she rides with Alec. This is emphasized in revision (1892) where her seat on the horse, being "precarious enough," is all the more palpably felt with the added phrase that she is precarious "*despite her tight hold on him*" (I.xi—my italics). And then we are told,

> She was inexpressibly weary. She had risen at five-o'clock every morning of that week, had been on foot the whole of each day, and on this evening had in addition walked the three miles to Chaseborough, waited three hours for her neighbours without eating or drinking…. it was now nearly one o'clock. Only once, however, was she overcome by actual drowsiness. In that moment of oblivion she sank gently against him. (70)

Perhaps the greater improbability is not that of her innocence but that the exhausted young girl could ever manage to stay awake at all (as some critics have maintained she should), let alone remain on guard on this fateful evening of her first sexual encounter.

Angel

This brings us to Angel Clare, the central male principal in *Tess*. He arrives on the scene at the outset of Tess's story, when he interrupts his hiking tour at Marlott to watch the May Day dance (Cerealia)—an ancient ceremony dedicated to the pagan goddess Ceres (Roman goddess of agriculture). Hardy's use of symbolic action is subtle and significant in this scene: Angel doesn't see Tess. He dances with another girl and catches only a glimpse of her wondering face as he departs.

Later, this idealistic, young parson's-son-turned-farmer—going back to nature in a way reminiscent of the dropout hippies of the 1960s and 1970s—reencounters Tess at Talbothays, and they fall in love. The first major obstacle is the class divide, but in his newfound socialistic philosophy, Angel feels he is a liberated man. This is not quite so, as his idealization of Tess reveals: he puts her on a pedestal, naming her variously goddess and virginal daughter of nature (the hazy atmospherics during these scenes function as an external correlative mirroring his lack of enlightenment). In a dual sense, then, he again does not "see" her. He views her as something else, a goddess woman. Physically, she is either dimly perceived in dawn hazes or irradiated by luminous rays of light—in short, obscured.

Angel harbors many illusions about himself and about Tess. His idealization of her is in part a psychological barrier to difference—sexual difference, class difference. Alternating between rarefying her and condescending to her, Angel treats her as a higher being (goddess) or a lower (child), but not as his equal, and emotionally distances himself from her without threatening his own sense of power and control. This is the manner of creating idols, by placing them on a pedestal. Tess is sensitively aware that she is not completely real to him.

> "O my love, my love, why do I love you so?" she whispered there alone; "for she you love is not my real self, but one in my image; the one I might have been!" (IV. xxxiii)

On the other hand, in true patriarchal tradition Angel not only expects a virgin bride, but he, the man, will be the making of her. He will give her his name (in marriage) so she will "escape" (his word) her own,[6] and if his attempts to teach her history meet only with a dreamy indifference, he is determined to have a "well-read woman." This, he "means to make" (IV.xxx).

Moving from ideological to cultural considerations and returning to the significance of the Cerealia scene, when Angel arrives he is immersed, as are his brothers, in reading *A Counterblast to Agnosticism*. Originally, Hardy had them reading "Answers to *Essays and Reviews*." This title and its topic would have been familiar to contemporary readers: it was a study born of the 1860s that was produced by several eminent scholars of Hardy's day who argued a historical reading of the Bible—a reading, that is, of the word of men, not of God. "Answers" would, then, present a counterblast to this historical-critical reading, a rejoinder based on the older tradition of the Bible as divine revelation. The age of Darwin inspired many such studies by scientists working in the new fields of geology and biology, each presenting a profound challenge to biblical history. *A Counterblast to Agnosticism* is significant, therefore, because it establishes Angel's religious background in relation to Tess's free-thinking paganism.

Later, part of Angel's confession to Tess discloses his newfound doubt in plenary inspiration (divine inspiration). He seeks to explain to her his reasons for adopting the farming life and for rejecting life as a parson; he hopes to stress that although he has been raised a devout Anglican and is now liberated from church doctrines, he remains, nevertheless, a strict moralist:

> Though I believe my poor father fears that I am one of the eternally lost for my doctrines, I am a stickler for good morals, Tess. I used to wish to be a teacher of men, and it was a great disappointment to me when I found I could not enter the Church. I loved spotlessness and hated impurity, as I do now. Whatever I think of plenary inspiration, I heartily subscribe to these words of Paul: Be thou an example—in word, in conversation, in charity, in spirit, in faith, in purity. (224)

This is the first edition.
The original version (the manuscript version) had read a little differently:

> "Tess, have you noticed that though I am a parson's son, I don't go to church."
>   "I have—occasionally."

"Did you ever think why?"

"I thought you did not like the parson of the church."

"It was not that, for I don't know him. Didn't it strike you as strange that being so mixed up with the church by family ties and traditions I have not entered it but have done the odd thing of learning to be a farmer?"

"It did once or twice, dear Angel."

The piety of the first-edition version (modified slightly in 1892 to make Angel sound less of a prig), together with its air of self-satisfaction and didacticism (which excludes Tess from the conversation), highlights many of his traits, not least his hypocrisy. As the bridal night episode will immediately disclose, an example of charity he is not.

There are few more unforgiving male lovers in Hardy than Angel. Although physically more beautiful than the fastidious Henry Knight (*PBE*), Angel does have a precursor in the latter who rejects Elfride for having been another man's lover. But otherwise, there are no parallels in Hardy's fiction. True, Cytherea in *Desperate Remedies* does inflame her mistress, Miss Aldclyffe, into jealously musing on the idea that she might have been kissed by other men, but this does not result in acts of cruel unforgiveness. Aside from these two examples, there is Fancy Day in *Under the Greenwood Tree*, who never lets on (Joan's true daughter, perhaps), and then Clym in *The Return of the Native*, who has the openheartedness to turn a deaf ear to rumors of Eustacia's liaison with Wildeve, until, that is, his mother is involved. Both Farfrae (*Mayor of Casterbridge*) and Giles (*The Woodlanders*) honor and respect their partners, as Henchard ultimately does, although each of the women has had previous sexual partners. Of all Hardy's male lovers, Jude is the most free-loving and the least hypocritical. Angel is Jude's exact opposite.

Alec

Alec d'Urberville, co-protagonist in *Tess*, is also Angel's exact opposite—not in terms of forgiveness, but sexually. Angel is relatively inexperienced, whereas Alec is the promiscuous seducer. By nature shallow and selfish, he evidently possesses a certain charm that isn't altogether lost on Tess (although she despises her own susceptibility). Interestingly, Alec redeems himself in the eyes of many readers by voluntarily providing for Tess and her family where Angel ruthlessly abandons her (it later transpires that his parents would have given her money, but this is poorly arranged and never implemented).

Hardy isn't interested in producing archetypes, hence there is as much complexity in Alec's characterization as there is in Angel's. He can, for example, be surprisingly tender: "Nights grow chilly in September" (72), he says, pulling off his overcoat and covering Tess (there is a mirror scene later where Angel does exactly the same). And, at the practical level, he gives Tess employment when asked and treats her well enough to induce her to stay on at Trantridge for three months.

Thus the polarities play out. The narrator observes that Tess is doomed to be coveted by the wrong man. Many readers would pluralize the noun in this sentence.

ROLE OF MINOR CHARACTERS

Certain minor characters who never actually appear in Tess's life carry a special significance in this novel. They hang in portraits on the walls and lie in tombs. They are her ancestors. These rollicking d'Urbervilles play a larger part in her short history than do Retty or Marian or Izzy, her dairy-farm companions at Talbothays. Hardy himself did not rate the importance of the d'Urberville pedigree too highly (thematically speaking), but critics have made up for it. Many, in common with Angel Clare, might abhor "the aristocratic principle of blood" but at the same time regard it, as he does, as making an "appreciable difference" to Tess's fate and fortune.

Significantly, Hardy places the responsibility for the whole pedigree business in the hands of a buffoon, the self-appointed antiquarian Parson Tringham. Even though he knows that "hunting up pedigrees for the new county history" is whimsical, he is serious-minded enough with Tess's father, the gullible Jack, to convince him with a name-dropping account that his "true" ancestry is blue-blooded. Believing himself to be "one of a noble race," the drunken haggler promptly orders a carriage, equipped with a "noggin o' rum" (on account), and rides home in style (I.i). His life will never be the same again.

Tess tolerates her father's untoward gentrification with humiliation, with embarrassment, and, eventually, with resignation, but her mother instantly makes plans. It is almost as if she hears Angel's words, that this will make an appreciable difference in Tess's life, although neither she nor Angel can know (as does the reader) that the appreciable difference will have tragic consequences. At any rate, on the strength of Tringham's farcical story and hoping for some kind of payoff, Joan promptly dispatches Tess to Trantridge to claim kinship with the wealthy Alec, who, after purchasing a titled name, has migrated from the industrial north. Alec is a fake—as is the whole notion of blue blood.[7]

In a desperate moment, even Tess falls back, on her ancestry upon aristocratic principle. When courage fails her as she struggles to broach her confession to Angel, she uses it to cloak her inner conflict: "I was told by the dairyman that you hated old families" (188). While feeling her way in a roundabout manner into a confession and also sidetracking Angel into his contempt for pedigree, Tess intuits his mind—one way or another he will hate *her*. Hardy uses this moment to expose Angel's hypocrisy. He does not hate old families at all, although his first reaction is to stand his ground. Delivering a rather pompous treatise on his high-sounding, newly acquired socialist principles, he then shifts the basis of his argument to the third person and, speaking on behalf of society (not himself), he tells Tess that people are "hopelessly snobbish" and will be impressed by her blue blood. This in turn will improve, he says, her chances of being accepted as his wife.

The condescending attitude bespeaks defensiveness. Concealed in his rhetorical efforts at exonerating himself from the snobbishness he ascribes to "society" there is a guilty satisfaction with the "pedigree." He cannot resist blurting it out. Tess, he insists, must now spell her name correctly:

"D'Urberville—from this very day."

"I like the other way rather best."

"But you *must,* dearest! Good heavens, why dozens of mushroom millionaires would jump at such a possession!" (IV.xxx)

Tess is agitated. "Now then, Mistress Teresa D'Urberville ..." [8] he begins, calling her by the very name she would rather not use—renaming her yet again.

The ancestors, the pedigree issue in all its implications, which Tess had earlier decided to repudiate as being not only fanciful but an impediment to her autonomy, the self-determination of her existence, rears its ugly head again. This time, however, it's not at the father's will but at the husband's. Angel now goes out of his way to choose what he calls "one of your ancestral mansions" for the honeymoon. The narrator tells us that the house,

> whose exterior features are so well known to all travellers through the Froom Valley [was] once a portion of a fine manorial residence, and the property and seat of a D'Urberville. (IV.xxxiv)

Two huge and hideous life-sized portraits of d'Urberville women are built into the walls on the landing. Their fixity adds to their ominousness. Tess is immediately oppressed by them although she tries to make light of it:

On the landing Tess stopped and started.

"What's the matter?" said he.

"Those horrid women!" she answered with a smile, "How they frightened me."

He looked up, and perceived two life-sized portraits on panels built into the masonry. (IV.xxxiv)

The fact that they cannot be removed is clearly intended to be significant: Hardy takes pains to have the narrator recur to their fixity a second time and in quite an artificial manner, betraying his schematics. The artifice is apparent in the irrelevancy of the conversation between Angel and the charwoman, where the latter is made to say that "Owing to their being builded into the wall they can't be removed" (217). Evidently this is intended as an omen—ominous at the level of plot and strategically symbolic.

Despite the gentle love play with Angel on that fateful evening, Tess is too "surcharged with emotion" to shed her intense feelings of dread and depression. No doubt the whole manner and style of her eventual confession is colored by these feelings. In the very moment of trying to start anew and on the brink of changing her life, she is again haunted by the "old" burdensome notion of a predetermining pedigree.[9] For, if Angel is to stand by his claim of the corruption of old families, he must and will view her story with less impartiality and less compassion. It is now "builded in" to his chosen honeymoon dwelling: her "tainted" blue blood is grimly staring down from the wall. It is a fixity.

Legends abound concerning ancient families, and the d'Urbervilles are no different. Another premonitory scene occurs (after Angel has abandoned her) when Alec turns up at Marlott while Tess is helping with the house move, and regales her with stories of a phantom coach, an abducted beautiful woman, and a murder. It is at this point that he offers to take care of the recently widowed Joan and all the children. He will make up for his wrongdoings of the past and will give them a home, will provide for them, and will send the children to a good local school. Tess dreads the idea of being beholden to him again and all that that means. And although she has no inkling of how things will turn out, the tragic fact is that Alec's words herald a ghastly repeat of the d'Urberville legend: the "abducted" woman and the ensuing murder will be played out, for real.

Meanwhile, the house move has gone wrong, and the family is homeless. They spend the night in Kingsbere church, the ancient d'Urberville seat. This is Joan's idea. Evidently she has brushed up on the laws of ancestry: "Isn't your family vault your own freehold?" (362) she asks Tess. Possibly this is the one and only benefit to be gained from having a pedigree: you get to sleep in the family vault alongside centuries of cadavers, skeletons, and dry bones.

The Kingsbere church episode becomes a nightmare of a different kind, but the symbolic meaning is clear. The ancestors are indeed inescapable, fixities. Paradoxically, while they feature in *Tess* as the most significant of the minor characters, they sustain their power not as living beings but as phantom, legendary characters, ghosting the story of Tess's life, as it were.

Among the other minor characters in *Tess of the d'Urbervilles,* there is the perennial (in Hardy) hypocritical preacher, the kindly, easygoing rustic—personified by Dairyman Crick in this instance—the mandatory gossip (who serves to highlight prejudices and destroy reputations), and, of course, the wonderful Hardy workwomen. Tess's companions, Marian, Retty, and Izzy, all share a fervent passion for the beautiful, sophisticated Angel Clare, and they each harbor fantasies about winning him. So devout is their worship that Retty tries to drown herself when he leaves to marry Tess. And in yet another moment of betrayal, Angel solicits Izzy to accompany him to Brazil; the poor girl has to wrestle with her conscience and her loyalty toward Tess before coming to her senses.

The role of these girls, at work and at play, serves to highlight certain preoccupations and conflicts in Tess that take place behind the scenes, in bedrooms and other domestic quarters, out of the orbit of her menfolk. Hardy chooses to dramatize these moments in action and dialogue, as opposed to employing narrative observation or descriptive paraphrase, thus illuminating aspects of her character via the tone and content of her own utterances and the perspective of other women. The hoydenish elements apart (the drunken Car Darch and her ilk), one consistent feature of Hardy's characterization of minor female characters is their solidarity. Loyalty, confidentiality, and intimate affection between women remain a constant in Hardy's oeuvre from first to last.

THEMES

The major theme of *Tess of the d'Urbervilles* is that of the fallen woman. The lore of the fallen woman has its roots in patriarchy, and because it is pivotal to nineteenth-century sexual ideology it warrants a brief, if oversimplified, history. Under the aegis of a social system based on private property rights, nineteenth-century society, under industrialization, witnessed a radical shift from village culture to a capitalist, metropolitan-based culture. This shift included the gradual erosion of the rural-based culture of fertility (vestiges of this appear in the Cerealia, in *Tess*), which was replaced over time by complex social codes high-ranking virginity. Due to mechanization, rural labor no longer needed to reproduce itself in high numbers (fertility), but instead, under an encroaching industrialization sought to secure capital and property (property included wife and children). Setting a high premium on virginity secured these patriarchal values by ensuring that a man's progeny was legitimately his own. Where once, under ancient village fertility lore, illegitimate offspring were absorbed into the community, under patriarchy they were stigmatized and were unable to make claims against their putative father's estate.

In *Tess* Hardy makes it fairly plain that Tess's illegitimate baby reverts to the community, as in ancient rural tradition. As she works in the fields, her infant is brought to her for nursing by others in the group who, evidently, provide nurture and care. But that she also experiences shame reveals the extent to which her village sensibility has been modified by urban codes and practices. The middle-class parson's son, Angel Clare, will be her first moral executioner.

Typically, the cultural model of the fallen woman is depicted in Victorian literature and artwork as a sickly outcast, a pariah. As in Gaskell's *Ruth* and Eliot's *Adam Bede*, she has no life after her fall. Hardy rebelled strongly against this stigmatization of the unmarried, sexually active woman. One of his most iconoclastic poems (attacking cherished beliefs), "The Ruined Maid," celebrates the fallen woman's rise to prosperity, and although Tess is not so fortunate, she does retain both personal integrity and heroic status.

Not only does she rebound to rebuild her life, but she actively engages in the world of work and community.[10] Indeed, in the eyes of unsympathetic critics, male and female alike, she is given far too much license—daring to baptize her baby, confronting church authorities over church burial, and having the nerve to think she could marry a respectable middle-class parson's son.[11] The closest that modern society has come to such a controversy is probably the racially mixed marriages of the early twentieth century and, more recently, same-sex marriage.

The theme of purity in *Tess of the d'Urbervilles* has always been controversial. Hardy is deliberately revising the Victorian urban legend that the fallen woman is permanently stained. He once told a correspondent that "pure woman" was a mere description, more or less as one would speak of, say, an accomplished lady or a man of wealth. Accordingly, he insists on demonstrating its factual basis in Tess's life and character. For example, she doesn't throw away her virtue because it has been defiled (as did the fallen woman in the public imagination, reputedly fit for nothing short of prostitution). She doesn't manipulate her abuser, play him for all she can get, plot to take revenge on him, cheat, or lie. And as we have seen, she doesn't even use her sexual charms to win Angel back in the bridal night scene. And if her act of removing the object of oppression from her life once and for all may be regarded as a crime of passion these days (unpremeditated, provoked, and executed in the heat of passion), historically it is martyrdom. It is a crime committed by women over the centuries against their oppressors in the knowledge that they will pay for it with their own lives.

SYMBOLS, ALLUSIONS, AND FIGURATIVE LANGUAGE

In *Tess*, as in *The Return of the Native*, the natural world is writ large as both representative habitat and literary metaphor. In each location, from Talbothays to Flintcomb-Ash, the physical reality of the natural world not only plays a part in the drama of Tess's life but also doubles as a literary device and an external correlative; that is, we read the external world as mirror to her inner consciousness, and occasionally the reverse. The world she inhabits exists in her own mind as often as it exists independently of it.

As regards the physical reality, it is not simply the miles she trudges and the rural labor she endures, but the kind of terrain she has to traverse and the kind of weather, even the kind of soil beneath her feet, that shape her character and her destiny. Fatigue is related not simply to fieldwork but also to the long distances she has to walk. A notable example is the scene of The Chase—the name given to the woodland region where Alec and Tess find themselves lost late at night and where she sleeps while awaiting his return. Physically, this is also the scene of her own chasing—she is driven to exhaustion, driven to surrender, and hunted down. Figuratively, and at a far more subtle level, where the narrator speaks of Alec's coarse tracing on her delicate tissue, there is also the suggestion of chasing, a term that applies to the act of engraving. She is "chased" to the most intimate, most hidden recesses of her physical being. The sense in which Alec has left his mark (his tracing) upon her, emotionally, physically, and psychologically, is compounded by the literal fact of his impregnation of her.

As regards locations, Talbothays is equally rich in symbolism. The Vale itself is a lush, fertile river valley and a dairy-farming community unbloodied by the slaughter of animals and blessed by peaceful productivity—the milking of cows, the skimming of cream, and the churning of butter. The climate is temperate: dreamy, summery days where the only sounds to be heard are the lowing of cattle in the meads and the songs of birds. The Talbothays story is ageless and mythic: the goddess of spring has returned, the world is made new again, and Tess, her instincts roused in sensuous affinity with the pulse and throb of natural things, flourishes.

But this is no romantic view of nature. The "real" is well detailed and palpable. Milk and butter can grow to rankness in this fertile vale, cattle can roam into the odiferous garlic grass, thus tainting their milk, or, when calving time is nigh, the cows can go dry and Tess the milkmaid can lose her job.

In terms of emblematic locations, a harsher reality strikes when moving farther afield to the lands of Farmer Groby, who departs from natural processes by
hiring a steam threshing machine. Flintcomb-Ash is definitely hellish. Critics
have made much of the "red tyrant" and the manner in which the mechanical
thresher is used to enslave field laborers to its unstoppable rhythms, driving the
workers senseless with noise, smoke, and fatigue. The image of the red tyrant is,
of course, aligned with Alec, who steps on cue into the scene to renew his pursuit
of Tess. Although critics tend to focus on the relentless tyranny of the industrial
machine in this episode, Farmer Groby is possibly the true culprit. When he hires
the thresher, he insists that his workers feed it nonstop throughout the day, even
by moonlight, to meet the greedy needs of his pocket. But the "red tyrant" image
is an obvious one: the patterning of the demonic machine, with its perpetual buzz
and hum and filthy pollution, exploiter of the economic underclass, is aptly linked
to the demonic male. Alec is, in truth, often thoughtful and caring, but in his
relentless pursuit and exploitation of the young Tess, he is tyrannical. Hence the
"red tyrant," as symbol, satisfies a certain aesthetic sense of apt analogue.

So too with Hardy's structuring of blood imagery. The pattern is clear and sat-
isfyingly appropriate for a young girl's growth to womanhood. The seven periodic
phases in Tess's short history, invite a parallel with both the female cycle and the
monthly lunar cycle and each Phase is marked with blood. In Phase the First,
when Tess is but 16 years old, there is the family disaster: the Durbeyfield bread-
winner, Prince, is accidentally pierced by a cart shaft, and as Tess tries to staunch
the wound she is spattered with blood. This is generally seen as the symbolic
precursor to the next bloodletting episode, when Tess herself becomes the bread-
winner at Alec's house and is brutally penetrated (in The Chase). In Phase the
Second, the "blood" issue from the Chase takes the form of Little Sorrow, who is
born frail and dies, losing his lifeblood. In Phase the Third, Tess comes to sexual
maturity, and in Phase the Fourth to a sexual consummation that never actually
takes place. Phase the Fifth features her mercy killing the bleeding, wounded
birds (the hunted creatures being linked, imagistically, with the legendary white
hart and the trapping of field animals at threshing). In Phase the Sixth her gaunt-
let assault on Alec draws blood, and in Phase the Seventh she seizes the carving
knife and pierces *him* through. Naturally and aptly, the periodic shedding of blood
from first to last attends her growth to womanhood.

At a completely different symbolic level, the roads and highways, the very
earth itself, pattern an extended metaphor of loss and recovery with a pleasing
degree of finesse. The night lane leading from Marlott, at the outset of Tess's
story, is treacherously narrow and winding and cannot accommodate both the
mail coach and Prince's cart; by contrast, the route she takes from Marlott to
Talbothays leads across a wide expanse of terrain on Egdon Heath—so wide and
vast. This is a turning point for Tess because she gets lost. After recovering her
route she suddenly perceives the world differently: "The new air was clear, brac-
ing, ethereal…. The Var waters were clear as the blue River of Life…. She heard a
pleasant voice in every breeze, and in every bird's note there seemed to lurk a joy"

(III.xvi). She bursts into song. She repudiates her past and eagerly steps forward to face the challenge of the new and strange.

With the ending of the Talbothays idyll, Tess is left to fend for herself again. Significantly, when she traverses the route back to the Clare parsonage it is bleak and depressing. The last few miles of this journey were "through a more gentle country," but "as the mileage lessened between her and the spot of her pilgrimage, so did Tess's confidence decrease" (297). And with diminished spirits, her outlook also grows dim. She now barely sees the landscape around her and grows pale with anxiety, beginning to wish "some accident that might favour her" (V.xliv). The signs are all there. Feeling miserably vulnerable, she retraces her steps from whence she had come.

On her last road, in her final phase, "Fulfilment," she is accompanied by Angel out across the plains to the sacred temple of Stonehenge. Deeply imbued with healing symbolism, mystical earth resonances, and astronomical and solar energies, the "altar" stone, where Tess sleeps while Angel watches over her throughout the night, not only heralds the final stage of her journey but bathes her, as in ancient pagan baptismal rites, with renewed purity.[12] "So now I am at home," she says (393). Arising from her last sleep with no trace of fear or alarm she turns to face her arresting officers.

> She stood up, shook herself, and went forward, neither of the men having moved.
> "I am ready," she said quietly. (V.lviii)

SETTING

The setting for *Tess of the d'Urbervilles* embraces the widest geographical area in Hardy's Wessex novels (with the exception of *Jude*) modeled on greater Dorset,[13] one of the maritime counties of southern England flanking the English Channel. Possessing an exceptional variety of terrain, a direct consequence of its complex geology, Dorset county encompasses the ancient oak-filled woodlands of Cranborne Chase (Chaseborough and the Chase); the heather-filled, gorse-covered heaths of the southeast along the coastal region (Egdon); the rolling chalk uplands of the Vale of Blackmoor (Flintcomb-Ash); the languorous river valleys and clay land of the Vale itself; and the lush, fertile southern vales stretching from Dorchester to Wool (Vale of the Great Dairies).

Hardy situates Tess's home village of Marlott (based on Marnhull, North Dorset) close to the Vale of Blackmoor (sometimes Blackmore Vale), a pastoral valley mazed by tiny lanes and field pathways. The "Marl" in Marlott refers to the white clay that, when hardened to a freestone, is used for local dwellings and churches. It is from Marlott that Tess wends her way, walking some 10 miles southeast to Alec's family home of the Stoke d'Urbervilles, at Trantridge, on the edge of the Chase. Once a royal hunting forest and the preserve of kings, the Chase provides habitat to rare birds and butterflies and, according to legend, to that most elusive of rare creatures, the white hart—the magical creature coveted by hunters but reserved only for the king's pleasure (white appears to be the color of choice in these early settings as befits the virginal Tess). It is in The Chase that Alec takes his pleasure of Tess.

When Tess then leaves home again, she heads for Talbothays, situated in the fertile Vale of Great Dairies and separated from the valley of her birth by "the intervening uplands and lowlands of Egdon" (III.xvi.102). Hardy makes full use of the diversity of his settings, based on Dorset's distinctive geological formations. Whereas Egdon features in The Return of the Native as an autonomous micro-cosmic world—remote, complete, and entire unto itself—in Tess it functions as borderland, as a plateau to be crossed from one region to another. The crossing is significant at two levels, topographically and psychologically.

Tess journeys more than 20 miles over hill and dale from Marlott to Talbo-thays and perceives the geological changes for herself. Having spent her child-hood in the Vale of Blackmoor, where the clay soil is heavy and the rivers run "slow, silent, often turbid; flowing over beds of mud into which the incautious wader might sink and vanish unawares" (103), she gazes with wonder upon the new and strange landscape spread beneath her as she breaches the heights over the Vale of the Great Dairies. Here, she perceives the air is light, not a dense blue as in her homeland vale, and the waters of the Froom are clear "with pebbly shal-lows that prattled to the sky all day long" (III.xvi.103). It is at this point that she shrugs off her burdensome past—the heaviness of her Blackmoor days now being replaced by the lightness of the new valley and the verdant lands of Talbothays, where she will meet her true love.

Later, in her banishment from Angel Clare and from everything she trea-sures, Tess makes her way 15 miles over highway and field, from Marlott to the harsh, exposed uplands of Flintcomb-Ash—the calcareous chalk lands of "stony lanchets or lynchets." Here again, the land tells its own tale, the stony terraces testifying to hardship and endurance, which is Tess's own experience during this phase. Over a thousand years earlier Viking and Anglo-Saxon settlers, con-fronted with dense woods and rough scrubland, cultivated strips of land by crop rotation on hillside terraces. The terraced strips were constructed in hilly areas where irrigation and drainage were assisted by a series of flat planes and ledges just wide enough to be tilled by ox and plow. This impoverished, lynchet-ridden land contrasts sharply with the fertile river valley where Tess finds love and happiness. As in tales of myth and heroism, she gravitates in banishment to the darker regions of the earth, just as she had earlier gravitated in hope to the Vale of the Great Dairies.

Had she made the 15-mile journey to the affluent Clare parsonage, itself suit-ably ensconced in the snug geological basin of Emminster, from Talbothays and not from Flintcomb-Ash, would she have succeeded in her mission? Possibly. For part of Hardy's purpose in Tess is to show how the profound assimilation of environmental forces borne by one sensitive soul impacts upon the human consciousness—its subliminal effect upon mind and spirit.

The model for Flintcomb-Ash is a cretaceous chalk ridge flanking the Vale of Blackmoor, and in the case of *Tess*, perspective is everything. From the vantage point of the weary, hungry working girls, this exposed, treeless, frozen "starve-acre" place is brutal. But viewed from the Vale of Blackmoor and in a different mood or altered psychological state, the same place presents itself as undulating hills of high elevation and dramatic contours. Beloved of *Tess's* author, this landscape enfolds Wessex Heights and the cherished settings of much of his poetry.

Stonehenge, on Salisbury Plain—Tess's last post, at it were—looms as the longest journey of all. It is situated some 40 or 50 miles north of Bournemouth (Sandbourne), a well-heeled resort on the coast. It is in Sandbourne that Alec keeps Tess as his mistress. Her trek to Stonehenge with Angel is a desperate attempt to flee Alec and the region of her captivity, but it ends in another kind of capture. There is a certain aesthetic rightness about the settings here: the well-heeled, middle-class town of Sandbourne at the southern outer limits of Wessex, from which she must flee, contrasts with the sacred pagan festival site to which she gravitates at the outermost limits of the north. Here she is offered shelter back in the natural world, under sun, moon, and stars.

In Sandbourne with Alec she is kept alive and prosperous but emotionally starved. Possibly, in some grim and terrible sense, this is where she must kill her oppressor if kill she must. In the latter setting of Stonehenge, she is eventually recaptured but is now spiritually fulfilled. She feels she is now at home. With its cosmic associations and mystical resonances of restoration and healing, Stonehenge would seem to be Tess's most appropriate destination. It also witnesses her shortest sorrow. Unlike the months of guilt and regret at Marlott over the death of Prince; or the endless weeks of frustration and despair at Trantridge, pregnant with Alec's child; or the misery of Flintcomb-Ash hoping Angel will return to her, Stonehenge is filled with peace and resolution. In its vast, all-encompassing power to bring heavenly bodies into its ambit, it draws Tess toward that ultimate state of equanimity—she is ready.

ALTERNATIVE READING: MASCULINIST CRITICISM

Masculinist criticism is primarily based on the experience of men and regards Angel Clare's repudiation of his background in Christian theology as a reflection of Hardy's own ethics founded on secular humanism. Christian theology and church pastoralism being, in Hardy's day, wholly patriarchal, it follows that he would be less inclined to accord to his female principals the religious ideas and practices he accords to the males.[14] This, incidentally, renders his characterization of Sue Bridehead, in *Jude*, all the more unique for her strong theological interests and counterblast agnosticism, which are his own.

Angel embraces scientific thought and believes he has moved on from his father's Evangelicalism (gospel followers and active evangelists) and traditional Protestantism. Like his author, he still appreciates some aspects of the church, although in his Talbothays days he doesn't attend a single Sunday service. He tells his father that he loves the church as one loves a parent, with admiration, but he cannot accept what he calls "an untenable redemptive theolatry" (the worship of a god that promises redemption, in return, as in Christianity). Despite this filial opposition that could be regarded as normal emotional growth toward separation from the parent and thereby toward autonomy, Angel feels he has a greater affinity with his father than does either of his pious brothers, the Reverend Cuthbert and the Reverend Felix (both of the Broad Church faction—liberal reformists who regard the Bible as myth and metaphor). Nevertheless, he confides to his father none of his ambitions to live the secular life. This comes as a complete surprise to Parson Clare when, taken aback by the arrival of one of Angel's scientific books, he confronts his son and is told the truth.[15]

Angel's heterodoxy—his breaking with the orthodox church and his father's faith—is not fully developed in his character with any depth. Agnostic humanism pledges a good deal more faith in humanity's cause than Angel is ready for. He is untutored and insecure. Although he is fair minded and kind, he is inexperienced and, in his struggle to develop manly authority and power, he becomes overly preoccupied with himself. He remains unaware that his quasi-agnosticism, which claims not to honor and glorify God but to honor and glorify man, fails him in the moment of being put to the test. He is still, Hardy's narrator tell us, "the slave to custom and conventionality" (265), and in common with youthful ideologues who might be propelled into shedding their first skin in their first season, he is easily "surprised back into his early teachings" (265): he has little philosophical understanding and limited psychological wisdom to sustain him in moments of crisis.

Angel is himself caught, in a way, in a crisis of manliness. Unlike his female counterparts, he cannot allow his weaknesses to show, and he cannot be indecisive or allow himself diminished authority. He comes from a family of men. The only sister he does have is considerably older and has long since left home for a foreign mission with her husband. His conflicts have roots in his manly pride and rigorous self-importance (in women, the equivalent ego is designated "vanity") as also in his lack of self-awareness and self-knowledge to which he, the Victorian male, does not accord much importance. He only knows he must appear in control at all times and thus lards his talk with intellectual theory.

Even in his condemnation of Tess he cannot allow himself to be seen as morally weak. It is not he who must forgive; it is she who has tricked him. He answers her pleas with an attack: "Forgiveness does not apply to the case…. How can forgiveness meet such a grotesque prestidigitation as that?" (228). As a theorist he has all the big-sounding words but not the moral fortitude and capacity for forgiveness his own father might have been able to summon under the circumstances. "Don't—don't! It kills me quite, that!" (228) she shrieks, and whether she understands what "prestidigitation" means (that he is accusing her of playing tricks on him, of performing a kind of sleight of hand), she does know from his grand words that he has deserted her emotionally. He has fallen back on authority and power and upon tyranny—using words to subordinate the one who cannot penetrate his bombast.

The saying goes that those who genuinely possess power do not have to display it. Angel becomes defensive in the face of Tess's power over him, but masculine codes dictate that he assert his authority over her at all times. He talks of making moderate reforms, but he has only a theoretical understanding of what might be involved. Surely his first set of reforms need to come from within?

At a different level of the *Tess* plot, masculinist critics have claimed that Alec is no rapist, that he has been attentive to Tess for months on end ("near three mortal months"), and that he has put up with her unreasonable rebuffs. She refuses to accept him as a lover, although he acts like one by giving the Durbeyfields a new cob horse to replace Prince and bringing toys to the children. Rather than perceiving this as exploitative (taking advantage of the fact that Tess was sent to solicit his help), the masculinist critic argues that Alec is motivated by kindness and affection as well as normal male desire. The critics compound this argument with reminders that on the night of the Chase he tenderly wraps Tess in his own jacket, thus going off into the cold night in a state of chill. Furthermore (the argument goes), Tess is complicit in her own fate, consensual even, because she allowed herself to fall asleep at the critical moment of male desire.

This would seem to bring masculinist criticism to the edge of male fantasy. A woman who lets herself fall asleep is giving in to male desire, not physical exhaustion? The same argument of compliance is applied to Tess's response to Alec when he asks whether he has offended her by his "love-making" and she answers "sometimes." "Sometimes" maybe her way of trying to negotiate a tricky situation, seeking to give Alec an honest answer (of rebuff) without risking his antagonism. However, the masculinist might well say she is urging his continued arousal and that "sometimes" is her way of making him work a little harder at seduction.

Misogyny is not out of the question among masculinists. That Tess doesn't leave Trantridge until she finds herself pregnant some three months after the Chase scene is taken as compliance: in her heart of hearts she really wants to stay with Alec. This overlooks the fact that she has been dispatched to bring in the family bread—her alcoholic father has a weak heart (he dies very shortly) and somebody has to support the little children. For Tess to abandon them while trying to please a cantankerous old woman and her harassing son would require serious cause: pregnancy would seem to be serious enough (although sexual harassment these days would suffice; to a young Victorian girl with fewer human rights, it might not).

The same masculinist rationale that claims Tess might fall in love with her rapist also argues that her self-loathing upon leaving him shows that she has been sexually awakened and loathes herself because it is not love. It appears that one crucial human dilemma the masculinist might have to experience personally is the depth of loathing and self-disgust a woman feels after having been sexually abused. Perhaps an analogy can be made with house theft when the sense of violation is profound and transfer that trauma to the burglarized body. As Hardy's narrator puts it, "An immeasurable chasm was to divide our heroine's personality thereafter from that previous self of hers who stepped from her mother's door to try her fortune at Trantridge" (I.xi). It would be hard to read the "immeasurable chasm" as sexual awakening.

NOTES

1. Hardy uses one of his favorite analogies here and speaks of this mental stretching as taking a witch's ride.

2. There is at least one incident in Hardy's life that is transferred to Tess's story. This is the scene of the barn dance, which features the young Hardy similarly caught waiting, hungry and tired, till three in the morning for the revelers to finish dancing (LW, 20).

3. Hardy claimed he was the lineal descendant of an ancient Norman family, in his case the le-Hardyes of Jersey. Note the similarity of Franco prefixes in le-Hardye and d'Urberville. William Masters Hardy, in Old Swanage: or Purbeck Past and Present (Dorchester: Dorset County Chronicle, 1908), provides a pedigree showing this lineage.

4. Thomas Hardy, Tess of the d'Urbervilles, edited by Simon Gatrell and Juliet Grindle (Oxford: Oxford University Press, 1983), 221–22. The editors claim that this edition is based on the manuscript and first edition, with added revisions. "Added revisions" nullifies the authenticity of the text as based on either Hardy's manuscript or his first edition. This kind of amalgamation of various texts is called an eclectic edition. An eclectic edition also contains assorted editorial interventions that have accrued to the original over time. The passage quoted here includes the added revision of the 1912 text.

5. The 1912 edition, Gatrell and Grindle, 222.

6. From the relatively recent time of property ownership in marriage, which includes the ownership of the woman by the man, patriarchal tradition required that the wife take the husband's name. Originally this meant taking his entire name, as in Mrs. Angel Clare. This strips the woman of her identity and history. Her name is annihilated, and she is rendered in many cases untraceable as a single entity. The Married Woman's Property Acts of 1882 and 1893, in giving married women the right to own their property (hitherto the husband owned her, body and soul, including her real estate), went some way to changing the public consciousness concerning a woman's right to her own identity and control of her own person.

7. The term "blue blood" is said to arise from a form of European elitism whereby the wealthier Caucasian classes would "prove" their superiority by showing that the blood ran blue in their veins. Darker skins did not show the blue veining as sharply (thus pointing not only to classism but also to racism). Hence, not only whiteness but the blueness of veins became a sign of high breeding, not simply a sign of genetic makeup and, of course, indolence (white skins were not supposed to be exposed to darkening by weather and labor in the fields). Indeed, it was the fashion for centuries for all those aspiring to the upper classes to whiten their skins with applications of powder, lemon, chamomile, sunshades, and dietary products. A "brown" skin betrayed inferior class and blood.

8. Note the town-country opposition in the family names d'Urberville and Durbeyfield. "Ville" (town) connotes the smog, overcrowding, and filth of the industrialized city, whereas "field" connotes the opposite: the fresh, free, and verdant life in the natural (unclocked) world.

9. The equivalent in predeterminism today would be when we speak in terms of things that run in the family, meaning "genetic."

10. Hardy wrote to his friend Frederic Harrison: "As to my choice of such a character after such a fall, it has been borne in upon my mind for many years that justice has never

been done to such women in fiction. I do not know if the rule is general, but in this county the girls who have made the mistake of Tess almost invariably lead chaste lives thereafter, even under strong temptation" (*Letters*, V1.251).

11. One anonymous reviewer so upset Hardy that he wrote to Walter Besant expressing anxiety about meeting this critic in his London club and asking whether he should resign. Besant replied to the effect that there was no need since his club didn't admit women.

12. The "altar" stone is a legendary cleansing stone reputed to have magical powers of restoration. Archeo astronomists attribute terrestrial energy and celestial significance to the Stonehenge ring. It was not only a temple used for festivals of renewal but also an astronomical observatory used to predict specific periods in the orbital cycle of the earth when energies were discharged by the sun, moon, and stars. The sacred festivals of renewal were held at those charged energetic periods, as predicted by astronomical observation.

13. The name "Dorset" is derived from the late-ninth-century *Dornsætum*, meaning "settlers of Dorn or Dorchester," the county town. "Set." (suffix) means "settlers."

14. Hardy puts into Angel's mouth a quotation he himself uses 20 years later in another context. Angel quotes from Hebrews 12:27 and tells his father that religious reconstruction is of paramount importance. He recommends "the removing of those things that are shaken, as of things that are made, that those things which cannot be shaken may remain" (116). Hardy uses the same phrase in the apology to *Late Lyrics and Earlier* (1922) when deploring the fact that superstition seems to be replacing Darwinism, except in "small bodies of various denominations," where there is evidence of "removing things that are shaken" (*Complete Poems*, 561).

15. This book is unidentified, but the incident is generally thought to be inspired by Horace Moule, Hardy's dearly loved friend who later committed suicide. Moule finally broke with his own father when Darwinist, Gideon Algernon Mantell's *The Wonders of Geology* (1848), arrived on the doorstep of the Moule parsonage.

6

Jude the Obscure (1895)

In April 1894, when the composition of *Jude the Obscure* was still in its early stages, the story began to veer toward nonconformity, causing Hardy, as ever, some concern. But in this instance he went straight to his publishers, *Harper's*, and asked to cancel the agreement. They declined. So, in a new spirit of compromise that his previous publishers would have applauded, Hardy agreed to bowdlerize as he went along, as he saw fit. This turned out to be a complicated business, and the result (for the serial) was a confusing, rather baffling plot. Making cuts and revisions for *Harper's*, some in blue ink, some in green, he had to keep reminding himself that the changes were for serial publication only. Despite these reminders, coherency and consistency were sorely disrupted. However, by the end of the year, the story was ready for publication. It appeared in London and New York in *Harper's New Monthly Magazine* first as *The Simpletons* and then shortly afterward under the title *Hearts Insurgent*.

Some of the alterations Hardy made for the serial version were, first, changing the relationship between Jude and Sue from sexual to platonic. The ramifications of this are, of course, complicated, but in brief, the babies are now adopted and Sue doesn't think of talking to Little Father Time about the facts of life; marriage between Jude and Sue becomes an issue only when Sue undergoes her religious martyrdom; Arabella doesn't deceive Jude with a trick pregnancy nor does she lure him into hunting for the Cochin's egg incubating between her breasts; and the pig-killing episode is muted as is the whole business of Sue's sexual revulsion for Phillotson. Crudely put, the novel is neutralized.

Compared with his four-year-long ordeal with *Tess*, this could be called a triumph, but Hardy was frustrated. He wanted to see the real thing in print. No sooner had serialization begun than he writes, almost apologetically, to his friend Grant Allen wishing he could send "the real copy of the story I have written for Harpers', as the form in which it is appearing there is a conventionalized one" (*Letters*, V2.69). But first he must find an appropriate title. He must, he feels, make a clear distinction between serial and novel. Writing to his publisher about the forthcoming "real copy" he says,

> please do not call it "Hearts Insurgent" but "A forthcoming new novel", (or some such words). This will give opportunity for a new title, the magazine form of the story being considerably mutilated. (*Letters*, V2.69)

What a long way Hardy has come from his censor-resistant days. He agrees wholeheartedly with Florence Henniker that censorship hinders "works from coming into existence"—it may even "prevent their being thought of, by exercising an unconsciously paralyzing influence" (*Letters*, V2.87)—but he shows no sign of paralysis. If censorship, or the prospect of bowdlerization is what hindered him with *Tess*, he has, indeed, triumphed. His restoration work with *Jude* is methodical and efficient, his book proofs are revised and corrected without delay, and he is in plenty of time for meeting the publisher's deadline. Yet ironically, this newfound sanguinity will be short lived. If Hardy had found "a way to the Better"[1] at last, *Jude* would all too soon return to him the very worst he had ever encountered in critical vilification. And he would never write another novel.

The first-volume edition, with its new title of *Jude the Obscure*, came out in November 1895 with Osgood-McIlvaine, as the eighth volume in its series of Wessex Novels—Hardy's very first collection. Reinstating and embellishing his original ideas and elaborating on his allusions, Hardy set about deepening the complexity of his characters: Jude would now see himself as Sue's seducer; Phillotson would be more repellant; Sue becomes more excitable, nervous, and conflicted with aberrant passions as opposed to being conventionally affectionate and passionate, and with a reverse momentum, the antireligious material is muted. Various aspects of sexuality are intensified (Jude and Sue now engage in a kiss instead of a clasp), and the marriage question is restored—those aspects that had been censored for the serial.

Then came the reviews. "Never retract. Never explain. Get it done and let them howl," Hardy tells himself, entering these warrior words into his pseudonymous autobiography, the *Life*. They are, ironically, Benjamin Jowett's words,[2] but Hardy adopts them here as he makes the following entry on the publication of *Jude*:

> The onslaught started by the vituperative section of the press ... was taken up by the anonymous writers of libellous letters and post-cards, and other such gentry. It spread to America and Australia, whence among other appreciations he received a letter containing a packet of ashes, which the virtuous writer stated to be those of his wicked novel. (*LW*, 288)

This was not the whole picture, of course. Although there was also the infamous book burning by the bishop of Wakefield, who announced in a letter to the papers that he had thrown Hardy's novel into the fire, Swinburne, for one, found *Jude* "equally beautiful and terrible in its pathos," and Havelock Ellis regarded it as a fine work of art. Then there was always the staunch poet and writer Edmund Gosse, who stood by Hardy through thick and thin. Relieved (probably) and appreciative (certainly), Hardy wrote his friend, "Your review is the most discriminating that has yet appeared. It required an artist to see that the plot is almost geometrically constructed.... As for the story itself, it is really sent out to those into whose souls the iron has entered, & has entered deeply, at some time of their lives" (*Letters*, V2.93).

But it wasn't good enough that his admirers encouraged him (as did Swinburne) to "hardly care about criticism or praise." Hardy was cut to the quick when he saw literary friends such as Margaret Oliphant going along with the bishop— Oliphant held that Sue's sexuality was even more disgusting than Arabella's with all the attention she drew to it. Deeply hurt by this betrayal from someone he regarded as a friend, Hardy was further wounded by hostility from across the Atlantic. "What has happened to Thomas Hardy?" cries *The New York World*,

> I am shocked, appalled by this story.... It is almost the worst book I ever read.... I thought *Tess of the d'Urbervilles* was bad enough, but that is milk for babes compared to this.... When I finished the story I opened the windows and let in the fresh air. (*LW*, 296)

"If he wished to retain any shadow of self-respect," Hardy told himself in the voice of quiet reason, he should "abandon at once a form of literary art he had long intended to abandon at some indefinite time." (*LW*, 309)
And so he did.

PLOT AND STRUCTURE

The structure of *Jude* is, as Hardy remarks, geometrical. "The involutions of four lives," he writes, "must necessarily be a sort of quadrille" (*Letters*, V2.105). A quadrille is a square dance with five measures for four couples. Hence the pattern is one of Jude and Arabella, Jude and Sue, Sue and Phillotson, and Arabella and Cartlett. The measures or figures might be seen (just to illuminate the pattern of the quadrille) as dancing to the tune of *advances* (wishes, dreams) and *reversals* (disillusion, depression), *side-stepping* (making changes, compromises) and *circling* (renewed hopes, renewed frustrations), and *returns* (a return to any one of the former measures).

This geometric patterning is also reflected in the journeys and changes of location, frequently undertaken by rail (linear routes), in keeping with Hardy's structure. These journeys map a crisscrossing course of lives—ambitions, hopes, dreams, and loves. The first steps are from the birthplace at Marygreen to the city of dreams at Christminster. Then there are crossroads to alternative settings—Melchester, Shaston, and Aldbrickham—where intimate relations between Sue and Jude are complicated by intervening relations: Sue with Phillotson and Jude with Arabella. The former is a reminder of Sue's need for a stable father figure; the latter is a reminder of Jude's need for sexual affection. The last stage of the journey brings Sue and Jude together in Christminster again, but this time as a family, with their children—and thence to the end of the road.

Hardy describes *Jude*'s parallel structure as follows:

> Of course the book is all contrasts—or was meant to be in its original conception. Alas, what a miserable accomplishment it is, when I compare it with what I meant to make it!—e.g., Sue & her heathen gods set against Jude's reading the Greek Text; Christminster academical, Chr in the slums; Jude the saint, Jude the sinner; Sue the Pagan, Sue the saint; marriage, no marriage; &c. &c. (*Letters*, V2.99)

On a more inscriptive level, Hardy's epigraph to the title epitomizes the plot structure: "The Letter Killeth" (2 Corinthians 3:6). The full quotation goes, "The letter killeth, but the spirit giveth life." What does this mean in terms of the plot of *Jude*? Specifically, it refers to the law of matrimony, but more generally it applies to the bureaucratic impact of church and state on individual lives.

At its most casual, matrimony is merely a convenience. Arabella feigns pregnancy to trap Jude into marriage and shortly afterward leaves him when domestic life turns sour. However, the legal contract remains. Worse, marriage to Arabella all but kills Jude's dream of Christminster, although when she deserts him and emigrates to Australia, "the spirit giveth life" and he renews pursuit of his goal.

The letter of the law, both legal and social, maintains a stricter governance over Jude's life with Sue. Reflecting on his union with Arabella, he labors under a conviction of wrongness when "a social ritual [makes] necessary a cancelling of well-formed schemes" (62). But when he meets Sue, matters become more complicated.

> He affected to think of her quite in a family way, since there were crushing reasons why he should not and could not think of her in any other.
> The first reason was that he was married, and it would be wrong. The second was that they were cousins. It was not well for cousins to fall in love, even when circumstances seemed to favour the passion. (II.ii.90)

On Sue's part, whereas she does "inspirit" Jude's life, she leaves him to marry Phillotson within days of learning from Jude that he was previously married to Arabella. Jude, in a parallel move, but motivated by misery and loneliness, returns to Arabella—at first to sleep with her for one night but later indefinitely, giving in to inertia, despair, and resignation. And when the reverse measure of divorce seems to provide a solution to the error of the contracted marriages, all parties involved are in some way compromised by the procedures.[3] The most expressive voice is that of Sue, who feels the potency of the marriage oath, the swearing-in of lives, prevails. Her sense is that divorce is not quite real and that you cannot simply unswear a promise. Yet she still feels matrimony to be a dreadful contract that might well extinguish all tenderness between the lovers: "I think I should be begin to be afraid of you, Jude, the moment you had contracted to cherish me under a Government stamp, and I was licensed to be loved on the premises ... [it] is foreign to a man's nature to go on loving a person when he is told that he must and should be that person's lover" (259).

The "letter" thus extends far deeper into the social fabric of the society in which Jude and Sue struggle to make a life together. It reaches into social conventions, into class attitudes, and, even at a literal level, into the mode of dismissal of Jude's application to study at the university. That particular letter, from the master of Biblioll College, explicitly encodes the status quo, which dictates that artisan workers keep to their reduced station in life and that only the privileged will gain a university education (thus perpetuating privilege among the privileged classes).

In like vein (but under the auspices of another institution, the church) the ecclesiastical "letter killeth" even more insidiously, stifling both heart and mind. If the individual human consciousness of Hardy's characters is not already circumscribed by the pervasive language and the rigorous edicts of church and state, the experience for Jude and Sue of trying to establish some kind of life together in a restrictive nonsecular society soon becomes a lesson in oppression. By way of emphasizing the tyranny of church indoctrination and the straitjacketing of its codes and practices, Hardy creates a juddering effect of reiterated "churchy" phrases throughout his text. From the episode of the Ten Commandments to Arabella's (second trick) public prayer mongering to Sue's final act of martyrdom, "that terrible, dogmatic ecclesiasticism—Christianity so called" resonates, agitating on and on.[4] It pounds Sue to spiritual death and Jude, with the words of Job drumming in his brain, to the grave.

CHARACTERS

Jude Fawley

Jude starts out in the story as a child—as a young boy of 11. This is unique in the Wessex novels: Hardy is notoriously absent on childhood. Orphaned and living with his aunt, Drusilla Fawley, Baker, the young Jude helps to augment the bakery business by doing odd jobs, scaring rooks for Farmer Troutham, and delivering bread for his aged aunt.

At the purely functional level of typology, orphans in Victorian literature operate as a literary device situating the "innocent abroad" in the midst of the action. This device usefully allows for a kind of purism of characterization. In setting the individual against society and the self against the community, the orphan remains unmarked by background or circumstance of birth, untouched by privilege or disadvantage of family influence and name, and in subtle ways remains exempt from the constraints and conventions of the culture by virtue of being beholden to no particular group or class. The story can then be told with a certain advantage through the perspective of the wide eyed "innocent abroad," who perceives the world in all its unfathomable mystery, absurdity, and wonder. This lone perspective, in turn, enhances the narrator's alternative roles, such as impartial bystander or omniscient observer, thus effectively establishing ironies of situation, contrasts in points of view, and the clash of perspectives so essential to a good drama.

In the absence of social and family constraints, Jude can, with justification, be said (and is said) to be born out of due time. He is not of his own age but ahead of his peers in thought and sensibility.[5] This is perilous insofar as adaptation is problematic—Jude is perceived as constantly vulnerable and struggling in a harsh, unjust world. But in terms of ideology and the representation of individual values (honesty, humanitarianism, fair-mindedness, compassion, and so on), set in opposition to society's corrupt values (class and sexual prejudice in particular), the conflict demands special attention in the sense of afflicting generations beyond Jude's own: the social, personal, and spiritual problems encountered in *Jude* cannot readily be dismissed as "history."

This "innocent abroad," then, is the boy Jude, who, understanding nothing of agrarian culture or the wheat trade, or of the domineering farmer exploiting child labor, sympathizes "with the bird's thwarted desires" and decides to feed them instead of scaring them away. He identifies with their orphanhood, their "living in a world which did not want them," and in a remarkable demonstration of fealty, he defies the farmer and sides with the very creatures he is supposed to be fending off. In a host of subtle ways, this opening premise acts as the paradigm, the exemplary pattern, for all that ensues in Jude's young life.

Jude's naivety as a grown man frustrates readers. Here is a skilled stonemason, a scholar manqué of deep sensitivity and gentleness who is incapable of reading in equal measure the world he inhabits and the woman he loves. His frustration becomes, in effect, our own. Preparing himself adequately for college admission and sustaining the effort eludes him, just as insight into Sue's contradictory nature defeats his understanding. He fails to comprehend these life tests and how to manage them. And perhaps his greatest weakness is his susceptibility to Arabella.

However, the fact that the child in the man is thrust upon the reader at the outset helps to ensure that he ultimately survives our harsher judgment. The pathos of his genesis pervades the text and establishes a tenderness of heart and willingness of spirit within the center of consciousness from the beginning. This will live on. Hence, frustrating as Jude may be, he remains very much the object of our forgiveness. Just as a book title resonates over the course of a reader's reading, so too the role thrust upon the reader (antagonistic, sympathetic) shapes a prior condition of receptiveness.

The premise of the opening has all the power and potency of first impressions. Suppose *Jude* had opened with the following passage:

In the long and intricately inwrought chain of circumstances which renders worthy of record some experiences of * * * * * and others, the first event directly influencing the issue was a Christmas visit.

What is our first impression? Well, to start with, a complicated, convoluted style does not herald a child's view of the world. "Intricately inwrought chains" points to something far more complex. There is a sense that something significant ("worthy of record") is about to unfold and that it is but the first of several events to unfold and that certain characters are involved in the chain of circumstances. If you guessed a tale of mystery and intrigue, you would be correct. This is the opening to *Desperate Remedies* (1871), Hardy's first published novel.

Reader expectations have been set up. The same strategy is applied to *Jude*. The novel opens with a simple, childlike sentence: "The schoolmaster is leaving the village, and everybody seemed sorry" (9). Whose perspective is this? It is little Jude's, the "sorriest" of them all. This may be fleeting as vantage points go, and certainly an alternative narrator now takes over and the "little boy of eleven" is relegated to onlooker. But the mark has been made, imprinted as first impressions tend to be imprinted: indelibly upon the minds of all involved.

The narratorial shift to an alternative narrator, like a moving camera, is important at this moment; without it, who would notice the tears welling up in the boy's eyes and his blushes—signs of a highly sensitive temperament? Nor would there be anyone to observe, with an eye for close detail, the young Jude's exhausted efforts to carry the water from the well (if he himself commented on it, the effect would be altogether different). The detailing is important here. Without it, we would not be urged to focus on the little boy's effortful task and the care he applies to it. Thus, in its various combinations, the narrative shapes a central consciousness of vulnerability, sorrow, and loss together with an external scenario of village life in all its simple rigor and trials of child labor.

The reader is now engaged in the life and times of Jude Fawley. The dream of Christminster begins to build at this very moment of loss with the departure of the deeply admired schoolmaster, on whose affections and teachings Jude has become dependent and who conveys his own dream to the impressionable lad. For a thing taken away from a child has to be filled in, replaced with another object: the schoolmaster leaves and the little boy fills the terrible loss and the unspeakable emptiness with Christminster.

It is this episode alone that establishes the nature of the fetish that Christminster will become. How else—without this childhood scene—would we understand the complexity of this fetish and what it means to Jude: his worship of Christminster, the magical powers he bestows on the city (his alma mater, as the motherless boy calls it), the spirits inhabiting the ancient college walls and quadrangles, and his irrational reverence?

Jude Fawley, the "innocent abroad," is not entirely unmarked by background, however. He may be orphaned, but his aunt instills in him a knowledge of his genetic makeup (called a family curse in Jude), which makes him "the wrong breed for marriage" (III.vi). Hardy doesn't exploit the genetic factor with any conviction—neither Jude nor the reader learns much more about this inherited defect, except that there have been broken marriages and tragedies among the Fawleys in the past. Readers may well feel that most families have broken marriages and tragedies in their past, and certainly this is the case in Hardy's oeuvre. Tess has the d'Urberville rape legend to haunt her, Eustacia and Bathsheba are orphans living with relatives, Susan Henchard is sold by her husband, Grace Melbury's mother is long since dead; and among the men, Troy is illegitimate and doesn't know his father, Gabriel Oak appears to have no family—neither do Wildeve, Henchard, Farfrae, Fitzpiers, and so on.

What the genetic factor, the family curse, does achieve in *Jude* is the psychological bonding of the cousins Sue and Jude. Learning that they share the same heritage,

> They stood possessed by the same thought, ugly enough, even as an assumption: that a union between them, had such been possible, would have meant a terrible intensification of unfitness—two bitters in one dish. (III.vi)

Then they throw off past bad marriages as sheer bad luck and go their ways, but the knowledge is there between them: the curse is written along their blood; it is their own private family secret.

Later, when Jude cannot bring himself to raise the delicate subject of Sue's bridal relations with Phillotson—are they good? are they bad?—Aunt Fawley does the job for him. She comes straight to the point. In a sense the family curse, the secret legitimizes the inquiry. "Do ye love un?" she demands of Sue. "What made 'ee marry him?" Then, without demur, she tartly observes that Phillotson is the kind of man "no woman of any niceness can stomach" (III.ix). Sue runs out and hides in the woodshed, weeping (at the truth of it), where Jude then finds her and comforts her. Aunt Fawley believes that the two young Fawleys are the "wrong breed for marriage"; this belief urges her questions; the questions drive Sue to a confrontation with the reality of her situation; this confrontation brings Jude to a closer understanding with her; and they are bonded.

Jude feels that he and Sue are mutually possessed. Aunt Fawley may have acted as a prompt, but Jude—already obsessed with having found kin in Sue—invests profoundly in their oneness. In common with his author, who also had a passion for his cousin (Tryphena), Jude is deeply drawn to the notion of what Hardy calls in another context "the family face." On first meeting, Sue had "looked so pretty that he could not believe it possible she should belong to him. Then she spoke ... and he recognized in the accents certain qualities of his own voice" (II.ii). Then, as he grows to love her, "She was nearer to him than any other woman he had ever met" (III.iv). The emptiness left in the young boy's heart is now beginning to be filled.

The seductive female animal that is Arabella exerts no hold on Jude beyond the immediate fact of physical attraction. Sue has quite the opposite effect. She has a profound hold on him even when they are not sexually intimate together.

Indeed, much that starves Jude, emotionally and spiritually, passes beyond his exclusion from the world of scholarship (which banishes him) into the world of kinship and belonging. He seeks Christminster in lieu of this belonging just as he seeks out the curacy when Sue abandons him. As he lies dying, the despairing words on his lips, his own epitaph as it were, are those decrying his own birth, denying his own act of belonging:

> Let the day perish wherein I was born, and the night in which it was said, There is a man child conceived.... Why died I not from the womb? Why did I not give up the ghost when I came out of the belly?.... For now should I have lain still and been quiet. I should have slept: then had I been at rest! (VI.xi)

Sue Bridehead

If Hardy had an array of models for Sue, from sister to cousin to Florence Henniker and beyond, his hindsight evaluation is colored, understandably, by the critical attention *Jude* received. In the early stages of composition, Sue, he said, was "nebulous," but when he was later told that she is "a marvellously true psychological study of a temperament less rare than the ordinary male observer supposes," he replied that it was "extraordinary" that this "comparatively common type & getting commoner, should have escaped fiction so long."[6] This hindsight view appears to have something in common with Alice in Wonderland's pert observation: "How do I know what I think 'til I see what I say?"

On the other hand, if Hardy was not conscious that he had drawn upon a comparatively common type until after he had drawn upon it, he certainly did not anticipate that such a drawing might provoke such a high degree of outrage. His erstwhile friend, novelist and critic Margaret Oliphant, was one of the more vociferous. Sue, she says,

> makes virtue vicious by keeping the physical facts of one relationship in life in constant prominence by denying, as Arabella does by satisfying them, and even more skillfully and insistently than Arabella—the fantastic *raisonneuse*, Susan, completes the circle of the unclean. She marries to save herself from trouble; then quits her husband, to live a life of perpetual temptation and resistance with her lover; then marries, or professes to marry him, when her husband amiably divorces her without the reason he supposes himself to have; and then, when a selfish conscience is tardily awakened, returns to the husband, and ends in ostentatious acceptance of the conditions of matrimony at the moment when the unfortunate Jude, who has also been recaptured by the widowed Arabella, dies of his cruel misery. This woman we are required to accept as the type of high-toned purity. ("The Anti-Marriage League," *Blackwood's Magazine*, January 1896)

One problem for Oliphant (as for many contemporary critics of *Tess*) is that premarital sexual activity in women and high-toned purity are antithetical. Although the word for sexual activity—"gross"—is applied across the board in *Jude*, as in Victorian society, signifying a libidinous nature at best and debauchery at worst, Jude evidently can be sexually active and still retain his moral rectitude. He is good in Oliphant's view and merely unfortunate. But, although Arabella is a "human pig," "worse than a sow," and a "beast," Sue, as a sexual being, is far more gross—she is "vicious" and "unclean." Why? Because she is an educated middle-class girl of refined sensibility, and Oliphant's expectations (and accompanying prejudices) of her are higher ("nice" girls don't) than they are of Arabella, who provides no model for the young British person.

Moreover, unlike Tess before her—whose sexuality (and purity) are closely aligned with the healthy, verdant life of the natural world—Sue belongs in the Victorian middle-class drawing room, as it were. She is part of life in the city—girls, women, and wives could all identify with her in a way they might not so readily with Tess. Worse, Sue is present in the bedrooms and chambers of her menfolk. Here she is seen sleeping, waking, and undressing. And most gross of all, she openly subjugates herself in grim prostitution to her marriage vow, to the man to whom she owes conjugal rights. The picture is vividly drawn: "her thin and fragile form" crouches "before him in her night-clothes" (VI.ix).

Given that both Jude and Phillotson are not only sexually active but also figure in similar states of undress in these scenes, it is possible that what considerably irked Hardy, with the critical attack on his representation of female sexuality in *Jude*, was that he had been battling the sexual double standard for the past 20 years in his fictional representations, yet it *still* holds sway. Margaret Oliphant ratifies this double standard. There is no "circle of the unclean" for the sexually hungry Jude or for the sadomasochistic Phillotson.

Returning to background and origins, if Jude was orphaned after his parents had separated, Sue was similarly situated (hence the Fawley curse of broken marriages, ill-omened in an age when divorce was inaccessible to the masses). Sue's parents had separated when she was a child, and for a while she was raised by her father "to hate her mother's family" (II.iv)—eventually moving to London, where she became what Aunt Drusilla Fawley calls "a townish girl."

As a child, Sue was evidently disobedient and wild: "a pert little thing ... with tight-strained nerves" (110)—frequently raising eyebrows with her tomboy habits and vivid, expressive renderings of poems. Far from being reserved or repressed, she would wave her hands around in unrestrained abandon "seeming to see things in the air" (111; this endears her all the more to Jude, who has the same propensity). But wild young girls grow up. They discover that lack of restraint can be misread as invitational to the opposite sex. They learn the hazards of possessing a seductive body.

To Widow Edlin's caution that she should save her pretty hands from rough work, Sue offers a light rebuke: "This pretty body of mine has been the ruin of me, already!" (VI.ix). Clearly, she can no longer experience her body as an instrument of pleasure without paying a high price, nor can she express herself with the carefree abandon and freedom of her girlhood. Instead she uses camouflage. She assumes the dignity and reserve of respectable womanhood as much to safeguard herself from ruin as to veil her vulnerability—notably her nervous tension, contradictoriness, and maladaptivity (constantly changing her mind). These traits mystify Jude but would be understood today as mood disorder, or personality disorder—the accompanying symptoms of emotional coldness and flattened affectivity being manifest in Sue's behavior.

Thus, when Jude first sees Sue—a gifted young artist illuminating texts in an ecclesiastical store, her head bent over her work, her manner quiet and dignified—he sees exactly what he wants to see: everything a proper young man can hope to see. He sees a "sweet, saintly" girl whom he will subsequently enshrine, adoringly. He will rarefy her and place her on a pedestal. She will be precious, untouchable, sexless, and ethereal—exactly the kind of woman a Victorian man might hope to marry.

Under Victorian codes and practices, the chaste "Madonna" type was polarized and stereotyped in the cultural imagination as the perfection of womanhood. Her antithetical opposite was the "Magdalen," the Arabella of the *Jude* world. The first was the womanly ideal and the kind of girl you married. The second was neither of these things, although she might be "had on the side." Interestingly, Hardy reverses the Victorian prescription and has Jude marry Arabella, not Sue.

Despite her outward decorum, Sue remains rebellious, attending church with her employer, Miss Fontover, merely for form's sake while secretly acquiring naked pagan statuettes and lying in bed at night, tossing and turning feverishly—the figurines glowing down on her in the darkness. As Jude gets to know her a little better, he will discover the pagan in the saint, the nonconforming rebel nascent in the "artless and natural" cousin, the lawless girl who escapes the oppressive teacher training school by wading across a river and making her way in sodden clothes, clinging wetly to her body, into his night chambers.

When Oliphant speaks of living a life of "perpetual temptation and resistance with her lover," she is referring to Sue's preference for living freely and openly with a man without cohabiting with him (when she does become sexual with Jude, it is only on an intermittent basis, according to her author). In her London days, Sue had lived in this manner with an undergraduate who later committed suicide (unrequited love, apparently), and when the unstomachable Phillotson proceeds to exercise his conjugal rights, she leaps from the window or hides in spider-infested closets. Clearly her sexual aversion to him is overwhelming. But from her nervous advances and retreats with Jude, desperately seeking approval and then turning on him when he loses his severity and "comes on" to her, she is not acting out of revulsion but repressed desire.

Repression keeps under restraint those feelings or thoughts that are felt to be in some way unsettling or threatening. Sue appears to feel safe when Jude is fatherly, even disapproving and strict, but alarmed when he turns amorous. And Jude, being keen, even clinging, often unwittingly stifles her impulses, which is perhaps the very thing she fears in a sexual relationship. Being a freedom-loving independent spirit, Sue might well fear that sexual possession will strip her of these qualities (a fear surely intensified by the threat, for a Victorian, of pregnancy).

Jude, on his part, is sexually tentative. He asserts himself by intellectualizing her feelings, rationalizing his own, bombarding her with words rather than caressing her with soft strokes, or what we nowadays would call foreplay. Hence he fails to arouse her, and her dormant sexuality remains unawakened—unawakened, that is, until it is too late, when, at the very last, she is excited to the point of feeling "O grossly!" (VI.Ix). These complicated crosscurrents may be familiar to many young men and women even today, and they certainly would have struck contemporaries as a "true psychological study of a temperament less rare than the ordinary male observer supposes" (*Letters*, V2.102).

Predictably, Sue responds negatively to Jude's wanting more of her than she can give. He constantly questions her, "What do you think?" "Why are you like this?" which the hyperactive girl finds frustrating, confusing, and irritating because there are no answers unless they are that she is frustrated, confused, and irritated. Capitulating to sex with Jude only after Arabella reappears on the scene (unsettling her composure—does she have a strong enough hold on Jude?), Sue is shown to be depressed, self-preoccupied, and withdrawn the following morning in a scene sensitively drawn by Hardy. Familiar only with rural ways—where country girls such as Arabella apparently respond, sexually, with gusto, with unrestrained animal spirits—Jude has no insight into or understanding of Sue's repressed sexuality. As Hardy shows with subtle touches of mood and nuanced gestures, she has not been orgasmic in her first sexual experience with Jude the night before.

It is ironic that the one deeply passionate kiss she gives him, which leaves her gasping, occurs too late in their relationship, when all is over between them. But then that kind of perversity is fitting to Sue's disposition and may well be what Hardy is thinking of when he speaks of a "comparatively common type & getting commoner." In an age when women's emancipation, their social and political rights, their greater freedom and independence lingered on the brink of emergence (from approximately 1870s onward), the threat to emotional security loomed just as large, if not larger, than did the promise of liberation. Sexual freedom was the promise. Fear and confusion were the threat.

The average middle-class woman was sheltered from early childhood, undereducated to be permanently dependent on men (from father to husband), and raised only for marriage and the inevitable childbearing years that went with it, which required, in turn, compliance and obedience to ensure continuing matrimonial support. She would have had no experience whatsoever (unless a maverick) of earning a living, of choosing a sexual partner, and of testing sexual needs and appetites, let alone taking the initiative or even exercising simple choices of lifestyle. Consequently, for women of Sue Bridehead's class and status, an important part of the new and rather alarming freedom in relationships meant testing and more testing. Provoking and deprecating, teasing and restraining, captivating and hindering, taking risks and camouflaging, playing, learning, and discovering—for women new to emancipation, these were behaviors that were comparatively common and getting commoner.

Sue's final martyrdom to Phillotson requires that she relinquish everything that signifies freedom of spirit (her free-loving anti-marriage views, her Hellenist, pagan interests and beliefs). Instead, she must adopt self-sacrifice and self-redemption, becoming, Hardy says elsewhere, "a penance-seeking Christian" (*Letters*, V2.98). In a clearer stroke of situational irony, Hardy has her start out working as an ecclesiastical scribe, illuminating text, and finish at the end by acting on, or acting out, the very words of belief, myth, and dogma she illuminated at the outset. In the eyes of the world, she is indeed the dutiful wife undertaking "sweet saintly business." Begging her husband's (Phillotson) forgiveness, using words of "sacrifice," "purification," and speaking of her "sin-begotten" children, she shreds her fine lace nightgown (from her days with Jude) into strips and burns them ceremoniously on the fire, choosing instead a coarse garment that Mrs. Edlin calls "sackcloth o' Scripture."

In significant inversion of the phrase Hardy uses in relation to *Jude*, referring to that "deadly war between spirit and flesh," Sue abandons the spirit (of love) and subjugates herself to the flesh (of conjugal life). The ghastly finality of this "deadly war," in the eyes of the world beyond the novel, met with resistance from one German critic. Had the portrait been drawn by a woman, she told Hardy, Sue would never have been allowed to break down in the end.

> Sue Bridehead … was the first delineation in fiction of the woman who was coming into notice in her thousands every ear—the woman of the feminist movement—the slight, pale, "bachelor" girl—the intellectualised, emancipated bundle of nerves that modern conditions were producing, mainly in cities as yet, who does not recognize the necessity for most of her sex to follow marriage as a profession, and boast themselves as superior people because they are licensed to be loved on the premises. The regret of this critic was that the portrait of the newcomer had been left to be drawn by a man, and was not done by one of her own sex, who would never have allowed her to break down in the end. (Postscript, TH. April 1912)

ROLE OF MINOR CHARACTERS

Arabella Donn

Arabella obviously has considerable charm. She lures Jude with that "unvoiced call of woman to man" (I.vi) from his devotion to his studies and later from his devotion to Sue—reasserting "her sway in his soul" (I.vi). This "complete and substantial female human" (I.vi: changed to "female animal" in later editions) not only is voluptuous, but also earthy: she incubates Cochin eggs between her breasts. In addition, she has an exceptionally fine palate: detecting additives in beer. But perhaps her greatest attribute is her psychological insight. She sees, for instance, right through Sue's bravado at their first meeting and intuits that the woman who enters her chambers is a woman who has not yet entered Jude's bed (so to speak). Sue is mortified that her "coarse" rival should find her so transparent. Evidently, Arabella is not quite so coarse after all—certainly not in respect of her fine reading of both character and circumstance in which she exceeds Jude, who is deficient in such insights. And, indeed, in many ways Arabella outwits Sue in sensitivity and perception—the latter admitting to Jude: "I—I can't help liking her—just a little bit!" (III.iii).

The reader, however, is made privy to aspects of Arabella, which mostly escape Jude: her plotting and planning behind his back, her vulgarity, her deceitfulness and artifice—the hair pieces, dimple making, and grooming habits in general. Interestingly, Hardy, unlike Jude, did not scorn dimple-making practices. He jots down in 1888 when making preparations for the novel a fragmentary note: "Rachel H—and her rich colour, and vanity and frailty, and clever artificial dimple-making" (LW, 215). Indeed, Hardy had to make a conscious effort to villainize Arabella, who did not altogether lack charm in her author's eyes. Her vulnerability, for example, in feeling that it is horrid not to have a place of one's own is later altered by Hardy to the more manipulative complaint that it is horrid not to have enough young men to play off against each other. Clearly, the first rendering would draw the reader's sympathy where the second would not, and he has to consciously work on reducing the sympathy. Much later, he comes across a phrase of Browning's that he scribbles in the margin of his own copy of Jude, next to Arabella's "inflated bosom," now annotated to her "breasts superb abundance." Eighty years old at the time, Hardy was still gazing at Arabella.

In passing, it is worth noting that Arabella's awareness of men's tickled fancy for dimples and her donning of hairpieces (which were high fashion in the 1890s) suggests a "modern miss" that somewhat conflicts with her rustic pig-keeping image in the novel. This is not a conflict that prevails, but it does exist. In the main, it is her duping of Jude, linked with the crudeness and brutality of the pig-killing, that most affects our reading of her characterization. "I suppose I have missed the mark in the pig-killing scene the papers are making such a fuss about," wrote Hardy to Florence Henniker:

> I fully expected that, though described in that particular place for the purely artistic reason of bringing out A's character, it might serve a humane end in showing people the cruelty that goes on unheeded under the barbarous régime we call civilization. (Letters, V2.94)[7]

It is fairly evident that Hardy is setting up an opposition here. Arabella is associated with animalism, with everything that Sue is not: fleshly where Sue is thin and fragile, earthy where Sue is fastidious, physically voluptuous where Sue fears all contact with the body, uninhibited where Sue is repressed, underprivileged where Sue is well educated (able to earn her own living as a professional), unscrupulous where Sue is overly scrupulous, a survivor in the world where Sue appears to encounter insurmountable hurdles at every turn, and the only thing they have in common is sensitivity of feeling and love for Jude.

There is some suspicion among scholars that the reason why Emma Hardy reacted so strongly (protesting publication) and with such hatred of Jude was because she was the original model for Arabella. Nobody, however, has commented on the common physical features: the carefully coiffured hair (to enhance its abundance); the fullness of figure, which, even in Emma's youth, is busty; and the slightly coarse facial features. But several critics feel that Emma may have duped Hardy into marriage by Arabella's method, although there are no extant letters or documents to support this. Arabella's impatience at Jude's proposing marriage certainly prompts a few devious behaviors; likewise, Emma's impatience over the four years of courtship with a nonproposing Hardy might also have prompted a few—she would scarcely be immune to the fears common to her generation of being left on the shelf after turning 30. Equally, her rage at Jude must also have been the rage of the dowdy, overblown wife whose husband has to make do with an unsatisfactory marriage (Hardy made no secret of his attachment to Florence Henniker), just as Jude is doomed to Arabella. Either way, the antimarriage theme of *Jude* would not have endeared the author's wife.

Arabella's most important structural function, aside from providing a foil to the female principal and a source of "fleshly" temptation to Jude, is to endow the narrative with insightful female perspectives on Sue. It is Arabella who perceives at the agricultural show that something is not quite fulfilled between the lovers just as it is Arabella who perceives that Sue is not yet sexual with Jude (as noted earlier), which drives the latter to consummate their union; and it is Arabella who is given the last word on Sue. First she lies, denying to the good Widow Edlin that Jude had ever asked her to contact Sue when he was terminally ill. But when the kindly old soul muses that Sue might now have found peace at last, Arabella bursts out with what is clearly the truth and, significantly, a truth that the widow should have known for herself: "She's never found peace since she left his arms, and never will again till she's as he is now!" (VI.xi)

Richard Phillotson

Originally Jude's mentor, who fills his childish head with dreams of Christminster, Phillotson takes on a more complex role as Sue's father figure and Jude's failed model. Kindly and good natured on the surface, Phillotson has an underlying streak of callousness that permits him to encourage Sue to take up a teaching career and then marry him while failing to help the young bride in his care, young enough to be his daughter, to develop intellectually or emotionally. On one typical occasion, knowing her to be troubled—"silent, tense, and restless"—he spends a preoccupied evening balancing the school registers before ascending to bed, mumbling to himself about ventilators. Finding Sue missing, he calls out for her—she's reading downstairs—and eventually hunts her out. He discovers that his unhappy wife has made up a sleeping place in a "lumber-hole" (spider-filled closet), and forcing open the door, causing her to cry out in fear and alarm, he angrily accuses her of "monstrous" behavior. She bursts into tears.

That he subsequently allows her to leave the marriage is to his credit—as his friend points out, he is legally entitled to lock up a recalcitrant wife. His action, though, in taking Sue back is revolting, especially his agreeing to her penitential offering to him of her body. Knowing of her sexual aversion to him, of her love and longing for Jude, he allows her to beggar herself, then carries her thin, shivering body into his bed. Thus he compounds the grossest form of her prostitution—the recompense for Sue being revulsion, shame, horror, self-loathing, and martyrdom.

In terms of structure and plot, Phillotson's role is to mirror Jude's struggle and his failed ambitions and, on the reverse side to highlight Jude's humanitarianism, compassion, loving kindness, and selfless love of Sue. At this point a timely reminder is due. Jude, in common with heroic predecessors such as Tess, does not survive: those who pay with their lives *sustain* their lives as proven models, beyond alteration and eternally inspirational. Thus, Phillotson must live and Jude must die, the former compounding the suffering of the latter while throwing into focus the merciless self-righteousness of Christianity, the iron force of ideology upon an impressionable mind. This tragedy, says Hardy, "is really addressed to those into whose souls the iron has entered, & has entered deeply, at some time of their lives" (*Letters*, V2.93). Phillotson is one such soul.

Aunts, Widows, and Quacks

Aunt Drusilla Fawley and Widow Edlin represent, for the last time in Hardy's novels, those salt-of-the-earth working women who people his fiction. Aunt Fawley and Widow Edlin are sister-women to all those earlier loyal maidservants and field workers: Unity in *A Pair of Blue Eyes*, Liddy in *Far From the Madding Crowd*, the dairymaids in *Tess*, Marty South in *The Woodlanders*, and not forgetting those devoted women who become lady's maids and companions—Elizabeth-Jane in *The Mayor of Casterbridge*, Grace (very briefly) in *The Woodlanders*, and Cytherea Graye in *Desperate Remedies*.

Aunt Drusilla is the strictest of the working women, but in common with her predecessors and with the kind Mrs. Edlin, she offers woman-to-woman support and a down-to-earth wisdom that fills the quieter, indoor spaces of the novel. As representations of decent, honest, kind-hearted human values, in contrast to the hypocrisy, sexual double standard, and other harsh realities afflicting the female principals they aid and support, these working women could well be marginalized were it not for the fact that they remain a constant living presence in the Hardy canon, from first to last.

Less than admirable but also a recurring presence in Hardy, Vilbert, the itinerant quack, appears in varying guises in the Wessex novels. In *The Woodlanders* he takes the form of a scurrilous lawyer; in *The Mayor of Casterbridge* he is female and turns up as the furmity woman, performing, as elsewhere with Mrs. Jethway and Susan Nunsuch, as the local gossip, druggist, or spell-maker. Vilbert's spells consist of love potions and female remedies (abortifacients in the real world), and he provides the sexually hungry Arabella with yet another partner for the time being.

THEMES

Although Hardy was, by the time of writing *Jude* in the 1890s, a confirmed agnostic, he would be the first to say that Christianity itself is not the target of attack in this, his last novel. A close examination of the attitudes and activities deriving from the influence of the church in *Jude* reveals, more specifically, an attack on prejudice, hypocrisy, and dogma. In respect of the last, and its impact on Sue, Hardy wrote in consternation to his good friend Sir George Douglas,

> that, having made Sue become a Christian, & recant all her "views" at the end, I shd be deemed High-Churchy in tone: you can imagine my surprise at the Guardian saying that everything sacred is brought into contempt, &c. in the novel! Did you see that The World nearly fainted away, & the Pall Mall went into fits over the story? (*Letters*, V2.98)

By "High Churchy" Hardy is referring to the tenets of the Anglican (High) Church, which stipulates, among other articles, that "Eternal Salvation" or deliverance from an undesirable state or condition is achieved only "by the Name of Christ" and by adherence to the holy scripture for salvation.

Hardy is being unduly apprehensive in this letter to Douglas. After all, in having Sue subjugate herself to the letter of church law (as also to matrimonial law and her husband's conjugal rights), he is making an exceptionally strong critical statement—in effect, that an educated mind, an intelligent young woman has to be reduced to a state of mental breakdown and must in effect go mad in order to embrace these church doctrines. Sue's subjugation is certainly obscene, and hostile critics dubbed the novel accordingly, "Jude the Obscene." As for the *Guardian* (an Anglican outlet), the *World,* and *Pall Mall,* Hardy must surely have anticipated an uproar from these establishment papers.

Jude's beliefs move in a reverse direction. His aunt Drusilla (and Sue, originally—hence her early imprinting of church doctrine) subscribe to a form of Evangelicalism (allowing for a more personal interpretation of the scriptures), but there is no indication that Drusilla and the youthful Jude pay more than lip service to these beliefs. However, Jude's scholarship (which introduces the motif of an elitist university system) necessarily leads him into theology and to the point where he considers becoming a church minister. In line with Sue, he only embraces the church with any wholehearted commitment when he has sunk into the depths of despair—from failure to gain entry to Christminster and failure to keep Sue.

Jude ends his days in a delirious rant in a scene that parodies the Crucifixion ("I thirst"), and muttering verses from Job (3:3, 4, 7, 11, 13, 18–20). "They know not their oppressor" moans the dying Jude (Jesus' words on the cross were "They know not what they do"). With the biblical words broken up into incoherent fragments by rowdy Remembrance Day shouts of "Hurrah" floating in from outside the sense is of profanity and dissolution. In ghastly mockery of the rites of Extreme Unction or the Last Sacrament, Jude is "anointed" not by sacred words or loving hands but by the yells of a boisterous crowd. Typical of Hardy's parallel structures in *Jude*, and in line with Sue's falling back on dogma as a drug (not a cure) for a broken mind, Jude, in delirium, descends into a hellish rant—the theme "The Letter Killeth" concluding with his crazed last rites, which are nothing less than a curse upon himself.

This brings us to another theme in *Jude*—humanitarianism. From the boy Jude's attempt to befriend the rooks, his protest over the pig killing, and his attack on the donkey beater to Sue's anguish over trapped creatures and beyond, *Jude the Obscure* approximates a veritable tract on humanitarianism. The call is for an end to needless suffering and oppression for all living creatures. "Though not a novel with a purpose," Hardy writes to Florence Henniker, "I think it turns out to be a novel which 'makes for' humanity—more than any other I have written" (*Letters*, V2.94).

A large part of this tract is devoted to an exposition of the struggle on the part of the young lovers to understand and to confront with sincerity and honesty their own sexual and emotional needs in a world riven with codes and practices circumscribing the love bond within the laws of church and state. If Arabella sets the bar at the outset for sexual activity at its most fundamental level of pure appetite (ironically highlighted by her tossing the most unappetizing part of the pig, the "pizzle," at Jude's head), Sue raises it to an uncomfortable level of nonnegotiability where Jude is concerned, and to prostitution, with Phillotson.

However, beyond the novel, with studies in sexology just beginning to burgeon (Havelock Ellis at the helm and Freud following close behind), Sue represents a product of her age and culture. She is on the brink of discovering her inner needs, not least the consequences of repression, while trying to find ways (perhaps for the very first time in women's sexual history—in literature) of openly talking to her man about these things. And Jude, in offering her considerable space in their relationship, does his best to facilitate this self-discovery and the struggle toward its articulation.

They fail in their efforts largely because the institution of marriage, its strictures and deficiencies, fails them. This forms a major theme in *Jude*. The 1890s had seen the genesis of a new age: the nuclear family—one man, one woman, one household, and a planned family.[8] "New" because, traditionally, households had comprised extended families (adult siblings, cousins et al., living under the same matrimonial roof), and family planning had not been common practice, beyond the abstinence of the partners. There were few laws of matrimony in the old days, as Mrs. Edlin testifies, and those that did exist were often ignored.

Now, when Sue speaks of being "licensed to be loved on the premises" she is referring to the prevailing marriage laws and power of the marriage license to give the husband conjugal rights over his wife. Whether he would have enforced these rights against the wishes of his wife in earlier times when adult sisters, brothers, aunts, and uncles all lived under the same roof is extremely doubtful. Live-in relatives would have provided effective checks and balances against abuse. And even if Jude wouldn't dream of enforcing his conjugal rights, Sue feels they corrupt the power base of the relationship. She fears she might be affected by them, that she would no longer feel free to withhold herself at will.[9] "Rights" in this respect signifies not freedom of choice but entitlements, and entitlements carry their own insidious force.

Sue's predecessor, Bathsheba Everdene in *Far From the Madding Crowd*, expresses similar concerns and thinks in terms of marriage as legalized prostitution. So, this is no new topic for Hardy, but it is a new theme. *Jude* takes two sensitive, vulnerable young people and exposes them to every conceivable aspect of matrimonial law, including divorce. Divorce (in the real world) was difficult for wives to obtain (they had to prove the near impossible: their husband's bigamy, incest, desertion, and so on in addition to adultery; see note 3). And even though property ownership had recently been reformed (1870s onward) to give women equal rights with their unmarried sisters, old attitudes die hard. Property ownership doesn't affect Sue and Jude, but preexisting attitudes prevail on all counts, adding to the second-class status of women and reflecting the imbalance of power in the matrimonial relationship.[10] In sum, the odds were stacked in favor of the husband. Understandably, Jude has no problem whatsoever with the marriage contract.

Despite his disclaimer in *Jude* that his own views "are not expressed therein," Hardy felt strongly about modern marriage, which is nothing better than a "survival," he tells Edward Clodd, "from the custom of capture & purchase, propped up by a theological superstition" (*Letters*, V2.92). He adds, in this letter to Clodd, as he also reiterated to his friends, that "the case of my people is one of temperamental unfitness for the contract, peculiar to the family of the parties." This may have been an effort at self-defense.[11] Indeed, the whole rather shaky apparatus of a family curse in *Jude*, of the Fawleys being genetically ill-fitted for marriage, may well have been designed from the outset as a device to deflect away from the author, the novel's open attack on the institution of matrimony. At surface level, the curse (which Hardy elsewhere calls a superstition) offers a reason for Sue's (and Jude's) decision not to marry, a rather weak rationale—if a curse can be so termed. But on closer inspection it proves irrelevant. The antimarriage theme exists independently of any curse. After all, regardless of their heredity, Jude and Sue cohabit and produce children and if anyone is cursed at all, it is Little Father Time, who is not born of the Jude-Sue union.[12]

One important reason for Hardy's need for a defense, for his attempts at various disclaimers and somewhat irrelevant "curses," was that he needed to protect his own domestic situation. He felt, with some justification, "that a bad marriage is one of the direst things on earth, & one of the cruellest" (*Letters*, V2.98). And the dire reality was that he had not only a bad marriage himself but also a very angry wife sitting at home bitterly raging over the fact that her husband had expressed the "cruellest" in a best-selling novel. So, what else could he do but try to deflect attention away from his personal views and his personal life by stressing that "the tragic issues of two bad marriages" in *Jude* are "owing in the main to a doom or curse of hereditary temperament peculiar to the family of the parties" (*Letters*, V2.93).

Sue's own rationale is that "the social moulds civilization fits us into have no more relation to our actual shapes than the conventional shapes of the constellations have to the real star-patterns" (205). She is thinking of the legalities that apply across the board to human love bonds and personal inclinations. In this respect it is worth remembering that until fairly recently one social mold required the bride to swear to everlasting obedience to the bridegroom. Another is that, upon divorce, he could sue his wife's new consort—the corespondent—for damages, just as Jude is cited by Phillotson. The corespondent could be sued for damages on the basis that the husband has been deprived of his property—that is to say, his wife, but Phillotson does not pursue this option, which would be a rather worthless action given Jude's state of perpetual poverty.

One of the wittiest anti-marriage diatribes in this novel is the description of Jude's marriage to Arabella:

> And so, standing before the aforesaid officiator, the two swore that at every other time of their lives they would assuredly believe, feel, and desire precisely as they had believed, felt, and desired during the few preceding weeks. What was as remarkable as the undertaking itself was the fact that nobody seemed at all surprised at what they swore. (I.ix)

SYMBOLS, ALLUSIONS, AND FIGURATIVE LANGUAGE

Of the opening passages, where Arabella tosses the pig's penis at Jude, Hardy writes to his friend Lady Jeune that: "Throwing the offal was, of course, intended to symbolize the conflict of animalism with spiritualism" (*Letters* V2.98). But to his literary friend Edmund Gosse he is not euphemistic. "The 'grimy'[13] features of the story," he says,

> go to show the contrast between the ideal life a man wished to lead, & the squalid real life he was fated to lead. The throwing of the pizzle, at the supreme moment of his young dream, is to sharply initiate this contrast. (*Letters*, V2.93)

"Offal" for the lady, "pizzle" for the man. Either way, the offal-pizzle is symbolic. The conflict between the ideal and the real "was meant to run all through the novel," Hardy writes. "It is, in fact to be discovered in every body's life—though it lies less on the surface perhaps than it does in my poor puppet's" (*Letters*, V2.93).

The clash between the ideal and the real (as between spiritualism and animalism), symbolized in the early scene where Jude is smacked in the ear by the pig's penis, touches on all aspects of Jude's life. "Yes, Christminster shall be my Alma Mater; and I'll be her beloved son, in whom she shall be well pleased" (38), is what he is envisaging when Arabella's projectile hits its target. But, if Jude's ideals are brought to an abrupt halt by Arabella's perfect shot (aptly resulting in his "shotgun" marriage), what do we make of the following?

A glance told him what it was—a piece of flesh, the characteristic part of the bar-
row-pig, which the countrymen used for greasing their boots, as it was useless for
any other purpose. (I.vi)

Is this not an antiphallic image? Surely the unappetizing—not to say redundant—sexual apparatus of the barrow pig, useless except for greasing boots,
works against the animal symbolism? For, in all respects, it is a useless appendage.
Although no critic has yet taken Hardy to task over this somewhat compromised
symbol, its implications for Jude are scarcely propitious.

We could argue, of course, that this is Jude's perception of things. It is his "glance,"
after all. Nevertheless, it does raise some interesting questions. The primary function
of symbolism is to reinforce the psychological, emotional, and sensual undercur-
rents of the narrative; the continuity of specific developments; the complexity of
those aspects of character and circumstance requiring nuanced touches as well as
a variety and subtleness of associations and allusions. Hardy's antiphallic reference
here certainly insinuates a psychological undercurrent while accentuating the harsh
reality of the animalism that forms a very real part of human nature to which Jude is
not exempt. One immediate concern would be that perhaps his failure to keep both
wives, Arabella and Sue, has something to do with his own sexual adequacy.

Either way, the animalism motif, supported by the pizzle incident, relies on
a host of related symbols and images for its sustaining force, not least that Arabella continues to be associated with pigs and butchery right through to the very
end. Added to these vulgar images are her occupations of bartending and public
hymning—the one catering to the body's need for alcohol and the other to feign-
ing respectability. Both activities revert to a preoccupation with the body—from
drugging it with inebriate substances to rendering its appearance pious. Then
there is her spiteful despoiling of Jude's precious books, her tearing of her bodice
to "prove" his abuse of her, and her later intoxicating of his near insensible body
in order to dupe him into marriage for a second time.

All of this provides a series of symbolic ramifications to the coarse pizzle-
throwing scene. Equally, the antiphallic image becomes an extended metaphor
when it is linked with, say, the allusion to Samson and Delilah at the inn where
Jude and Arabella stop for tea but drink beer instead. (See Judges 16:19.) Delilah discovers that Samson's power lies in his uncut hair. Shorn, he is impotent.
This allusion is reinforced by subsequent references to Jude's resemblance to
a shorn Samson (I.xi & VI.vii). Indeed, biblical allusions abound—and Jude's
head is also full of them. Interestingly, he transfers them to people and objects
indiscriminately and often inappropriately—thus perpetuating his illusions, his
dreams of the ideal. Most are transferred to Sue, inappropriately because she
is not only pagan but also Voltairean (Voltaire was highly critical of church
dogma).

In the immediate moment of the pizzle scene, however, the animalism motif prevails over any suggestion of sexual inadequacy (or of a shorn Samson), and Jude's
thoughts and feelings turn not upon the redundancy of the phallic member but

upon his own sexual arousal. This consequential factor following from cause to effect extends the symbolic action into the larger arena of the novel. To wit, he is held by sexual compulsion, "held to the spot against his intention" (40). And shortly afterward, studying his books and struggling to keep his attention on the Greek Testament, he not only "felt as a snake must feel who has sloughed off its winter skin" (43) but is so overwhelmed with desire that it is as if "a compelling arm of extraordinary muscular force seized hold of him" (I.vii). There couldn't be a much more graphic image than that! One can only surmise that if, later, Jude loses his sexual potency, it is intermittently related to heavy drinking and psychological stress—for he does produce offspring.

Thereafter, harsh reality hits this incurable dreamer at every turn: Christminster, seat of learning, is also Christminster in the slums; Phillotson the mentor is Phillotson the failed scholar; sainted Sue is pagan Sue, and so on. The opposition of the ideal and the real forms the center of interest in this novel and the very heart of Jude's history. Between finding Sue/Christminster and losing Sue/Christminster, the episode with the musician epitomizes this opposition. Seeking out the Wessex composer one day in the hope of discussing his beautiful compositions, Jude is subjected to a long, disillusioning talk about funds and commerce and is shown the door when it becomes apparent that he has no money.

A tempting symbol of harsh reality is Little Father Time. But he is so thoroughly an embodiment of "the coming universal will not to live," and his personification is so plainly limited to an antirealist figuration, that he becomes what Richard Nemesvari calls "a closed signifier." A symbolic object or action must, of necessity, represent, typify, or recall an idea or quality already present in the work in question. A symbolic character must possess qualities analogous to that idea or quality. In one sense, Little Father Time is father to the man insofar as he manifests the suicidal urge that will later shape Jude's own demise, but this is not thematic. He is ultimately representative only of himself.

Music, and musical instruments—notably, the piano—are, however, also symbolically significant. The novel opens with Phillotson's departure and the ensuing problem of what to do with the piano. It is temporarily stored in Jude's home and later draws Sue and Jude into a tender moment of intimacy that, in common with other such musical moments, excludes Phillotson from their charmed circle. Ironically, the instrument of exclusion is Phillotson's own.

Nature's creatures also feature symbolically in *Jude*. The contrasts Hardy speaks of to Gosse are many and include the birds Jude protects (although he cannot protect himself), the pigeons Sue releases from captivity (although she cannot release herself), the donkey Jude saves from beating (but is himself "beaten"), and the trapped rabbit that draws cries of anguish from Sue (who is herself psychologically trapped).

Among other symbols, there are the railways. These both connect and separate the lovers while also overextending them, taking them farther than they had intended to go. Significantly, for Sue, railway stations provide a more modern meeting place than Jude's (suggested) cathedral; and to be sure, the former is free from tainted associations, unlike the latter, from which emanates the "Letter that killeth." Then there are the crossroads, as it were, of "spirit and flesh," when Jude alights from the Aldbrickham train after spending the night with Arabella only to realize that the road he is walking "is the very road by which I came to Christminster years ago, full of plans" (III.ix). The plans are, of course, also imbued with symbolic associations, as are biblical words and phrases that, as noticed earlier, crowd into Jude's head in contrast to Sue's, which gathers clusters of pagan images.

Classical images are also abundant, amplifying perspectives and lending depth and complexity to character and situation. Hardy puts his classical resources to melodramatic use in the service of the Fawley family curse. Sue speaks of it, in a somewhat inflated manner, as the curse of the House of Atreus, and Jude recurs to this allusion in invoking Agamemnon: "Things are as they are, and will be brought to their destined issue."[14]

Interestingly, in the age of Mendel and the advent of rapid advances in heredity research, Hardy relies not on the biological sciences but on the Greek classics to shed light on the Fawley curse. This reliance does not serve to illustrate the tragic outcome of genetic inheritance, which the murdered babies could be said to exemplify, but Jude's manner of externalizing it.

SETTING

Jude the Obscure is divided into six parts, each denoting a particular setting. Beginning with the Fawley[15] birthplace at Marygreen, then shifting to Christminster, Melchester, Shaston, "Aldbrickham and Elsewhere," and then back to Christminster, each destination marks a specific period of development in character or plot. The main locations are situated in north Wessex, and most are urban settings separated at the farthest possible distance imaginable from Hardy's own birthplace and domicile.

Marygreen is a sparsely populated, remote spot surrounded by hills and set in clear contrast to the thronged city of Christminster, based on Oxford about 15 miles away. Jude's first glimpse of the city of gleaming spires is gained when he ascends from the valley of his home to the hilltop of the old ridgeway, "the Icknield Street and original Roman Road through the district" (19). Mounting a ladder to the roof of the Brown house, he gazes on the distant halo of his dream city.

The old ridgeway from Alfredston (based on Wantage, the birthplace of King Alfred in 849) carries most of the traffic in *Jude*, notably Jude himself on his frequent returns to his native village. This is also where he walks in courtship with Arabella and then settles down to married life in a "lonely roadside cottage" (58). Here, Arabella later returns, devising ways of getting him back, and here, Sue kisses Jude—too late—with a passion she has never shown before. Farmer Troutham had beaten Jude in these very fields, and the milestone on which Jude carves the word "thither" flanks the road farther along. The gibbet upon which one of his ancestors was hanged, according to legend, stands close by—in fact, not a single character, not even Phillotson, escapes connections with this primeval track.

Christminster is vividly represented in the novel and is too complex and too detailed to discuss here. As dream city, Christminster is Jude's New Jerusalem (he thinks of himself as Christ-like), and it is here that he wishes to become a scholar, but instead he learns the bitterest lessons of his life. The college he applies to, Biblioll College, is held to be based on Balliol (founded in 1263), which was one of the first to open its doors to the working classes.

Jude meets Sue in Christminster, and when she leaves to go to training school in Melchester (modeled on the cathedral city of Salisbury some 60 miles from Oxford), Jude takes up quarters there and works on the restoration of the ancient cathedral. Moving farther south, Shaston, a historical contraction of the medieval town of Shaftesbury (about 30 miles from Dorchester), provides home and schoolhouse for Phillotson and his benighted wife, Sue, and verges closer upon Hardy's own territory near Dorchester. Aldbrickham, modeled on the commercial town of Reading (back on the road to Oxford), provides yet another venue for Jude and Sue. Living there, Jude pursues his work as monumental mason, and when he and Sue visit the Wessex Agricultural Show, Arabella spots them there. This is probably their happiest time. As ever the setting is urban.

Stoke-Barehills (based on Basingstoke—another sizable town) is the last of the fixed abodes for the lovers, who thereafter adopt a nomadic life for a few years following Jude's discharge from his church work. They wander far and wide at this point, working in distant towns such as Sandbourne (Bournemouth), Casterbridge (Dorchester), Exonbury (Exeter), and Kennetbridge (Newbury), where Arabella finds Sue selling cakes at a market stall. They finally return to Christminster, where they live in poverty and end in tragedy.

Sue, emotionally destroyed by the tragedy, leaves to remarry Phillotson, now back in the village of Marygreen, and the now sickly Jude, no longer caring whether he lives or dies, treks five miles through the rain to see her one last time. He retraces his steps to his native village, across the ridgeway, till he comes to the milestone where he had carved his name. Rain soddened, he stumbles past the gibbet of his ancestor and onward to his beloved Sue. Exhausted, ill, and spent, he later returns to Christminster to die.

ALTERNATIVE READING: FEMINIST CRITICISM

Feminist criticism has, theoretically, moved beyond issues of patriarchy. But there are still adherents of that school. In contrast to postmodernism, which tends to oppose the idea of seeing language as a stable, closed system, some recent feminists have placed considerable authority in the patriarchal text—that, for example, what Jude wants is implicit in his view of language (learned from books) and that his sense of reality (Christminster) is shaped by the biblical text. Psychoanalytic theory, by contrast, would reverse this and argue that Jude "wants" first and foremost and gains illumination, inspiration, and, inadvertently, influence from the patriarchal text after the fact.

This same feminist vantage point situates Jude as the author's mouthpiece. Indeed, this is a preoccupation in one particular feminist camp that seeks to show that the author *is* the character, that the men who gaze on women in Hardy's fiction represent the Peeping Tomism of the author, or that the admiring eye of the hero, casting an appreciative eye over the woman he desires, reflects the voyeuristic (scopophilic) activities of his creator. Hardy creates a good many female characters who gaze appreciatively on the male body, or upon each other, but this form of scopophilia, or even lesbianism, is not ascribed to the author.

An alternative school of criticism would claim that an author is not circumscribed by his or her sexuality—that a writer can create male as well as female characters who are autonomous, not projections of himself or herself. It is worth noting in this context that when Hardy first published *Far From the Madding Crowd* as an anonymous author, he was taken to be George Eliot (who, despite her male pseudonym, is a woman). This mistaken identity would appear to support the autonomous school of thought.

In line with the notion of "character as mouthpiece," Jude is seen as the passive agent of ideology rather than as a seeker in his own right: instead of summoning the Christminster "ghosts" as much-needed father figures, mentors, and supporters of his cause, Jude *listens* (passively) to the "ghostly presences." These are considered by feminists who promote this theory to be unconvincing presences because they have been conjured by Hardy for his own purposes—whatever these might be—and have nothing to do with artistic characterization, only with autobiographical fiction. It might be added here that Sue Bridehead's capacity for conjuring presences, for seeing "things in the air," is also a gift Jude possesses; hence, there appears to be a conflict of feminist theory with textual evidence in this respect.

In foregrounding the patriarchal text, the reliance is on the biographical text, regarding *Jude* as radically shaped by Hardy's own feelings about the body (albeit that these feelings are indeterminable). A far more persuasive feminist approach treats Jude's dilemma of identity not only as a thing in its own right (not as a mirror to the author's feelings) but also as an issue to be debated in the context of his conflicting responses to his cousin, Sue Bridehead. This theory seeks not so much to establish the authenticity of character (Jude's or Sue's) as to analyze the construct of identity itself in relation to the feminine, notably Sue's role as catalyst for the text's critique of sexuality and class.

Linking up with Bakhtin's dialogical model of an individual's engagement with the world (the struggle between inner self and the external not-self), this feminist analytical approach pursues the authoritative word, Jude's reading the texts of the "Fathers," in the context of Sue's otherness. She represents all that Jude wishes to rebel against. Indeed, he knows her before he meets her. And he knows her to be his other—she is the tomboy to his "poor useless boy" (as Aunt Drusilla describes him). Sue, on her part, values Jude's "useless" otherworldliness. Even his failure of ambition is a virtue in her eyes (unlike many heroes in Hardy, Jude is a good person).

Jude, in turn, constructs his identity with decreasing attachment to the authoritative texts that initially shape his thoughts and aspirations and more in relation to Sue's interpretation of them. Hence, the external not-self is assimilated to the self's ultimate identity. In contrast to the feminist theories cited at the beginning of this segment, Jude immediately feels himself to be in the presence of kin when he enters Christminster. These are not patriarchal presences or Thomas Hardy's autobiographical projections, but Jude's own siblings in spirit—those "other sons of the place." This reading situates Jude precisely where he wants to be. Christminster's alienation effect (pertaining to Bakhtin's external, authoritative world) exists only in relation to the internal persuasiveness of Jude's own consciousness, in which he dwells with Sue. In this manner, by this method, the reader comes far closer to identifying with Jude and his tomboy "other"—far closer than the alternative theory cited at the outset permits.

If there are varying levels of reader sensitivity in feminist criticism—some alienating, some captivating the reader—the most extreme is the kind that positions readers in an antagonistic role. Several male feminist critics have recently projected onto the reader their own experience of what they call homicidal voyeurism and sadism—this perspective, they claim, derives from their own personal experience of *Jude* (and in one case, of *Tess*). For example, it is no longer that Aunt Drusilla can recount innocent tales of Sue as a child wading into the pond with "her shoes and stockings off, and her petticoats pulled above her knees" (110), but that readers are indulging in erotic pedophilia. The critic's assumptions are that we (readers) are deriving vicarious satisfaction from such scenes—Sue wading stockingless (erotic pedophilia) and Farmer Troutham beating Jude (sadism).

No critic to date has yet explained why this should come under the umbrella of feminist criticism (aside from the fact that it publishes in that name). The question arises: does the erotic pedophilia reside in the text or in the reader's mind independent of the text; or, is the innocence of the text defiled by the guilt of the reader? "No doubt," writes Hardy in the 1912 postscript to *Jude*, "there can be more in a book than the author consciously put there, which will help either to its profit or to its disadvantage as the case may be."

NOTES

1. From Hardy's poem "In Tenebris II": "if a way to the Better there be, it exacts a full look at the Worst." *Thomas Hardy. The Complete Poems*, edited by James Gibson (London: Macmillan, 1976), 168.

2. "Ironically" because Jowett (Greek scholar, Church of England clergyman, master of Balliol College, vice-chancellor of Oxford (1870–93), and a highly influential teacher) is held to be the model for the master of Biblioll College in *Jude*—the man who so brutally shatters Jude's dream of entering the university.

3. Divorce as a secular, legal measure was relatively new for the masses. Before the 1857 Matrimonial Causes Act, divorce had been a slow and expensive business available only to the wealthy and influential because it required a private Act of Parliament. The new 1857 act allowed the husband to petition through the law courts on the basis of

his wife's adultery. The wife did not have the same rights. She had to prove her husband had committed adultery coupled with incest or bigamy or cruelty or desertion. Hence Jude takes the action against Arabella, and Phillotson takes the action against Sue.

4. Hardy's full phrase reads: "The older one gets, the more deplorable seems the effect of that terrible, dogmatic ecclesiasticism—Christianity so called (but really Paulinism *plus* idolatry)—on morals & true religion: a dogma with which the real teaching of Christ has hardly anything in common" (*Letters*, V2.143).

5. Hardy marked in his Bible the following verse from Job, whose words are the last Jude utters: "Why is light given to a man whose way is hid, and whom God hath hedged in?" (Job 3:23).

6. Author of *Keynotes*, George Everton (Chavelita Clairmonte) wrote this to Hardy. See Millgate's note to Hardy's letter to Clairmonte (*Letters*, V2.102).

7. Hardy wrote to an animal protection group, saying "it occurred to me that one of the scenes might be useful in teaching mercy in the Slaughtering of Animals for the meat-market—the cruelties involved in the business having been a great grief to me for years" (*Letters*, V2.97). Subsequently his "A Merciful Man" was published in the *Animals' Friend* (published by the Society for the Protection of Animals, December 1895).

8. See Annie Besant and Charles Bradlaugh, in *The Fruits of Philosophy* (London: Freethought Publishing Co., 1877), Charles Knowlton's book advocating birth control. Besant and Bradlaugh were sentenced to six months for obscenity, although the sentence was waived.

9. In this context Hardy writes to Gosse: "One point illustrating this I cd not dwell upon: that, though she has children, her intimacies with Jude have never been more than occasional, even while they were living together (I mention that they occupy separate rooms, except towards the end), & one of her reasons for fearing the marriage ceremony is that she fears it wd be breaking faith with Jude to withhold herself at pleasure, or altogether, after it; though while uncontracted she feels at liberty to yield herself as seldom as she chooses" (*Letters*, V2.99).

10. The 1893 Married Women's Property Act afforded married women full legal control of all their property owned before or after marriage, whether by inheritance or by their own earnings. But new laws and old customs are frequently at odds. Feminist Millicent Garrett Fawcett recalls losing her pocketbook in the late 1890s and not being able to trace it. It was eventually recovered—registered by the Lost Property Office in her husband's name as his property.

11. For the full text, see Hardy's letter to Clodd (*Letters*, V2.92).

12. Under British church and state laws of consanguinity, cousins can marry, unlike the 24 states in the United States where this is banned.

13. Edmund Gosse's review in *St. James' Gazette*, November 8, 1895, begins, "It is a very gloomy, it is even a grimy, story that Mr. Hardy has at last presented to his admirers."

14. The House of Atreus features in the tragedies of Aeschylus, Sophocles, and Euripides, who depict generations of god-defying characters who commit horrible crimes against each other. Agamemnon is a son of the House of Atreus.

15. The actual village of Great Fawley lies close to Little Fawley, a hamlet in the county of Berkshire.

7

The Poetry—An Overview

Hardy was first and foremost a poet. He considered his fiction to be secondary to his achievements in verse, and, indeed, his status as the Grand Old Man of English Letters and his influence on modern poetry rests securely on these achievements. However, without the fame and furor of his novel-writing years, which by the turn of the century had brought his name into prominence among the literati and the common reader alike, it might well have proved very difficult indeed to gain the attention of potential publishers.

He had been writing poetry from the outset: "Domicilium"[1]—a retrospective vision of the Bockhampton birthplace, the speaker of the poem echoing the voice of his grandmother—was begun as early as 1857, when he was but a lad of 17. Three years later he started composing poems for a collection but met with dispiriting rejections from editors. By the end of his career as a novelist, in 1896, with 14 novels and 40 short stories to his name, he had also written 50 known poems but had published none.

Hardy was, by now, a man of independent means and could afford to return to poetry, his greatest love. He would, he said,

> abandon at once a form of literary art he had long intended to abandon at some indefinite time, and resume openly that form of it which he had been able to keep alive from his early years, half in secrecy, under the pressure of magazine writing. (*LW*, 309)

Critics deplored this move. But the visionary Hardy was, as ever, one step ahead of them: he was to compose over a thousand poems, all told—most of them published in his lifetime.

His career as a poet—nearly 70 years in all—spanned the Victorian, the Georgian and Edwardian periods, World War I, and beyond into the 1920s. No other poet writing in the English language reached so extensive an audience in his or her own lifetime. Hardy touched the lives of thousands and influenced poets from his own generation right through to the millennium years—from Siegfried Sassoon, who took *The Dynasts* into the trenches of World War I; to Edmund Blunden, for whom Hardy's "loving kindness" remained a lifelong inspiration; Walter de la Mare, who sought to emulate his pastoral mode; Cecil Day Lewis, who admired and aspired to his experimentalism; W. H. Auden, for whom Hardy was his "first master"; to one of his most devoted followers, John Betjeman, who also sought to forge links between the rural life and modern metropolis.

Back in 1896, Hardy's return to poetry was largely influenced by the endless censorship troubles he was still enduring as a novelist:

> Perhaps I can express more fully in verse ideas and emotions which run counter to the inert crystallized opinion—hard as rock—which the vast body of men have vested interests in supporting. To cry out in a passionate poem that (for instance) the Supreme Mover or Movers, the Prime Force or Forces, must be either limited in power, unknowing or cruel ... will cause them merely a shake of the head ... If Galileo had said in verse that the world moved, the Inquisition might have let him alone. (*LW*, 302)

Overall, despite various academic attempts at categorization, Hardy's poetic oeuvre has persistently defied definition. This has been both problematic (especially for traditionalists) and glorious. "The immense rambling country house of his *Collected Poems* has so many rooms that one could live in it forever," Mark Van Doren once said—marveling at his rediscoveries as he "peered" with the poet "at every visible shape, human or unbreathing" (*Autobiography* [1958], 167–68).

Hardy's vision and poetic influence live on to this day, as modern poets Philip Larkin and Seamus Heaney would vouch. But of all his qualities, it is his integrity, candor, courage, and sincerity that, through the ages, have brought the accolades: "Hardy," Larkin says simply, "taught one to feel."

THE DYNASTS (1904–1908)

Of all his works in verse, Hardy's monumental Napoleonic epic drama, *The Dynasts*, remained from first to last the magnum opus of his dreams.[2] He had started research on the Napoleonic Wars as a young man in London in the 1860s with his mentor and close friend Horace Moule advising and encouraging at every point. Thirty years later, after ending his career as a novelist, Hardy renewed his endeavor and subsequently published *The Dynasts*—Part First in 1904, Part Second in 1906, and Part Third in 1908.

The Dynasts is structured along the principles of Hardy's philosophical concept of the Immanent Will—a nonhuman, nondivine force lacking consciousness—acting as a kind of celestial machine upon the witless lives of men and women. Thus Napoleon, deluded by notions of power, ambition, and self-will, cannot achieve the dynasty he seeks.

With its vast array of voices and 297 characters, *The Dynasts* concludes on a choral note of muted hope that the Immanent Will *may* develop consciousness and *may* become aware of the pain and suffering borne by all creatures on Earth. The chorus chants:

> But—a stirring thrills the air
> Like to sounds of joyance there
> That the rages
> Of the ages
> Shall be cancelled, and deliverance offered from the darts that were,
> Consciousness the Will informing, till It fashion all things fair!

(Part Third, After Scene)

The Dynasts was not well received at first. Critics didn't know what to make of its unique structure and content, much of which is innovative, and, in terms of poetic form, highly unconventional. It employs a variety of ballads, rhyme schemes, assorted jigs, reels, morris dance tunes, and other folk rhythms. Yet by 1910 with the Order of Merit award (where it received honorable mention), the 1914 success of the Granville-Barker staging in London, followed by Oxford University's Dramatic Society production in 1920 (choosing *The Dynasts* in preference to a work by Shakespeare), and the acclamation of 100 younger poets including W. H. Auden, D. H. Lawrence, Ezra Pound, Dylan Thomas, and Siegfried Sassoon, it was clear that Hardy's masterpiece had arrived.

WESSEX POEMS AND OTHER VERSES (1898)

Wessex Poems (WP),[3] the first of Hardy's eight collections of verse, comprises 51 poems—one-third of which date back to the 1860s. The first edition features 30 of Hardy's own illustrations.[4] Describing this collection in his preface as a miscellany, Hardy recalls that many of the pieces were

> written long ago, and others partly written. In some few cases the verses were turned into prose and printed as such, it having been unanticipated at that time that they might see the light.

This "turning into prose" had been detected by Coventry Patmore in the early 1870s in *A Pair of Blue Eyes*, which he admired deeply for "the poetry infused in the prose."

Hardy goes on to justify his use of dialect: "Whenever an ancient and legitimate word of the district, for which there was no equivalent in received English, suggested itself.... It has been made use of, on what seemed good grounds" (*CP,*

6). "The Bride-Night Fire" in *Wessex Poems* is a fine example of this. From the outset Hardy had always been a devout champion of dialect, as manifest in the novels, and he never ceased to perfect his skills in rendering the "ancient" words as a vibrant, salt-of-the-earth living language.

Grouping of Poems in *Wessex Poems and Other Verses*

Circa 1860–1874

Thirteen poems in this sequence are dated 1866, the year of Hardy's breakup with his first love, Eliza Nicholls. "Amabel" and the "She to Him" sonnets are youthful, change-of-heart verses. "At a Bridal," "Her Dilemma," and "Neutral Tones"—"the tedious riddles of years ago"—are similarly experimental but bear motifs of mischance and lost opportunities in love. Of the three poems, "Neutral Tones" is held to be the most accomplished in its search for meaning in nature mirroring an exploration of inner, complex emotions.

"The Temporary the All (Sapphics)," "In Vision I Roamed," and "Hap" anticipate Hardy's developing cosmology of a godless, indifferent universe ("Purblind Doomsters … Crass Casualty"), whereas poems such as "Heiress and Architect," "At an Inn," and the disturbing "A Confession to a Friend in Trouble" take a retrospective look at a self-indulgent caprice, the disillusionment of a hope-filled, clandestine meeting, and a self-honest, moral dilemma, respectively.

Circa 1878–1883

Hardy clusters a contrasting series of poems at the center of this volume. His life-long interest in the Napoleonic Wars shapes "Valenciennes," "San Sebastian," and the antiwar poem "The Peasant's Confession"—"the great Napoleon, who for years had strewn/Men's bones all Europe through." "The Sergeant's Song," which appears in chapter 5 of *The Trumpet-Major*, was later set to music by Gustav Holst. The locally set ballad "The Dance at the Phoenix" (Hardy liked this poem) is a fine example of narrative art; it resembles a folk song as does "The Casterbridge Captains." "The Burghers" also has a Wessex setting, where the speaker-husband sets out by night to intercept his wife with her lover to slay them. He is startled, though, by her move to save her lover, to fling her "faint form shieldingly/On his, against the vengeance of my vows." "Blanked by such love," he now sees himself as nothing more than a "licensed tyrant." He is transformed by this epiphany: instead of murdering them, he takes them in, gives them money and provisions, and sends them on their way. This echoes many a Hardyan theme of role reversal, where the woman becomes the valiant knight and saves the helpless male (see also *A Pair of Blue Eyes*).

Circa 1885–1890

"The Impercipient (At a Cathedral Service)," which in the manuscript is less opaquely titled "An Agnostic (Evensong—Cathedral)," expresses the heartfelt cry of an unbeliever feeling excluded by the believers around him. "A Sign Seeker," a musing existentialist verse, heralds a group of personal poems: "I learn to prophesy the hid eclipse/.... To weigh the sun, and fix the hour each planet dips."

In contrast to his customary verbal and metrical experimentation, Hardy keeps "Thoughts of Phena: At News of her Death" very simple, soft, and beautiful, evoking the speaker's sense of emptiness and loss: "Not a line of her writing have I, /Not a thread of her hair, /No mark of her late time as dame in her dwelling, whereby/I may picture her there." The yearning voice, protesting the sense of loss in the negations, "Not," "Not," "No," echoes in the lonely-sounding cries of the long-drawn-out vowels. "Thoughts of Phena" is contrasted by another bereavement poem, "Middle-Age Enthusiasms," dedicated to "M. H."—Mary Hardy, his adored sister and childhood companion—which moves beyond feelings of loss to a kind of denial, an alienating nullification of the past.

One of the most important and most ingeniously structured poems of the 1890s period is "Nature's Questioning." In a significant circularity of form, the poem begins and ends with a personal meditation. "When I look forth" concludes at the last "No answerer I. ..." A movement within the speaker's orbit of reverie signals a philosophical discourse appropriately focusing on some "Vast Imbecility, /Mighty .../impotent ..." that has left humanity in a state of incompleteness ("are we live remains /Of Godhead"?). Appropriate because, in pulling the speaker into its own orbit of impotency, it ratifies the sense of universal incompletion: "Earth's old glooms and pains/Are still the same."

Wessex Poems concludes with one of Hardy's most oft-quoted short verses, "I Look into My Glass," where the speaker projects his intense emotional hunger onto his dispiriting, aging reflection in the mirror. He cries out against "Time," which "Part steals, lets part abide; /And shakes this fragile frame at eve/With throbbings of noontide."

POEMS OF THE PAST AND THE PRESENT (1901)

During this early period of his return to verse, Hardy felt "an awkwardness in getting back to an easy expression in numbers after abandoning it for so many years" (*LW,* 310). While "abandoning it" he never had, that crucial dimension for a writer—a sense of audience—would have been remote to him as, for all those years, he projected voice, ideas, intellect, and imagination onto an entirely different medium, to an entirely different listener—the reader of the novel. "Numbers," too—symbols, abstract units, figures of representation, word forms, and so on—operate rather differently under a nonmetric system. Likewise, the highly censored medium of the novel provided Hardy with an audience he could not always identify with. So, "awkwardness," yes, after working against the grain of his own poetic temperament for twenty-odd years as a novelist. He had felt unheard for far too long. Few major poets have suffered this prolonged sense of muteness. The "getting back" must have felt rather like being released from shackles (how, now, to recover that easy gait?).

"An easy expression" for Hardy did not mean conventional sounds and traditional metrics. Ease of expression meant challenging those very forms by innovation, experimentation, and invention. Language, he believed, was constantly mutable—as in the conceptual framework laid down by the Greek philosopher Heraclitus: no one steps into the same river twice.

"Much," writes Hardy in the preface to his second published volume of verse, containing 99 poems,[5] "is dramatic and impersonative." By "dramatic" he is referring to the play of action, the conversion of thoughts and ideas into dramatic scenes. By "impersonative" he means the adoption of a persona or speaker in the poems who represents, in his or her own right, with his or her own voice, manner, body, and style, *another* person, thing, or idea. Think ventriloquism: the speaker is not one and the same as the poet-puppeteer but is "impersonative," performing a different role and owning a separate identity.

Hardy makes no apology for the lack of cohesion in this collection:

> Unadjusted impressions have their value, and the road to a true philosophy of life seems to lie in humbly recording diverse readings of its phenomena as they are forced upon us by chance and change. (*CP*, 84)

Poems of the Past and the Present (PPP) received many favorable reviews, although there were some complaints about his "ugly" neologisms, his attraction to the charnel house, his gruesome morbidity, and so on. The collection sold well, requiring a second printing within a few weeks of publication. And the following year, when Hardy switched from Harpers to Macmillan, there was a further reprint, with corrections, in the form of Volume 19 of Hardy's *Works* (Uniform Edition), another in 1907, another (Wessex Edition) in 1912, and yet another, with minor corrections (Mellstock Edition), in 1920—*Collected Poems* appeared in 1920 and 1923.[6]

Grouping of Poems in *Poems of the Past and the Present*

War Poems

After a short philosophical "Reverie," Hardy goes straight to a selection of 11 war poems.[7] "Embarcation" fittingly sets the sequence in motion (this poem is inscribed, incidentally, on the starboard walls of the new Cunard liner, Queen Mary II): "Wives, sisters, parents, wave white hands and smile, /As if they knew not that they weep the while." Three "departure" poems follow where the focus is on the loved ones left behind. Next, "At the War Office, London" elicits the anguish of the "hourly posted sheets of scheduled slaughter," but the most renowned in this series is the antijingoistic "Drummer Hodge." Here the speaker tells of a "homely" Wessex lad who now forms "a portion of that foreign plain" in the veldt lying not under his own familiar skies but alone and unknowing under "strange-eyed constellations" where he has been thrown into a mass grave, "uncoffined."

Moving from one tragic young casualty of war to "The Souls of the Slain," Hardy expertly orchestrates the voices of the dead, "the spirits of those who were homing" but who never come home. They are plunged, instead, into the "engulphing, ghast, sinister place" of the ocean, where they remain "in the gloaming," part of the "sea-mutterings." A meditative poem, nuanced with fine detailing ("The thick lids of Night closed upon me"), ironies of rhyme ("Sweethearts"/"fleet hearts"), and juxtaposition ("war-mightiness"/"homely acts"), "The Souls of the Slain" is immediately followed, sadly and ironically, by a song ringing with waiting hope and high expectations for the homing men: it is the "Song of the Soldiers' Wives and Sweethearts."

Several of the war poems, including "Drummer Hodge," have proved controversial. The antiwar poem "A Christmas Ghost-Story," first published in the *Westminster Gazette,* questions the Christian "Law of Peace" from a nonpartisan standpoint—later amended by Hardy following critical commentary from readers to the more partisan, "your countryman." The antiwar tone remains. The war sequence concludes with "The Sick Battle-God"—a "lurid Deity" who no longer has a role to play because modern wars return no heroes and bring no rejoicing. Rather, the "many-sidedness of things" erodes all need to imagine any kind of God battling on one's side.

Poems of Pilgrimage

Hardy's journeys to Italy and Switzerland in the late 1880s (at the time of *The Woodlanders*), in which he visited the burial grounds of his literary predecessors, yielded a variety of poems. The most notable, "Shelley's Skylark," reverses the Shelleyan sentiment of "Ecstatic heights" inspired by the exquisite song of the bird. Instead, it celebrates simply the dust, "The dust of the lark that Shelley heard,/And made immortal through times to be;—/Though it only lived like another bird,/And knew not its immortality." It is the bird itself and not the effect of the bird upon the human senses that "Shelley's Skylark" evokes and with such extraordinary compassion for the "little ball of feather and bone" that Shelley's own ecstatic sentiment appears almost fanciful and self-indulgent by comparison. In his inimitable way, Hardy interrogates the immortality extolled by his esteemed predecessor and returns it to the meek life that inspired it.

Several "Rome" poems and assorted celebratory verses follow—"These umbered cliffs, and gnarls of masonry" is one finely textured phrase—resurrecting ghosts from the past and the broken grace of great ruins. "Lausanne: In Gibbon's Old Garden: 11–12 p.m." bears the inscription: "27th June 1897 (The 100th anniversary of the completion of the 'Decline and Fall' at the same hour and place)." The speaker here communes with Gibbon, who first asks, "How fares the Truth now?'" and then quotes Milton's words: "'*Truth like a bastard comes into the world/Never without ill-fame to him who gives her birth'*"—but there is no answer. Hardy's speaker remains mute. For one who suffered firsthand and sorely from "ill-fame," whose bowdlerized novels muted what he considered to be the "Truth now," the silence is eloquent.[8]

Miscellaneous Poems

This sequence contains 67 poems of which the group of cosmological verses provides an important elaboration of the theme broached in "Nature's Questioning"—the impotency, indifference, or cruel lack of awareness of the Immanent Will (as Hardy chose to call the Supreme Mover, or God). Of this group, "ΑΓ–ΝΩΣΤΩΙ ΘΕΩΙ" (Agnosto Theo), which appears later in the collection, directly addresses an unknown god. The opening cluster includes "God-Forgotten," in which an indifferent deity admits to having "no remembrance" of the Earth. "It perished, surely"? And anyway, "I lost my interest from the first." The speaker pleads that "Earth's race" still exists, but the only response to this is that there is no need to "heed their tainted ball."

In "The Lacking Sense" the "force" (Time) is blamed for effecting crimes against humanity, "Whereat all creation groans." But in "The Mother Mourns" the roles are reversed: Nature itself is the accuser, blaming mankind for all ills.

Several of these poems, including "Doom and She" and "The Sleep-Worker," cry out, as does Jude in Hardy's last novel, against Nature's brutal law, whose "coils" are "wrought unwittingly." As several scholars have noted, the notion of a world bereft of beneficent forces remains a theme pursued by several notable Victorian poets. Hardy's distinction lies in the power of his sincerity and compassion. Even so, running "counter to … crystallized opinion" and "cry[ing] out in a passionate poem" provoked one contemporary reader to write to him saying he seemed like "some terrible old prophet crying in the wilderness." Again, the "crying in the wilderness" is also Jude's role (born ahead of his time)—a reminder of how closely Hardy's prose narratives and poems so often interact: "He had mostly aimed," he writes in the *Life*, "to keep his narratives … as near to poetry in their subject as the conditions would allow" (*LW*, 309).

Love Lyrics

In the miscellany there are many love lyrics, of which "A Broken Appointment" is possibly the best known. Reputedly inspired by Florence Henniker, this soft-singing sonnet opens and closes the first stanza with a heartbeat refrain: "You did not come," "You did not come." This rhythmic pattern recurs in the second stanza: "You love not me" and (the final interrogative) "You love not me?"—the two-beat measure treading and retreading the pacing steps of the waiting lover. The disappointment is palpable: "Was it not worth a little hour or more/ … Once you, a woman, came/To soothe a time-worn man." Yet, leaving with the interrogative, "You love not me?"—which echoes, but questioningly, the earlier line "love … can lend you loyalty"—hope lingers on. A sweet song of love and loyalty ("Between Us Now") immediately follows as if in direct response to the plaintive question left unanswered in "A Broken Appointment."

Here, very briefly, is an indication of the sheer variety of what follows in this subsection. The triolet "How Great My Grief" expresses love and longing; "I Need Not Go" reverses the "Broken Appointment" situation of the waiting lover ("New loves inflame me"); "The Coquette, and After" provides a retaliative contrast (wishing that "your free heart should ache for me!"); "A Spot" poignantly recalls a past love; and "Long Plighted"—jadedly wondering whether it is worthwhile trying to revive old desires—drifts, despite itself, toward tenderness. These are succeeded by "The Widow Betrothed"—she eclipses her lover in favor of "the call of motherhood"; "His Immortality," which looks inward to a shriven heart; "The To-Be-Forgotten"—mourning "oblivion's swallowing sea"; and "Wives in the Sere," which echoes the theme of Hardy's novel *The Well-Beloved,* where the unattainable "wives" seem "Something beautiful to those/Patient to peruse ..."

These heart-searching poems contrast significantly with the harshly bitter, self-annihilating "Tess's Lament" (augmenting Tess's voice in *Tess of the d'Urbervilles*) and those that encompass broader social issues in this collection, notably the oft-quoted, iconoclastic[9] "The Ruined Maid" and "The Levelled Churchyard"—poems spiked with cutting irony and satire.

Birds and Insects

Another subgroup of poems treats with creatures great and small. The most notable, "An August Midnight," points to the existentialist Hardy for whom a tiny moment—the meeting of five insects (moths, longlegs, flies) banging aimlessly and self-destructively on the speaker's night lamp—provokes the humble thought that "They know Earth-secrets that know not I." The philosopher-poet is stirred by the minutiae of life to muse on the nature of being.

A number of other poems follow, philosophically contemplating birds, flowers, fields, a caged thrush, game birds, and comets—crowned by the highly acclaimed "The Darkling Thrush." This is Hardy's most anthologized poem. First published in the *Graphic,* subtitled "By the Century's Deathbed," and, in common with "An August Midnight," "The Darkling Thrush" celebrates the mystery of things unknowable but possible, as befits a poem written at the turn of the century. Significantly, as with many of Hardy's juxtaposed poems, it stands between "The Last Chrysanthemum," which asks why this doomed flower should bloom out of season (while resisting the survival-of-the-fittest explanation), and "The Comet at Yell'ham," which ponders the ephemeral mystery of the "fiery train" with its "strange swift shine" and its unpredictable recurrence.

Philosophical Verses

Still contemplating the mystery of the unknowable moment, the much-lauded poem "The Self-Unseeing" recalls a childhood experience of dreamy bliss that memory manages to retrieve out of a former state of unawareness: "Yet, we were looking away!" This poem is followed by the three philosophical "In Tenebris" poems, the second of which carries a phrase familiar to all Hardyans as encapsulating his meliorist philosophy:[10] "If a way to the Better there be, it exacts a full look at the Worst" ("In Tenebris II")—the capitalized words maximize their own capital, as it were.

Poems of the Past and the Present concludes somewhat inconclusively with a medley: *Imitations, Etc*, six incidental poems after Heine, Catullus, and so on, and *Retrospect*, three fantasy poems of which "ΑΓΝΩΣΤΩΙ ΘΕΩΙ" (aforementioned) carries most weight. The lack of finish to the collection and the sense of indeterminacy well befits "*the Present*" element in the volume title. This gesture at unending, so to speak, not only is very Hardyan but deliberately points onward, to the future. This is reinforced by the last words on the last page, which are set in the future conditional tense: "I/Would raise my voice in song."

TIME'S LAUGHINGSTOCKS AND OTHER VERSES (1909)

Hardy stresses yet again the disparate nature of his collection, and this time he offers an apologia arguing for no apology. "Dramatic monologues by different characters," he claims, render "the lack of concord" immaterial. Hardy's need to restate an apologia in this, his third volume, suggests that editors and critics were pressuring for homogeneous collections. Hardy did not succumb to this pressure. Most of his subtitles indicating groups of poems in this collection are entirely arbitrary. Many of the lyrics are narratives, many of the narratives are lyrical, and most of the themes and motifs intersect with one another, or complement one another, and even contradict or appear to negate one another. If there existed headings that could adequately subdivide and categorize the 94 pieces in this volume, the chances are that few of the poems would prove to be the boundary-breaking works they actually are. Poems can be likened to human emotions in that they resist categorization, they are too complex to be defined under simple headings, and they can rarely be signposted within fixed boundaries. Categories and headings aspire to the absolute. Hardy's poetry does not.

There was also, coincidentally, a lack of concord in Hardy's private life during the years of *Time's Laughingstocks:* his deteriorating marriage had become virtually moribund. Emma had moved into the attic at Max Gate, and when she did appear, it was often to disappear. Once, at this time, she vanished without warning (taking the Channel crossing to Calais), without canceling a garden party she had arranged at Max Gate. Aside from these startling assaults on Hardy's patience and anxiety, she would spend her time lodging complaints—"renew[ing] her assault on the world of letters," as Michael Millgate puts it.

Time's Laughingstocks[11] contains almost double the amount of poems published in *Wessex Poems,* and at least a quarter of them had already appeared in distinguished literary periodicals. The reception to Hardy's first two collections had swung from the adulation of many contemporary poets to the vilification of traditionalists. As James Gibson notices, Wordsworth and Coleridge had suffered similarly with *Lyrical Ballads* when attempting to bring poetry back into the lives of everyday men and women a hundred years earlier. "Most of Hardy's critics," explains Gibson, "were unable to appreciate that there was a new voice in the land" (*Oxford Reader's Companion to Thomas Hardy* [*ORC*], 421).

Several modern scholars regard *Time's Laughingstocks*[12] as Hardy's true debut volume. *The Dynasts* (1904–8)—dubbed "The Iliad of Europe"—evidently contributed much to its achievement and success not simply by enhancing Hardy's reputation as a poet but, as Dennis Taylor points out, by helping to hone his poetic skills and his metrical development and facility in longer stanza forms. Of the 94 poems in *Time's Laughingstocks*, at least 60 rate among Hardy's greatest.

Hardy's beloved mother had died at age 90 in 1904. Mother and son had been close, spending a lifetime of Sundays together. Hardy was filled with the inconsolable sense of her absence—"The gap," he writes, "is wide, & not to be filled" (*Letters*, V3.119). No doubt he went some way toward narrowing the gap when invoking her presence, her memories, and her yesterdays in such retrospective poems as "A Church Romance," "The Roman Road," "After the Last Breath," "Night in the Old Home," "One We Knew," "A Wet Night," and "She Hears the Storm." For Hardy, with his deep psychic sense and powerful vision, a bereavement gap would rapidly fill with near-palpable presences. Even so, he would miss his mother's ready repartee, her quick-minded responses (so much faster than his own, he would say), and her "extraordinary store of local memories, reaching back to the days when the ancient ballads were everywhere heard at country feasts, in weaving shops, and at spinning wheels" (*LW*, 345). Thus the loss was also the loss of an era, a cultural heritage, and a community of folklore. Psychologically speaking, his mother's death heralded another kind of dispossession, that of his own lifelong identity as the "chosen" son. Cherished by a maternal heart—tender beneath the stern frame—this firstborn son never lost the solicitude of a mother who had almost lost her child at birth. He was, in her eyes, forever fragile—and as he grew to fame he must surely have been the "Beloved Son in whom she was well pleased."[13]

Groupings of Poems in *Time's Laughingstocks and Other Verses*

Time's Laughingstocks

The narrative poem "A Trampwoman's Tragedy" opens this collection (following "The Revisitation"). Hardy considered this balladlike tale one of his greatest achievements in form, and indeed the refrain that repeats, in each stanza, the preceding line cleverly mimics the jogging of the motley group of friends as they "beat afoot" (stanza one) and "jaunted on" (stanza two) "Ay, side by side" (stanza three). By the fourth stanza the speaker has overstepped the mark, as it were, by teasing her "fancy-man" and flirting with "jeering John." Thus, as jealousy and passion begin to rise, an ominous heart-pounding is infused into the refrain: "My man and I," "My man and I," (stanza 4) intensifies to

"O deadly day,/O deadly day!" (stanza 5), and by stanza 9 the dastardly deed is done: "with his knife,/And with his knife." Twice stabbed it would seem. The refrain now adjusts to a dying fall, the impetus descending slowly, seeping away like the lifeblood of the luckless lover. "Alone, alone!" the trampwoman is left—"alone I stray/Haunting the Western Moor." The metric patterning is beautifully done.

Although, prior to the publication of *Time's Laughingstocks*, Hardy had encountered opposition from the media and could not publish "A Trampwoman's Tragedy," as also the succeeding "A Sunday Morning Tragedy" (which treats with abortifacients), both poems have remained remarkably popular to this day.

"The House of Hospitalities" recalls soft memories of past Christmases with his mother: "I see forms of old time talking,/Who smile on me," while "Reminiscences of a Dancing Man" celebrates Hardy's love of the "wild, whirling" quadrille. From private to public, current affairs inspired "The Rejected Member's Wife" (first published in the *Spectator* as "The Ejected Member's Wife"), which, in a typical Hardyan reversal, looks at the losing electoral candidate (not the winner) to evoke the ephemeral life of a celebrity.

More Love Lyrics

The retrospective Hardy returns here with 26 poems, including "The Dawn after the Dance" (1869), "To an Actress" (1867), "Her Confession" (1865–67), "From Her in the Country" (1866), "At Waking" (1869), "The Minute Before Meeting" (1871), and "To an Impersonator of Rosalind" (1867)—youthful verses reworked by the mature poet of half a century later. A later poem of 1883, "He Abjures Love," ironically (given the group heading) rounds off this cluster. "Love" is here personified and gendered masculine—a "daysman" to whom youth has given too much credence and too much glory. The connotations of "daysman" are ephemerality, as in day laborer (hired for the day) or daylily, a plant that flowers for only a day. The speaker of the poem chastises himself for giving way to "heart-enslavement," to "daysman" fevers, for allowing himself to be "Enkindled by his fires." He is now mortified by having been "Too many times ablaze/With fatuous fires."

A Set of Country Songs

This sequence of 18 poems overlaps (as noticed earlier) in some cases with the *Love Lyrics*. "Rose-Ann," "The Husband's View," "To Carrey Clavel," and "Julie-Jane" come under the latter category but remain *Country Songs* because set in dialect: "Julie, O girl of joy,/Soon, soon that lover he came./Ah, yes; and gave thee a baby-boy,/But never his name...." The country song ballad "At Casterbridge Fair: 1. The Ballad-Singer" is a favorite among translators, including Romanian: "La Tingul de la Casterbridge."[14]

Pieces Occasional and Various

Family and folklore again supply the inspiration for some of these poems ("By the Barrows" and "One We Knew"), while others crosscut to the Wessex novels: "The Dead Quire" and "The Rash Bride: An Experience of the Mellstock Quire" recall *Under the Greenwood Tree*: "quiring her at the casement seemed romantic to the boy" but, unlike the "quiring" of Fancy Day, catching a shadowy glimpse of a man standing in her room behind her quashes all romantic notions. "The Roman Road" recalls *The Return of the Native* with the description of the road dissecting Egdon Heath: "As the pale parting-line in hair"; and "The Pine Planters (Marty South's Reverie)" speaks directly to *The Woodlanders*.

Hardy not only has a special talent for evoking the female voice (making him unique among male poets) in writing a poem of childbirth—"In Child-bed"—but he also is extraordinarily skilled in designing a poem's structure so that form *alone* reveals content. "The Dear" is a good example: it elicits from an incoherent dialogue with a maiden "One fain would guard" the sorry fact that she is deranged. She remains oblivious, but the reader gradually becomes aware of this while simultaneously being placed in her shoes—implicated in the incoherence of the dialogue and that nothing makes any sense. Another apt example is "New Year's Eve," where a dilettante God, preoccupied with producing pretty colors, sums up his efforts with, "I have finished another year." The speaker is dumbfounded: "what's the good of it"? but God isn't listening, thus permitting of no answer. Hence the act of not listening, of leaving questions unanswered, becomes the tenor of the poem. Oblivious as to ethics or meaning or logic, God simply continues with his activities "rapt" and "unweeting." That God's disordered activity is "logicless" and that it has no rhyme or reason is expertly ironized by the structure of the poem, which employs a metric order so regular, timeworn, and classic that it is in fact aptly mechanical (did Hardy have Paley's clockwork universe in mind—a mechanistic contrast to the "unweeting" deity of the poem?). Additionally, the perfect arrangement of closely patterned vowel sounds and end rhymes set in a strictly ordered rhyme scheme of a,b,a,a,b suggests that in comparison with the aimless dauber of pretty colors, a "higher" (poetic) mind is now at work.[15]

Other poems on this theme are "A Dream Question," in which God cares not a jot for what his creatures say, "Before Life and After," and "God's Education," where God is accused of cruelty. Back to earth, the long poem "Panthera" also challenges the status quo, contrasting "One Ralph Blossom Soliloquizes" and the case of a man brought before the town of "Budmouth" (circa seventeenth century) to implement his maintenance of his seven women lovers (Blossom was exempted from seven counts of alimony costs on the grounds that he was dying of a sexually transmitted disease). In the poem the women call to him, most of them with affection and with no regrets whatsoever. The last lines of the poem are Anne's: "wherefore should you burn down there?/There is a deed under the sun, my Love,/And that was ours./What's done is done, my Love./These trumpets here in Heaven are dumb to me/With you away. Dear, come, O come to me!"

There is no doubt that Hardy's return to verse afforded him the freedom of expression he had long yearned for as a novelist. Although establishment critics continued to vociferously express their displeasure, Hardy's words still held him in good stead, that "if Galileo had said in verse that the world moved, the Inquisition might have left him alone."

SATIRES OF CIRCUMSTANCE: LYRICS AND REVERIES WITH MISCELLANEOUS PIECES (1914)

In 1913 Hardy was passed over, in favor of the more conventional minor poet, Robert Bridges, for poet laureate. According to some critics, the influence of the clergy played a part in this decision. Whereas the academy, led by Aberdeen and Cambridge universities, were quick to offer Hardy honorary degrees, the establishment, especially in its clerical quarters, held firmly to traditional values, codes, and practices.

Ironically, Hardy had an aptitude for occasional verses and would have made an effective laureate, albeit that he would have had to curb his antiestablishment views. His fine tribute to his long-standing friend of 40 years, the eminent man of letters, George Meredith, was composed impromptu in one day and published three days later (in the *The Times*, collected in *TL*). And "The Schreckhorn," written in honor of Leslie Stephen (editor and friend of 20 years), collected in *Satires of Circumstance* (*SC*), is an exceptionally fine example of character figuration: the mountain merging with the man who loved to climb it—"this silent adamantine shape." Furthermore, Hardy regarded his poems based on real-life incidents as a unique kind of achievement, unique because the imagination could be constrained if circumscribed by a prior set of images and ideas. A good example of this achievement is "The Dance at the Phoenix" (*WP*), to which Hardy would refer with some pride as being "based on fact"—adding that it was a poem that Swinburne liked.

A curbed Hardy is not, of course, an attractive (let alone plausible) notion, so perhaps, in this instance, thanks should go to a conservative clerisy. How else would such masterpieces in *Satires of Circumstance* as the antiwar "Channel Firing" have been written?—"All nations striving strong to make/Red war yet redder. Mad as hatters/They do no more for Christés sake/Than you who are helpless in such matters." Or "The Convergence of the Twain (Lines on the loss of the 'Titanic')"?—whose shape moves across the page in stanzas topped and elongated like a ship viewed bow to stern and set in 11 progressive movements (short stanzas). These are odd, irregular in number as befits the topic, and shaped as triads—aaa, bbb, right through to kkk at the 11th movement (11th hour, the uneven hour?) when everything stops: "And consummation comes, and jars two hemispheres."

No doubt a laureate would have had to eulogize and elegize what Hardy ingeniously re-creates as a monumental convergence of two massive forces, the collision of "two hemispheres"—man's hubris and nature's supremacy. At an alternative level of signification, this catastrophic "consummation" rather uncannily prophesies the outcome of World War I.

England had declared war on Germany in August 1914, but Macmillan insisted on going ahead with *Satires of Circumstance*; 2,000 copies with 107 poems were printed at that time (35 previously published in periodicals), followed by a reprint with corrections and revisions in March 1915.[16] Hardy, who wrote no preface to this collection, told his friend Edmund Gosse that it was, as with previous collections, a mixture of "unstable fancies, conjectures, and contradictions." He added shortly afterward that many of the pieces

> do not precisely express my attitude to certain matters nowadays—or rather, they express what I would now prefer to leave unexpressed. They had, however, been printed in periodicals in past years, so I could hardly leave them out of the book though they seem to myself harsh beside the others. There is too, in me, a little of Pilate's feeling: "What I have written I have written." (*Letters*, V5.66)

Hardy was never quite reconciled to the placement of the Satires in his collection. As titleholder they might have opened the volume, but possibly his growing nervousness about their harshness provided him with good reason for placing them off-entry—further along at the center of the volume. In later editions he changed this and positioned them at the end of the collection.

His nervousness was not ill-founded. Critics took him to task over them. The *Academy* thought some of them "too horrible," the *Sunday Times* found them too pedantic in wording, and for the *Daily Telegraph* they lacked music. Hardy "places life on the operating table," wrote the *Globe*, "and with an uncannily skilful knife, lays it bare to the public gaze, a shuddering, trembling mass of anguished nerves, inexpressibly vile and appalling." But poets felt differently. For Lawrence Binyon, Hardy's poems had the effect "of little, deeply-bitten etchings," and for fellow poet Lytton Strachey, who was a devout admirer of Hardy's modernism, particularly his experimentalism, there were admittedly "cumbrous expressions, clumsy metres and flat, prosaic turns of speech," but these were "in reality an essential ingredient in the very essence of his work":

> The result is a product of a kind very difficult to parallel in our literature.... What gives Mr Hardy's poems their unique flavour is precisely their utter lack of romanticism, their common, un-decorated presentment of things. They are, in fact, modern as no other poems are. (*New Statesman*, December 1914)

Virtually ignored by reviewers were the most "musical" of the verses in the collection, the "Poems of 1912–13." Emma Hardy had died in 1912. Remorse, regret, and perhaps even a terrible, guilty sense of relief overwhelmed Hardy, and he instantly set about repairing some of the emotional damage inflicted on him by his difficult marriage. Writing a cluster of poems reifying the Emma he had once hoped to love, Hardy invoked emotions both sincere and moving, albeit projected onto a chimerical figure: the Emma he had longed for but had, in life, never found. As Hardy had shown in *The Well-Beloved* (rewritten in 1897), the creative imagination readily projects desire onto new objects, into new directions more longed for than actualized in real life, and when presence becomes absence, the imaginary beloved can be shaped at will to fill the painful gaps the insufficiency of "real life" had opened up. This is the context of the "1912–13"poems.

That Hardy juxtaposes the "1912–13" love poems with others treating with unhappy marriages and the "deeply bitten" Satires reveals something of his divided consciousness at this period. He could, after all, have composed (or retained) the "Emma" poems for a later volume where, standing alone, or set in more sympathetic company, they would not have been compromised by their bedfellows. But he did not. And since Hardy never positioned any one of his poems unthinkingly or casually, it would benefit the reader to consider each poem as an autonomous work in its own right and then to reconsider it in the literary context the poet has provided.

Groupings of Poems in *Satires of Circumstance: Lyrics and Reveries with Miscellaneous Pieces*

Lyrics and Reveries

The 30 poems in this group number among the most famous personal poems Hardy ever wrote. "After the Visit" is given pride of place and is dedicated to "F.E.D." Florence Dugdale and Hardy were married in 1914, following many years of close companionship that helped to sustain him during the final, troubled years of domestic life with Emma. "To Meet or Otherwise" follows, evoking the "human tenderness" and "faltering progress" of those companionable years. Next is the popular poem "When I Set out for Lyonnesse: 1870"—a falling-in-love "magic in my eyes!" romance inspired (with hindsight?) by Hardy's first meeting with Emma at the rectory at St. Juliot, Cornwall.[17] Then comes "The Sun on the Bookcase: (Student's Love-Song: 1870)"—set at the same date as "Lyonnesse" and portraying the kind of conflict the fictional Jude undergoes as a young scholar poring over Greek texts yet erotically distracted by thoughts of Arabella: "And I have wasted another day..../But wasted—*wasted*, do I say?/Is it a waste to have imaged one/Beyond the hills there, who, anon/My great deeds done,/Will be mine alway?"

That deadly war of spirit and flesh reconfigured here as the light that "smears" the bookcase (echoing Arabella's smearing of Jude's precious books), that "wasted day" that anticipates more fulfilling days of "great deeds"—all of this is familiar to Jude, whose grand dreams are rudely interrupted by Arabella, the "imaged one ... who anon.... Will be mine." Were such dreams also interrupted for one young poet by one maturing woman seeking a husband? Whatever the inspiration for the "Student's Love-Song," Hardy has chosen this spot for its inclusion among a sequence of poems treating with loves old (Emma) and loves new (the two Florences), loves past and present; hence its relevance is intriguing.

The magic circle is completed by "A Thunderstorm in Town: A Reminiscence: 1893," which, by all accounts, was inspired by Florence Henniker: "I should have kissed her if the rain/Had lasted a minute more." This fascinating cycle of intersecting relations—one man and three women, or more aptly, one poet and three lives—develops further, becoming even more complex in the process.

Two poems of yearning follow. First, "The Torn Letter," juxtaposed with "A Thunderstorm," describes years of longing: "That ache for you, born long ago/ Throbs on." Second, "Beyond the Last Lamp" recalls "thirty years of blur and blot," harking back to a pre-Henniker period when Emma and Hardy were still struggling with their difficult marriage. Are the phantom figures representations of a domestic demise? Does the ghost of broken hopes inform the anguish of those who "Held in suspense a misery/At things which had been or might be"?

That said, it is almost impossible to precisely date a Hardy poem, and equally inappropriate to ascribe the experiences and feelings evoked therein to those who inspire them. Hardy would start and stop a poem over the years much as he would plant shrubs at Max Gate and cut and prune and graft for growth and fruit—"graft" being the operative word.

"Wessex Heights," dated 1896, would seem to make it a Henniker-inspired poem: "As for one rare fair woman, I am now but a thought of hers,/.... Yet my love for her in its fullness she herself even did not know;/.... and now I can let her go," but Hardy never did let her go. And on her part, she remained as loyal and loving as a dutiful wife (of another man) could be, constant until the day she died. Indeed, in this very year of 1914, which was also the year of Hardy's second marriage (to the other Florence), his thoughts (to Henniker) turned on "old times—very romantic ones—when I was younger than I am now, though you seem the same as you were then" (*Letters*, V3.134). Clearly, the force of her inspiration was as strong as ever even if *her* thoughts had turned on what must have seemed to have been Hardy's lack of constancy.

But despair and dejection afflict any intimate relationship, and theirs was no exception. Typically, when Hardy seeks to project fear and insecurity, or darker feelings of any kind, he chooses a graveyard setting. This is the situation in "In Death Divided" (dated 189—), where the speaker experiences total alienation from the beloved. Yet love and loyalty flow like an undertow, silently and invisibly drawing the two together in an unheard "common lullaby." "The eternal tie which binds us twain in one/No eye will see/Stretching across the miles that sever you from me."

A disparate cluster of some of the most important poems in the Hardy canon are gathered together here, beginning with "The Place on the Map," figuratively, a revelation of pregnancy; "The Schreckhorn"; "A Singer Asleep" (a tribute to Swinburne); "A Plaint to Man," in which God gripes about being invented (Man's "unhappy need of creating me"); "God's Funeral," in which God recalls the good old days when people prayed to him and assured him he was really there; and of the remaining dozen, the seminal poem "The Year's Awakening" and the retrospective "Under the Waterfall" are probably the most notable.

Poems of 1912–1913: Verteris Vestigia Flammae

Significantly, unlike most of Hardy's important poems, not one in this group of 21 verses was published in periodical form prior to volume publication. Whether this points to their inappropriateness as love poems coming from an unhappy marriage, or whether Hardy prepared them specifically for his fourth collection, *Satires of Circumstance*, remains indeterminable. While biographers, eager for material, may prefer to read them autobiographically, the poet Middleton Murry, one of the first to perceive that they were *not* the poems of a "man giving way to memory in poetry," views them as the voice of "a great poet uttering the cry of the universe." Certainly their overall long-suffering gentleness goes some way to counterbalancing the waspish Satires, so in this respect they contribute importantly to the general tenor of *Satires of Circumstance: Lyrics and Reveries*. They are melodious even while encompassing a wide range of emotional experience.

"The Going" opens the sequence with a theme all too familiar to the real-life Hardy—Emma's sudden disappearance (this theme is repeated in "Without Ceremony"). Unlike her habit of vanishing without warning and returning unannounced, in this instance she dies. "That such a swift fleeing/No soul forseeing—/Not even I—would undo me so!"

Biographers have disputed Hardy's real-life amazement—not "foreseeing"—claiming that he must have known Emma was dying. This claim fails to take into account his inurement. With her unannounced disappearances, Hardy would probably have become hardened to what amounts to long-term manipulative behavior. Shocks repeatedly inflicted diminish in impact over time. Hardy would surely have learned to rely on the fact, if only for his own sanity, that she always returned, eventually.

"The Going" mirrors something of this dilemma. There is indignation in the speaker's stance. The opening phrase, "Why did you give no hint ..." is shaped to a refrain for stanzas 3 ("Why?") and 5 ("Why?"). At the same time, his sense of being up against the wall, so to speak, is evoked in stanzas 2 and 6. Tone, tenor, and mood testify to an accumulated frustration, anxiety, and shock of the years. But being repeatedly abandoned is one thing; to be denied a return is something quite else—justifiably, the speaker feels completely destroyed.

"Your Last Drive" turns upon the alienation of the spouses and, in common with "The Walk," poignantly acknowledges that "I drove not with you," just as in the latter poem "You did not walk with me." In "Rain on a Grave," a fine example of a "grafted" theme (as also "Lament"), the speaker invokes the experience, as in *Far From the Madding Crowd*, of waters spouting on a grave "in ruthless disdain"; in common with the mourning lover in the fictional account, who plants flowers on the dead girl's grave only to find them "pelted" by "summertime spills," the speaker wishes he, too, could be underground.

"The Haunter," "His Visitor," and "The Phantom Horsewoman" adopt an alternative perspective and voice—the world seen through the eyes of the dead woman's ghost to whom the "dim faces" are "strangers quite, who never knew my rule here." Poems designed as retrospective include "I Found Her Out There," "A Dream or No," "A Death-Day Recalled," "Beeny Cliff," "After a Journey," "At Castle Boterel," "St Launce's Revisited," and "Where the Picnic Was." This cluster of poems reifies a version of the beloved the speaker had once longed to love and, reinventing her to bloom again as a girl (she was nearing 30 in real life when Hardy met her), frequently childlike, he situates her in bewitching Cornish settings of pure romance. The poems are enchanting while pointing to their own illusoriness. "The Voice," by contrast, creates no such picturesque settings, no poignant dramatizations but instead cries out in lonely anguish to the "Woman much missed"—responding to the "woman calling."[18] "The Voice" has intense power, heart-wrenching honesty, and haunting emotions. There is no schematic setting, no artifice, no conjuring a well-beloved figure, and no trace of self-delusion. It is one of the most moving bereavement poems in existence.

Miscellaneous Pieces

"The Wistful Lady" opens this mixed bunch of 38 pieces with the lady's warning that when she dies she will "hover round/And show herself .../To any newer Love." Unhappy unions provide the theme for "Had You Wept"; "The Cheval Glass"; the long poem "A Conversation at Dawn"; and "She Charged Me"—the speaker is berated so bitterly and so remorselessly about a past love "I knew/... That the curtain would drop upon us two."

Current affairs inform "A King's Soliloquy: On the Night of His Funeral," in which the spirit of the dead king (Edward VII) reflects that if he had his life again he would "prefer the average track/Of average men." The satirical "The Coronation" adopts a similar schema (one of Hardy's favorites)—the dead talking—portraying past monarchs inquiring from their tombs about the preparations for George V's coronation. The dead also speak in "I Rose Up as My Custom Is," where, talking to a "former Love," the poet learns to his discomfiture that poets make the worst husbands since they lack "the wherewithal to pave their way."

In the poem "In the British Museum," the voices of antiquity are trapped in the "time-touched stone," but in the next, longer poem, "The Obliterate Tomb," being written in stone is no safeguard against being obliterated. Still on the subject of stone, or masonry, the long poem "The Abbey Mason: Inventor of the 'Perpendicular' Style of Gothic Architecture," dedicated to Hardy's first employer, John Hicks of Dorchester, appropriately sets the celebratory lines in rhyming couplets as close in shape to the perpendicular style laid down (made recumbent) for the entombing of one who had worked all his life with edifices, transoms, and the laying down of stone. Hardy's own aesthetic philosophy is reflected in the idea of "Petrified lacework—lightly lined/On ancient massiveness behind," recalling his dictum about artwork, that "the seer should watch that pattern among general things ... and describe that alone" (*LW*, 158).

Many of these verses testify to Hardy's talent for creating great poems out of ordinary domestic situations. "The Death of Regret" unravels the fickleness of human memory, "In the Days of Crinoline" (using her skirts to conceal more than her duped husband suspects) plays on domestic unrest as does "The Moth-Signal (on Egdon Heath)," which recalls *The Return of the Native* and the practice of night signaling between clandestine lovers. "Seen by the Waits" follows the "restive" motif, but here carol singers catch a glimpse of an unsuspecting woman dancing joyfully in her chambers—she has just been told "That her roving husband was dead:/Why she had danced in the gloaming/We thought but never said."

Several poems in this section are more fitting to the Satires group. A good example is "In the Servants' Quarters," which dramatizes Peter's denial of Jesus, setting it in the servants' hall among the gossiping maids who cross-examine the accused, exposing him as a liar: "His face convulses as the morning cock that moment crows."

Satires of Circumstance in Fifteen Glimpses

These glimpses were composed in 1910–11 during the last two years of Hardy's marriage to Emma. Aside from the ballad-tragedy "The Sacrilege," "The Jubilee of a Magazine," and a few other sober pieces, the glimpses are actually more pathetic than harsh—rarely doing justice to the great poet's ingenuity and imagination. "At Tea" depicts the oblivious but "happy young housewife" serving tea to the pretty visitor as the husband yearns furtively after the latter (his first and former love). In the poem "In the Room of the Bride-Elect," "she" regrets, too late, her choice; in "At a Watering-Place," "his" secret caresses of another man's fiancée are relished as he watches them walking out together. "In Church" echoes "Seen by the Waits" except that here it is the unsuspecting preacher who is observed in a telling moment—likewise in "At the Draper's," where "he" accidentally comes across his unknowing wife as she chooses luxurious widow's weeds.

One group of poems, featuring misdeeds and wished-for deaths, has cemeteries for the setting ("By Her Aunt's Grave," "In the Cemetery," "Over the Coffin," and "In the Moonlight")—these must have stung Hardy's conscience when, shortly after writing the verses, he found himself standing over his own wife's coffin. Several of the most pathetic of the verses seem to be the plaints of a deeply unhappy poet. There is "his" "narrow escape" (as the speaker sourly puts it) as he catches out his erstwhile love in a shrewish temper with her mother ("Outside the Window"). Then there is a bitter little piece where the "type of decayed gentility" affects not to be "selling" but rather acting in the interests of art ("In the Study"). Yet another finds the new bride cruelly taunting the groom with "it's he I embrace while embracing you" ("In the Nuptial Chamber"), while "The Satin Shoes" tells of a young bride's descent into the madhouse. And yet another, "In the Restaurant," asks that "she" passes her unborn child off as her husband's. All told, it is easy to see why Hardy regretted these verses, which "express what I would now prefer to leave unexpressed" (*Letters*, V5.66).

MOMENTS OF VISION AND MISCELLANEOUS VERSES (1917)

With hindsight, Hardy observed that at the time of writing *Satires of Circumstance,* "the scales had not fallen from my eyes," but "when I reprinted them they had." Scholars have debated the meaning of this and most have concluded that by "scales," Hardy is speaking partly of the weight of his domestic shackles, partly of his consequent lack of loving kindness in a loveless marriage, and partly of the strange ghosts his bereavement visited upon him—inflicted upon a deeply disturbed mind. He may even have feared, sensitive soul (and often paranoid) that he was, that those wishing others ill will in the Satires represented externalized forms of himself. This would be harsh self-judgment indeed, but bereavement guilt and regret affect the mind in dark and complicated ways.

Hardy must have wished Emma many times dead and as many times afterward must have suffered the most terrible remorse. Moreover, after concentrating on reifying (in verse) the woman he had once hoped to love—a woman mirrored in desirable identities that are girlish and childlike, fragmented in events that are frozen in time or ephemeral, and often introduced by speakers who are spellbound—many a mental carapace, many a "scale" must have fallen from his eyes as he pursued these chimeras. There was not only the factor of self-delusion to confront but also his own part in the failed marriage. The mythic aspect of his early romance with Emma, the marriage preserved in a domestic cocoon from which no vital life emerged (not even progeny), the years of patient forbearance miserably empty of love—these contingencies alone might well have armor plated an indifferent marriage partner. Much of Hardy's descaled vision, as it ranges across transcendent impressions and visionary transformations of past events and present epiphanies, is reflected in the highly personal collection that is *Moments of Vision* (MV).

Several critics have held that *Moments of Vision* alone would have earned Hardy the accolade of "great poet." This fifth collection of his verse, comprising 159 poems, was published by Macmillan three years after *Satires of Circumstance.*[19] Some of the pieces in *Moments of Vision,* together with 211 from previous collections, had been chosen by Hardy in 1916 for a Golden Treasury edition of *Selected Poems.*[20] Hardy had always hoped to publish in the Golden Treasury series and was pleased to be able to tell a correspondent that

> the selection, so far as it goes, is satisfactory, bearing in mind its conditions & limitations—that it is primarily a drawing-room table & birthday book—& that therefore the "strongest" (to use the journalists' word), & more controversial poems had to be omitted. Moreover, as it was published before "Moments of Vision" came out it contains no pieces from the latter book (except two or three taken from the manuscript of it) & so omits many, possibly among the best I have written—such as Near Lanivet, To the Moon, The Duel [a man's poem only!] The Photograph [ditto], It never looks like summer, The Figure in the Scene, During Wind & Rain, etc., etc. (*Letters,* V6.96)

"Two or three taken from the manuscript" ended up being nine poems in all. Hardy was quite understandably forgetful of such details: it was around this time that he confessed, when giving a correspondent the meaning of the word "griff" ("a claw: also a griffin"), that "I had no idea that I had used it!" And in mistakenly alluding to "Lines to a Movement in Mozart's E-Flat Symphony" as "The Minuet," he had obviously forgotten that he had substituted "Movement" for the manuscript title of "Minuet" (Purdy, 196). These slips of memory are surely to be expected of one approaching 80 years of age who has also achieved the feat of publishing two substantial volumes of verse containing over a hundred new pieces in the space of three short years.

Moments of Vision was well received with the usual complicated mix of establishment disapproval and art world admiration. Hardy wonders (to Gosse) "why they [critics] quiz the author rather than review the book" (*Letters*, V5.253). This is, yet again, self-forgetful. Why? Because Hardy himself expressed a greater interest in those poems in which he had overcome the limitations set by the "real" upon his poetic imagination and which called up a certain time, place, event or feeling in the author's mind. In these instances, he'd felt a special "affection for the incident or feeling that gave rise to the poem" (*Letters*, V5.258). But no doubt, with his critics, he was balking at the fact that quizzing the author can lead not only to misrepresentation and errors of quotation and of journalistic license, but also to an appearance of inside information, of special, privileged knowledge. "Reviewing the poem," by contrast, demands genuine insight, innate wisdom, and profound understanding.

Of "establishment" criticism, Hardy writes to his dear friend Florence Henniker:

> Did you see the super-precious review of the verses in the Westminster Gazette? It amused me much (having no weight or value as criticism) as it was obviously written by a woman. It condemned the poem entitled "The pink frock" because the frock described was old-fashioned & Victorian! The publishers have sent me some fifty reviews—all of them, save 5 or 6, deplorably inept, purblind, & of far less value than the opinion of one's grocer or draper, though they were friendly enough, I must say. I always fancy I could point out the best, & the worst, in a volume of poems, which none of these did. But perhaps that is my self-conceit, for I have had no experience as a reviewer. (*Letters*, V5.250)

"The Pink Frock" (MV), incidentally, satirizes the cultural stereotype of the "doll-woman"—a stereotype Hardy swore to demolish in his fiction. It is a subtly clever poem wittily situating the speaker and the reader in a satiric monologue, as it were, of heartless vanity. The speaker mimics, *assumes* the thoughts of the stereotype, set in a kind of petulant, foot-stamping rhythm: "O my pretty pink frock,/I shan't be able to wear it!/Why is he dying just now?/I hardly can bear it!" The sophisticated structuring of the verse and the pouting effect of the repeated *p*'s in the first and last stanza indicate that the speaker is an exceedingly skilled rhetorician intent upon reproducing the stereotype (based on an immature, thoughtless girl) of an empty-headed doll-woman. Evidently, Hardy's critic missed the mark altogether—being preoccupied with garments "old-fashioned & Victorian!" (no wonder Hardy placed an exclamation mark there).

With the more insightful critic, Hardy was gracious and gentle: "I am honoured," he told Samuel Chew (professor, Bryn Mawr College), "by your remarks on 'Moments of Vision'" (*Letters*, V5.251); "I am much obliged to you," he wrote poet John Drinkwater, "for writing and sending your very generous review of Moments of Vision in the Manchester Guardian—a newspaper I highly value" (*Letters*, V5.258); and to author Harold Child, "A friend writes from Cambridge to say that yours is just the review he would have written if he had had the brains & literary skill" (*Letters*, V5.295).

But to the less insightful, in this instance the *Daily News* journalist Robert Lynd, Hardy was less than gracious, wondering out loud at "the ignorance of my critic, wondering why the editor put me into such incompetent hands!!" His fury is controlled but he cannot resist saying

> You will be surprised probably when I mention it. The lines you quoted, & now reprint, of the poem "On Sturminster Foot-Bridge" as being as musical as a "milk-cart" are an attempt (& I am told by poets a not unsuccessful one) at Onomatopoeia, in which the words are made to reflect the clucking sound of water when blown up-stream into holes on the bank; so that, to those who know, your ridicule of them must have been of a reflected kind. (*Letters*, V5.319)

Well, Hardy was right, of course. Like the "purblind" reviewer of "The Pink Frock," poor Lynd had completely missed the (structural) point—the formation of onomatopoeia, which mimics the sounds that resemble those associated with the action, or that seem naturally suggestive of its qualities.

However, when it happened to be a personal friend who showed professional incompetence, Hardy was, naturally, deeply upset. Reviewing for the *Fortnightly* (February 1920) longtime friend Frederic Harrison (Positivist philosopher) stepped out of line and took liberties no friend should take: Why, he complains, Hardy's "monotony of gloom?" "Byron, Shelley, Keats," he writes,

> were all exiles from home, decried, destined to early death abroad. And yet their pessimism was occasional. But Thomas Hardy has everything that man can wish—long and easy life, perfect domestic happiness, warm friends, the highest honour his Sovereign can give, the pride of a wide countryside.

Hardy was deeply affronted. It was not just that his domestic life, his "easy life" was used to fuel a literary critique that, by rights, should be focusing on his art, and this at a time when he was still composing bereavement poems (a friend should have known better), but also that his art, his poetry, was to be no longer regarded autonomously as poetry but as some kind of "gloomy" confessional booth.

According to Florence Hardy, that was the end of his friendship with Frederic Harrison. But this was not so (Florence was a notoriously unreliable witness).

Hardy was, undoubtedly, deeply wounded, but egotistical and unforgiving he was not. Within weeks, he was again engaged in intellectual rapport with Harrison, and they quickly resumed their friendship.

Grouping of Poems in *Moments of Vision and Miscellaneous Verses*

"Moments of Vision"

"Moments of Vision" is the title poem, opening the collection (which has no formal subdivisions aside from a group of war poems at the end; see the next subdivision). It adopts a platonic theme of a mirrored universe and is followed by "The Voice of Things" (see also "For Life I Had Never Cared Greatly" and "The Masked Face")—similarly meditative, but notable for Hardy's use of the pathetic fallacy: "The waves huzza'd like a multitude below." He was evidently taken with this phrase and reiterates in "The Wind's Prophecy": "The waves outside where the breakers are/Huzza like a mad multitude." Other meditative poems in this collection include "To the Moon," which muses on the human condition, concluding that "God ought surely to shut up soon." In a contrasting lunar poem, "On a Midsummer Eve," the moonlight sheds just enough of a glow for "a faint figure"—a phantasm—to emerge in the dusk who speaks "a tender verse for me." In "A Kiss" the speaker knows that nothing ever completely disappears (just as sounds, past and present, simply await a receiver) but remain forever in the ethereal atmosphere: hence "that kiss is gone where none can tell/It cannot have died; that knew we well."

One of Hardy's most well-loved philosophical poems is "The Oxen." This seasonal poem expresses spiritual doubt but also draws the speaker into an affinity with unknowable things where hope still lies (see also "The Darkling Thrush"—*PPP*). Of the most celebratory of Hardy's poems, "Timing Her" is also the most erotic. "Written to an old folk-tune," it builds in tempo, sound patterns, and imagery to an intense climax after nine soaring stanzas.

Poems of War and Patriotism

This group of 17 poems on World War I is placed at the end of *Moments of Vision*. Hardy's meliorist philosophy of "the gradual bettering of human nature" was severely tested by the events of 1914–18. They left him feeling completely shattered. Indeed, Florence Hardy felt that the war years had aged her husband by 10 years: "I think he feels the horror of it so keenly that he loses all interest in life."[21] The most heart-heavy poem in this group is "In Time of 'The Breaking of Nations'" (the phrase is from Jeremiah 11:20). Here the speaker perceives, in a terrible sense of the obliteration of the countless lives lost, that none of their names or annals will endure; only the timeless stories of the plowman and the lover will remain—"War's annals will cloud into night/ere *their* story die" (my italics).

Hardy deplores the war fever, the jingoism, and the sheer insanity of "Empery's insatiate lust of power" ("In Time of Wars and Tumults"), possibly foreseeing the century's worst—*two* World Wars and their catastrophic repercussions. In "A New Year's Eve in War Time" the speaker has an apocalyptic vision where Time is personified as a rider: "Death astride came/To numb all with his knock—."

Apparently, Hardy wished to leaven his own exit here and abandons war in favor of a finale containing two contemplative verses, "The Coming of the End" and "Afterwards." "Afterwards" is one of Hardy's best-known poems and most favored of themes: the refreshing simplicity of a pastoral life lived with the "dew-fall hawk" alighting on the "wind-warped upland thorn" and the mind turning, serenely, upon the "full-starred heavens that winter sees."

Time and Memory[22]

The poignant "The Faded Face" offers the speaker a glimpse of her youthfulness, and he wishes he had known her when those "lips [were] rosy red." In stark contrast, "Life Laughs Onward" evokes so much joy that "My too regretful mood/Died on my tongue." Verses following related themes of time and memory include pieces as various as "The Man Who Forgot," "I Travel as a Phantom Now," which combines anti-God sentiments with personal regrets (as does "In the Seventies"), and "At the Piano," where phantoms intervene when he glances away from the woman playing. And, pursuing a different theme, the mystery of her unspoken memories is pondered in "The Riddle." For further variety, add the celebratory "Joys of Memory," "Why Be at Pains?" "The Wind Blew Words," "The Occultation" "The Ageing House," "A Merrymaking in Question, " and "At Middle-Field Gate in February," with its characteristically Hardyan cinematic touches. As the polarities of past and present, life and death, and youth and age crowd in on the speaker's mind, a seasonal mist falls upon the external world, and the "cosmic" perspective, or aerial vision, is replaced by a zoom-lens shot (so to speak) focusing on dewdrops on the field-gate: "Like silver buttons ranged in a row." The sense is of the harmonious interconnectedness of all things great and small, inner and outer, visible and invisible.

Weather and seasons, for Hardy, frequently function symbolically, and this is beautifully accomplished in the crowning achievement of his renowned time poem, "During Wind and Rain." Time is one of his most persistent themes—time interrupted, hazed, fragmented, thwarted by memory, or overarched by an external consciousness that countenances it, as in this poem. Several dreamy scenes are hazily evoked as if from faded photographs (there is no color whatsoever in this poem), and as vivid lives slowly emerge, a choric voice, taking its cue from "their dearest songs," interrupts at the end of each stanza, much as a sudden consciousness of time would interrupt a thought or action. Overseeing the weathering events—the obliterating effect of wind and rain over the years—the choric voice hazes those vivid lives back into the mists of time. Two less well-known poems, "The Change" and "Where They Lived," work along related themes. The first employs a similar choric voice—"Who shall unroll the years O!"—and the latter follows the same passage-of-time progression.

A delightful poem featuring a woman's hair (only Hardy!), called "The Tresses," is matched in exuberant mood by "Great Things." This revival of pleasure celebrates cider drinking. Less spiritedly, but decidedly close to zestful, is his treatment of heredity. In "She, I, and They" the speaker mourns the fact "That we should be the last/of stocks once unsurpassed," as also in "Heredity." "The Pedigree" adopts a more philosophical stance merging platonic mirror worlds with phantasmagoria. An underestimated poem, "The Pedigree" has some enchanting lines: "In the deep of the night" the moon lets in "a watery light …/And green-rheumed clouds were hurrying past where mute and cold it globed." And when the illusion of the mirror begins to fade, "the stained moon and drift retook their places there."

Poems of 1871–1898

This group of "Emma" poems, including "Why Did I Sketch," "Love the Monopolist," and the tragi-ironic "The Figure in the Scene," which depicts the beloved as existing only for a day despite the "Genius"—the conjuration of her form—is tentatively attributed by scholars to an earlier Hardyan phase based on the poem's topical matter. "First Sight of Her and After," with its hint of enchantment—"moonshades on the way," "Sky-glancing travellers say"—catches the mood of "When I Set Out For Lyonnesse" (SC). It also posits the same problems of dating (see note 17), especially given the hindsight sensibility accruing to phrases such as "The first of many [days]" and "the pattern grows." More temporally specific is "We Sat at the Window," subtitled "Bournemouth, 1875." This evokes a historical immediacy, a sense of the here and now in which the endless "witless" downpour aptly externalizes the tearful mood of two disillusioned souls "in their prime,/And great was the waste, that July time/When the rain came down."

"Overlooking the River Stour" is generally held to be a reflection on the Sturminster Newton days when, Hardy says, husband and wife enjoyed their happiest time. But the poem holds out little joy, aside from the beautifully detailed flight of swallows and water birds and the obvious satisfaction taken by the artist in observing the magical minutiae of the natural world. Less satisfaction is taken in domesticity and "the more behind my back," to which the speaker never turns—"these less things hold my gaze!" Another poem that bespeaks a similar distancing is "The Last Performance," whereas the retrospective "It Never Looks Like Summer" hints at an early temperamental disparity; his joy in "Beeny by the sea" is not well matched by her moody "drear."

"Near Lanivet, 1872" was a great favorite of Hardy's. Was this due to his fascination with the macabre? "She leant back … [and] laid her arms … stretched out … as one crucified"—"'Don't,' I cried." Or was it the element of prophecy? "If no one is bodily crucified now,/in spirit one may be!" A biographical reading would probably situate the poem at a later date of composition if it assumes knowledge of the "bodily" torment of Emma's mental breakdown coupled with the agonies of an unhappy marriage. These considerations aside, Hardy would surely have delighted in the poem's balladic form, which expertly develops the crossroads/

crucifixion motif to conclude with the apt image of the hourglass of time, which, itself, provides a miniature figuration of two "open palms" connected by a stem. Readers might be prompted to the question—when did time actually run out for this sorry pair and has the crucifixion of the spirit already been determined or is it premonitory?

Family and Friends

Hardy's best-beloved sister, Mary, closest companion of his childhood and youth, died in December 1915, and he spent a sad winter in the deepest depression. "Logs on the Hearth: A Memory of a Sister" is one of several tributes to her—the tomboy perched on the apple-bough, "laughing, her young brown hand awave." That last wave, that ambiguous gesture that signals both greeting and farewell, purposefully resists representation but is customarily endowed by Hardy with rather more beckoning signification than dismissal. He transfers it to several allied, ambiguous gestures in his poems such as the last turn, the last backward glance.

Mary is one of the very few family members who inspired laughter and joy in Hardy. However, the haunting "Molly Gone" is more poignant than glad— "No more summer for Molly and me," "No more singing by Molly to me." "In the Garden" and "Everything Comes" are also poems of love and loss, albeit established in a generic sense (not as overt tributes). It would be hard to pinpoint the inspiration for some of these verses (unless specified, like "The Last Signal," which is a tribute to the dialect poet William Barnes), although the sheer love of life expressed in "He Fears His Good Fortune" conveys the feel of a blissfully happy childhood (with Mary) rather than amorousness emotions for another.

"The Five Students" brings together several family members and friends (Emma and her sister, Horace Moule, and Hardy himself) rather as a snapshot catches an oddly assorted gathering and frames it as a group—"Five of us; dark He, fair He, dark She, fair She, I." Hardy sustains the sense of oddity by employing this kind of awkward phrasing. Going one step further, "Conjecture" wonders at the curiosity of life—what if "there were in my kalendar/No Emma, Florence, Mary?"

"At Mayfair Lodgings" recalls a youthful love inspired by the revelation that she, the "one I had rated rare," had recently died in the house across the street, "And neither of us knew." Returning to the days of childhood, "Afternoon Service at Mellstock: (Circa 1850)" depicts a time when the daydreaming boy, psalming in church, lets his mind wander off out of doors to be at one with the trees, the clouds, and the birds. There are interesting rhythms and images here that echo those in the more famous "The Darkling Thrush" (PPP): "So mindless were those outpourings! —/Though I am not aware/That I have gained by subtle thought …" A more enthusiastic tribute to psalming (which Hardy the man actually grew to love) occurs in "Apostrophe to an Old Psalm Tune" (1916), where the speaker is delighted that the psalm "hailed me … waylaid me."

"To My Father's Violin" might be more aptly titled "To My Father's Corpse." Just as the "The Shreckhorn" (SC) honors Leslie Stephen and fuses figurations of the mountain with the man who loved to climb it, so Hardy's tribute to his father merges the instrument with the man who loved to play it: "your strings a tangled wreck,/Once smart drawn,/Ten worm-wounds in your neck."

"In a Museum" and Other Verses

"In a Museum" is the first of several verses in *Moments of Vision* to celebrate associations: in this instance the speaker is entranced by the idea of the ecstatic song of "a musical bird" linked in his mind to "a contralto voice I heard." In a typical Hardyan reversal, as in "Shelley's Skylark" (*PPP*), where the title leads readers to expect exultation but there is none, the exalted bird appears in the unlikely setting of a museum, where the singing voice thrills, "In the full-fugued song of the universe unending."

Birds remain a constant feature in Hardy's poems. Also of note are "Her Love-Bird," "The Robin," and the disturbing "The Caged Goldfinch." "The Blinded Bird"—yet more horrifying—provides an appalling reminder of the eye gouging of caged songbirds so they could not tell night from day and would thus sing continuously. Hardy's intensely committed, lifelong compassion for nature's creatures could have made this a poem of ghastly brutality, of unspeakable loathing for humankind's inhumanity to the innocent and defenseless. Instead, "Blinded ere yet a-wing/By the red-hot needle" (gouged as a fledgling), the poem turns and throws every thinkable Christian tenet back at speaker and reader alike. In a rhetorical monologue, the biblical voice of outrage cries, "Who hath Charity?" "This bird," comes the rejoinder, in psalmic style. "Who suffereth long and is kind." "Who hopeth, and endureth all things?" calls the biblical questioner—now unstoppable. "Who thinketh no evil, but sings?" "Who is divine?" And by way of an answer, the antiphonal voice ends the poem with a quiet simplicity wholly befitting to its subject—two small words: "This bird."

"Copying Architecture in an Old Minster" (subtitled "Wimborne") associates the Minster with both time and circumstance as "the call to ghosts" raises voices from the past and offers a caution of things to come. Voicelessness, by a swift Hardyan irony, is the subject of "To Shakespeare: After Three Hundred Years," which commemorates the unknowability of that "radiant guest" (Shakespeare) who left "no intimate word or personal trace." An earlier poem begun in 1898, "Lines," has the dedication "To a Movement in Mozart's E-Flat Symphony"—the E-Flat is a romantic work and one of Mozart's last from which Hardy takes his cue. The speaker, evidently in his last years, harks back to "Junetide's prime," when "Love lures life on"—romantic recollections expressed in lines thick with alliteration (repeated progressive sounds), which mirror the pattern of exposition, development, and resolution of a symphonic movement.

The associations triggered by the statue in "The Statue of Liberty" lead to unexpected ironies; those triggered by "relics of householdry" yield warm, tender recollections of family life, and "Midnight on the Great Western" recalls *Jude* and Little Father Time's arrival by train. "In a Waiting Room" is also set in a railway station, but here the bright children "spread a glory through the gloom."

Photographs are, by their very nature, crowded with associations. The speaker in "The Rival," a woman, is threatened by her own youthful photographic image, whereas in "The Enemy's Portrait," the image is painted (and equally threatening), as also in "Looking at a Picture on an Anniversary." More disturbingly, and with a brutal self-honesty, "The Photograph" enacts a virtual burning at the stake: he watches "furtivewise/Till the flame had eaten her breast, and mouth, and hair." There are unsettling erotic-cum-homicidal overtones to the ritualized act of enflaming and devouring the face and body parts of the woman.

Poems of Mysticism and of the Surreal

Aside from his poems on phantasms, ghosts, and voices of the dead (including "An Upbraiding" and "The Choirmaster's Burial"), one of Hardy's most celebrated themes is surrealism—the occult, the paranormal. "Something Tapped" pursues the latter phenomenon—presences that arise and vanish in a heartbeat. "By the Runic Stone" tells, very simply, of something mysterious that subtly changes two people sitting by the Runic Stone (a stone marked with ancient rhymes—runes—possessing transformative qualities). The shade of a human presence makes itself felt in the widely popular poem "The Shadow on the Stone," where broken rhythms cleverly push the (metric) arrangement out of synchrony (as befits a theme on the paranormal). "The Upper Birch-Leaves" also yields up spirits as does "While Drawing in a Churchyard," but these spirits manifest as arboreal, not human, presences. "Transformations" takes a more organic approach and depicts the absorption of human spirits into air, sun, and rain, transforming each to "the energy again/That made them what they were!"

LATE LYRICS AND EARLIER WITH MANY OTHER VERSES (1922)

Hardy's eyesight began to fail as he turned 80 in 1920. Increasingly, he relied on his newfound friend Sir Sydney Cockerell[23] (curator of the Fitzwilliam Museum) for help with correcting proofs for *Late Lyrics*, "since my eyes are not so good as they were, & misprints have a way of stealing past them in a most mysterious manner" (*Letters*, V6.117).

He was quite clearly under considerable strain as he struggled with this publication (his health never robust at the best of times), and whereas his second wife, Florence, assiduously provided him with secretarial services, she was, by nature, dour, not the most enlivening of companions. Hardy did, though, feel deeply grateful to her for understanding and championing his idea of working toward a betterment of the human condition. Acknowledging her invaluable support in the ninth poem in *Late Lyrics*, dedicated to F.E.H. and titled "I Sometimes

Think," he expresses the loneliness of one crying in the wilderness—but then effects a reverse turn in the final stanza. In skillfully stilted rhythms, he evokes the bustling motion of domestic work, a flurry of haste and effort: "For one did care,/ And spiriting into my house, to, fro,/Like wind on the stair,/Cares still, heeds all, and will, even though/I may despair."

As Hardy prepared *Late Lyrics*, his sixth collection of verse, he wrote dejectedly to his longtime friend Florence Henniker:

> I have collected most of the poems of mine that have been written since the last volume came out five years ago, & they are to be published anon—about the middle of May, I understand. It is no pleasure to me to appear again in print; but I really did not know what to do with them: a good many having already been printed in magazines, &c., about which people were continually writing to know when they could be got in a volume. In the book there will also be some very old ones, which I had overlooked in making previous collections. (*Letters*, V6.120)

"No pleasure" appears disingenuous, but the truth is that Hardy was still weak from a recent illness and generally depressed. He goes on to tell his friend Gosse, "I don't altogether jump at the chance of appearing on the literary stage again; but I don't know what else to do" (*Letters*, V6.115). This dispirited comment reflects his concern about what he called his "stray" verses: he had been publishing widely in periodicals of every stripe, thus his poems could be reprinted or reproduced often without his knowledge—to reclaim them for a collection was in effect to secure the "stray" for the safety of the fold.[24]

But he felt incredibly weary. When the University of St. Andrews wrote at this time to offer him an honorary degree of doctor of laws, he replied that he was too fatigued to make the trip to Scotland (so it was conferred in absentia). Seventeen years earlier he had jumped on the train to Aberdeen—"almost as far as the Pyrenees," he quipped—to receive his first honorary degree in person.

Late Lyrics contains 151 poems—as usual, a mixed bunch with about half "written lately" and the earliest dating 1866.[25] The collection opens with an apology ("more piquant" than "preface," Hardy decided), over which he had had many misgivings. Thinking the apology unworthy, he had asked Cockerell's opinion as to "whether I shall prefix it to the new volume or not. I don't wish to, & should not at all mind destroying it" (*Letters*, V6.116). Cockerell urged him not to destroy it.

What was Hardy's concern? If his reiterations to friends and colleagues are indicative—repeatedly stressing that he had written the apology during his long illness, "It was that which caused [it] … I wrote in bed" (*Letters*, V6.131), he told Gosse (among others)—then it appears he was as discomfitted about its literary health as he was about his own physical disorders. And indeed, it is prolix. In several hundred words it makes a case for free speech; in several hundred more, counterarguments to allegations of his pessimism. Eventually, in the last few hundred, it presents a defense of poetry, and a very fine defense too. Unlike the preliminaries, the defense is apropos, solid, and strong: "Poetry and religion touch each other," he writes, "or rather modulate into each other; are, indeed, often but different names for the same thing … the visible signs of mental and emotional life" (for the orthodox, this would have been inflammatory all by itself). Thus religion, he continues, should embrace "the principle of evolution"; "joining hands with modern science" it could, with dignity, strength and "scope for transmutability," "keep the shreds of morality together." Poetry, meanwhile, would continue to infuse into the world "the breath and finer spirit of all knowledge; the impassioned expression of science" (many ecclesiastics would have objected that infusion of "the breath and finer spirit of all knowledge" should be attributed to religion rather than to poetry).

Hardy's misgivings about the apology were prophetic. And it was the religious element that caused the most trouble. For instance, some critics misunderstood his support of the New Catholicism (which, at that time, embraced evolutionary theory) and assumed Hardy the agnostic to be no more. He expressed his anxieties to his good friend, Lady Grove:

> I find some people gather from it that I have become strictly orthodox (rather funny, this!) when I thought my meaning to be clear enough that some form of Established ritual & discipline should be maintained in the interests of morality. (*Letters*, V6.162)

In general, however, Hardy felt that reviewers "have been civil enough" about *Late Lyrics*, although this civility must have been decidedly relative.

A new friend and admirer, the poet Siegfried Sassoon, proffered his civility with grace: he was trying to review *Late Lyrics*, he said, and found it difficult to express his admiration "coherently." A far more serious controversy arose over the iconoclastic "The Wood Fire." In this poem, a bargain buyer of cheap logs has purchased "executioner's" wood—useless for anything because "split by the nails" and the "cuts and stains thereon." The speakers jest together about one recently crucified who had called himself king. The poem anticipates the satirical humor of Monty Python some decades later—you can almost *hear* the voices.

Hardy tells one correspondent:

> An old friend of mine … who has grown cantankerous of late—Maurice Hewlett, said that "The Wood Fire" was "revolting": almost at the same time that a quite old fashioned rector near here told me he was interested in it because it was "probably what happened"—seeing nothing shocking in it at all. (*Letters*, V6.163)[26]

That Hardy managed to retain any sense of humor at all, given that Hewlett had established himself as a devout follower and friend, is a sure sign that he had recovered some of his high spirits and certainly his sense of mischief.

Grouping of Poems in *Late Lyrics and Earlier with Many Other Verses*[27]

"Weathers" and Other Verses

The opening poem of any collection provides the formal handshake to that volume. "Weathers" is distinctively and wholeheartedly Hardyan. First and foremost, it sings. And it sings in pure harmony—man and nature in intimate, reciprocal accord, yet with the latter setting the pace and the former following its rhythms, respecting its patterns, and abiding by its signs: "nestlings fly" and "rivulets overflow" and "rooks in families homeward go,/And so do I." The message is simple but timeless, and the expressiveness is beautiful. But the lesson remains, to this day, still to be learned.

"Summer Schemes" follows shortly afterward, zestful with renewal; "Epeisodia" imbues nature with desire and love, "the leaze is smiling,/On and on beguiling"; "At Moonrise and Onwards" invokes Hardy's fondest celestial body but rarely (for him), conventionally feminizes it (the moon). "Going and Staying" recurs to another favorite theme, time, which, incidentally, features far less in this collection than previously. "Read by Moonlight" is poignantly regretful, as is "Her Song." "A Wet August" echoes the radiancy of "Weathers," and the musical "To a Lady Playing and Singing in the Morning" startles the idle listener with a joyful song of "evening time."

Other colorful songs include "I Look in Her Face," "Could I but Will," and "If It's Ever Spring Again," which, despite the omen in the title, abounds with promise. Then there is the romantic "A Maiden's Pledge: (song)" and the plaintive "The Selfsame Song" (echoed in another tender poem, "First or Last"). "A Bygone Occasion" recalls "delight,/Though tears may throng!" and in "Two Serenades," a gentle irony pervades in contrast to the bouncing dance tune of "Meditations on a Holiday." "The Colour," another spirited song, is "remembered from a Wessex folk-rhyme" and rings out with the delightfully familiar tempo and nuance of a children's playground song.

This astonishing collection of bright songs—"astonishing" for a poet hailed for his dark pessimism—also features a club song (a pub song?) titled "I Knew a Lady," which concludes with a twist, a typical Hardyan irony, as does "O I Won't Lead a Homely Life," where "she" opts for being a fiddler's wife because she thinks life will be musical rather than "homely" but, ironically, "never at home played he." "The Rift," subtitled "Song: Minor Mode," is one of several poems employing specific musical tonalities—among others there are "Nocturne" ("Murmurs in the Gloom") and "Scherzando" ("A Military Song"). These verses are well matched by those celebrating the human voice, notably "On Stinsford Hill at Midnight," where a woman sings "airily"; "At the Entering of the New Year," where "The contrabasso's measured booming" heralds the New Year; and most lauded of all, "The Maid of Keinton Mandeville." This favorite was inspired by a singer at Sturminster Newton who transported Hardy one summer's eve with her rendering of Henry Bishop's "Should he upbraid."

Where Hardy gets balladic, he does tend to get sad ("The Woman I Met"), although this is fully justified in the renowned "The Chapel-Organist," which treats with serious issues of sexual discrimination destined to have a tragic outcome: the gifted organist is stripped of her position by church dignitaries who are anxious about her reputation and that she has "too much sex in her build." She, who also owns a rare contralto voice that beautifully enhances the church services, is utterly broken by this seconding of her talents to her physical appearance—"Men's senses had libelled my soul." These words will strike a familiar note to feminists currently working on the sexual double standard—the woman being blamed for men's desires. And there is also a very modern ring about "The Beauty," where she pleads not to be praised for her beauty—"these things harass me!" She begs instead to be treated as a person, a friend, for "My beauty is not I." In "An Ancient to Ancients" (a poem reminiscent of Dante's *Inferno* as notable personalities pass before our eyes), the speaker is not a woman but is clearly sensitive to the kind of tyranny inflicted by the male gaze in "The Beauty." Recalling "sprightlier times" ("now clean forgot") "Where once we rowed, where once we sailed," he adds, "And damsels took the tiller, veiled/Against too strong a stare" (it may come as a surprise to some modern readers to learn that the veil is and was worn by women not to shroud them but to defend their privacy, to forfend "too strong a stare").

As *Late Lyrics* progresses, some of the songs of joy turn to sorrow, although "Growth in May," set at the center of the collection, renews the mood of "Weathers" with its springtime freshness, colorful wildflowers, and luxuriant jungles of grass and "lush stems"—its abundance of nature's bounties. If poems of this ilk do not surprise the pessimist-mongers, they should surprise those unaware that Hardy is not in his springtime but now in his 80s.

More appropriately, perhaps (given Hardy's advanced age), "The Country Wedding," subtitled "A Fiddler's Song," ends in a graveyard, as does the ballad "The Second Night." In lighter vein, a sour-minded squire takes center stage in "The Children and Sir Nameless," where he gets his comeuppance at the hands of the schoolchildren who had once annoyed him with their noisy romps in his park at Athelhall (could this be an artistic transference of, and self-accusatory stab at, Hardy's own annoyance one day when the gardener's boy was romping noisily outside his study window?).

"Her Apotheosis," subtitled "Secretum meum mihi" (Faded Woman's Song), features an aging theme with a difference. Hardy customarily mourns the cruel tricks played by age, but here there are surprises. There are the usual encroaching years when "no lures bewitched," but then, with an unexpected turn, "age" enters the scene seeming like "an iris at that season" who "Ringed me with living light" (an iris has resplendent blossoms that prettily curl against the stem). This celebratory approach contrasts the grim face of age in "At the Dinner-Table," which employs the Oscar Wildean motif of parallel images as in "The Picture of Dorian Gray." Likewise (by way of contrast), there is the familiar theme (in Hardy) where the husband, in "A Wife Comes Back," pursues the alluring chimera of his ex-wife only to meet with "an ancient dame" who coldly greets him "with features frozen and numb." Perhaps the most ingenious of Hardy's "age" poems is "The Two Houses." This was originally commissioned by Ezra Loomis Pound (Hardy and Pound were mutual admirers) and published in Pound's *Dial* in August 1921. "Two Houses" engages the adjacent dwellings, the ancient and the modern, in a neighborly conversation that leaves the younger of the two "awestruck and dumb" at the prospect of its vapid ignorance—it is as "void as a drum."

Country Churchyards

If ballads are sometimes sad, graveyards for Hardy are not. There is considerable tenderness in two of his churchyard poems. "A Woman's Fancy" tells of an empathy so strong that she seeks to be buried with a man she's never met—a motif repeated in "A Gentleman's Epitaph on Himself and a Lady, Who Were Buried Together." Then, in "She Revisits Alone the Church of her Marriage," a middle-aged wife is so touched by the immutable quality of the place, and that it is the sacred spot where once her dreams were shaped, that the very permanence of it all jars her sense of her own changeableness (in marriage) and gives her pause for thought. On the other hand, the seeker after solace in "They Would Not Come" finds nothing to console him in the house of prayer; instead, the desolation of its emptiness "bruised the heart of me!"

Hardy once explained that from his days as a young architect when churchyards brought fulfilling activities of church restoration, they retained strong associations of pleasure. And, of course, there is no knowing how many extracurricular activities he might have enjoyed in the idyllic settings of Wessex country churches. Certainly romance features in "Side by Side," where an estranged couple gets seated, quite by chance, in the same pew. Then there is the well-loved transcendental poem, "Voices from Things Growing in a Churchyard" (linked with "Transformations," MV), which is overtly sexual. The stanzas build on the various songs of the spirits from poor Fanny Hurd, who once flitted among the daisies; to Bachelor Bowring, who now delights in his new role as "a dancer in green"; to Thomas Voss, who produces "berries of juice"; to Lady Gertrude, shiny in her satiny sheen; to Eve Greensleeves, who "in olden time" was "kissed by men from many a clime," where now she is kissed "by bees"—as if in celebration of her erstwhile "nectar."

Occasional Verses

The Railway

Occasional poems encompass a wide variety of circumstances in Hardy. Lost opportunities provide the themes for "Faintheart in a Railway Train" and "She Did Not Turn," whereas in "At the Railway Station, Upway," a little boy with a violin takes pity on a handcuffed convict and plays a tune for him whereupon the prisoner promptly bursts into song. Another unusual railway moment occurs in "After a Romantic Day," where nothing romantic happens; on the contrary, the railway bears him through "An earthen cutting" into the city with "no scope for view" except for a shaft of moonlight. Such is the extraordinary mind of the visionary poet that this was romantic, it was "enough/For poetry of place"—and "The visions of his mind were drawn."

Special Events

The Summer Exhibition at the Royal Academy takes nature indoors in "At the Royal Academy"—"Woodland and meadowland—here hung aloft,/Gay with limp grass and leafery new and soft." Early and Late Victorians alike, for whom nostalgic memories of pastoral England still haunted their newly acquired metropolitan consciousness, refreshed their city-jaded appetites by regularly attending the great art exhibitions, where the sight of cascading streams, flower-filled meadows, and verdant green woodlands restored their hopes and sense of vigor. However, to welcome the New Year, Hardy looks instead to a centuries-old crossroads. In "By Henstridge Cross at the Year's End," he cleverly employs the theme of roads not taken—contemplating the signpost and rejecting, in turn, the road to London, to Bath, and so on—to evoke the tracks yet to be forged: "We are for new feet now."

Dedications

Two poems celebrate the poet John Keats. One is "At a House in Hampstead," subtitled "Sometime the Dwelling of John Keats," and the other is "At Lulworth Cove a Century Back," where Keats landed in 1820 on his way to Rome and evidently composed the sonnet "Bright Star! Would I were steadfast as thou art." To another artist, known personally in his younger days, Hardy offers "The Opportunity." Dedicated to "H. P.," this verse is a reminder that Hardy had been strongly attracted to his first illustrator (of *FFMC*), Helen Paterson. "We got married," he once said with deep regret, "but not to each other" (*Letters*, V3.218). Another special person celebrated in a poem that appears to pass the notice of critics is the mason in "The Old Workman." "Why are you so bent down before your time,/Old mason?" asks the speaker. Says he, "Those upper blocks..../... ruined me." The stone hefting has cracked his back, but he remains justifiably proud of his work: "I fixed it firm up there," he says with quiet pride, "to stand storms for ages, beating around/When I lie underground"—and "nobody even knows my name."

War Poems

Of the war poems in this collection, "'According to the Mighty Working'" questions the postwar peace, while "Jezreel" recalls the "Seizure by the English under Allenby, September 1918," and "After the War" tells of a "war-seamed" hero who returns home to his beloved to find "That I am the living,/And she the dead!" "'And There Was a Great Calm,'" carrying the subtitle "On the Signing of the Armistice, 11 Nov. 1918," continues the war theme under a highly personal Hardyan imprint, whereas "The Spirit of Pity" is not assured "that earth was bettering slowly." By contrast, a very tender poem titled "Outside the Casement," subtitled "A Reminiscence of War," is taut with the tension of the war news brought home. Every phrase is a strain: "in was brought/That message fraught"; "the question pressed/Like lead on each breast." Then, at the end, when she tries to keep on smiling, there is a gaping emptiness in the echoing, openmouthed sounds of "before" and "evermore"; ultimately, the grotesqueness of sitting in a room and waiting for war news stiffens that last smile, "she smiled us another smile," and turns it to a grim fixity.

"To a Well-Named Dwelling" and Other Verses

Hardy had a fondness for the marks left by humans and animals upon ordinary, everyday objects—the battered pewter mug, the well-trodden field track, and the worn stone steps at the doorway. In *Late Lyrics* he turns his attention to a "glad old house" to bless it for simply existing ("To a Well-Named Dwelling") and, in "The Milestone by the Rabbit-Burrow"—subtitled "On Yell'ham Hill"—the rabbit's burrowing and messaging is neatly mimicked by a bumping rhythm, as in the signals it would send by thumping. Reading "their glancing eyes," the rabbit notices that certain stones "distress/the frail and lame,/And the strong of frame" in equal measure, so he innocently infers that the marks on the stones "Declare how far" "no gins are" (a "gin" is a brutal limb-breaking trapping device). Back in the world of domestic interiors, "The Lament of the Looking-Glass" also adopts the vantage point of the subject, which, in this case, does not simply reflect the human face but, in surrealistic vein, also mirrors "phantoms of the night."

On the other hand, "The Garden Seat" humbly remembers those who once "sat thereon," and the ancient joints of "The Little Old Table" creak out "a history" from long ago as knees or elbows (human joints) touch it: "Whoever owns it anon/and hears it, will never know" its story. The idea of knowledge preexisting in inanimate forms also shapes the motif of "The Marble Tablet," which prompts a paradox: the engraving on the headstone "Shows in its cold white look" no look of her—"Not her glance, glide or smile." Yet the very fact that it stands, "still marble, date-graven," signifies the fullness of a life lived of which no one might otherwise have any knowledge. "Haunting Fingers" ("A Phantasy in a Museum of Musical Instruments") endows the musical instruments with voices, celebrating music-making in moody contrast to the bleakness of "In a London Flat," which is reminiscent, in the view of some critics, of T. S. Eliot's *Waste Land*, published in the same year as *Late Lyrics*.

Family and Friends

Hardy continues to mourn and to memorialize his beloved sister Mary. In "The Sun's Last Look on the Country Girl," the face of the sun no longer gazes on the once-bright face of the girl—a radiance has gone from the earth. Moving from sun to landscape, "Sacred to the Memory" is taken from the inscription Hardy designed for her on her tombstone at Stinsford Churchyard. But in the poem, these conventional words are shown to be but the paler carvings of a fuller script "lined/Upon the landscape high and low/wherein she made such worthy show." Typical of Hardy is the manner in which both landscape and tombstone exist as texts mirroring one another and the lost sister.

The "L. H." of "The Passer-By" reifies a youthful love of Hardy's, Louisa Harding (see also "To Louisa in the Lane," WW), whereas "An Old Likeness" commemorates a missed opportunity (thought to refer to Rosamund Tomson—deeply admired by Hardy), as does "The West-of-Wessex-Girl," the "blithe" girl who "never

I squired" (possibly an imago of the girlish Emma that Hardy had once hoped to love). "The Marble Tablet" (referred to earlier) recalls Hardy's memorial stone erected to Emma, and, more hauntingly, "A Man Was Drawing Near To Me" sustains a touching dialogue with "When I Set Out for Lyonnesse" (MV). Other mythic motifs related, in a general way, to Emma occur in "On a Discovered Curl of Hair," "The Marble-Streeted Town," "A Woman Driving," and "Best Times." More vividly, "A Duettist to Her Pianoforte" evokes the music-loving Emma.

The cats and dogs at Max Gate were deeply loved friends. As with his sister and his wife, Hardy carved their headstones himself. "Last Words to a Dumb Friend" mourns the accidental death on the railway line of Snowdove, Hardy's adored male cat. Interestingly, the vital life of this pet inspires more concrete detail and evocative imagery than do many mourned human lives. From the "Foot suspended in its fall," to the "expectant" stance awaiting "the stroking hand," to having "his little pathways" raked out, to smoothing "away his talon's mark," this beloved "speechless thing" conjures such a vivid presence that, as the speaker lets his gaze wander out across his garden to the pets' cemetery, to Snowdove's burial mound, he sees him still, "Bounding to the window-sill."

HUMAN SHOWS, FAR PHANTASIES, SONGS AND TRIFLES (1925)

Human Shows[28] was an unceremonious affair compared with Hardy's earlier productions. His original, rather *unimaginative* title to the collection of 152 poems had been "Poems Imaginative & Incidental," but he was struck with its dullness and decided to change it to *Human Shows, Far Phantasies, Songs and Trifles.* Although visitors and friends still found him energetic with no sign of memory loss, his health was frail, depression dogged him, and his eyesight had deteriorated so badly that he found, to his intense frustration, that he was blotting his own writing even as he wrote. He was becoming increasingly dependent on the services of Florence and the newly engaged secretary, May O'Rourke.

As with *Late Lyrics,* the diligent Cockerell (now elevated to "My Dear Cockerell") had undertaken the proofreading and was, in fact, expanding his artistic activities. Hardy writes to his staunch friend that he has

> sent off the final proofs at last, & must thank you for your list of suggestions as to words here & there. I adopted some—about half I should say—& considered the others carefully. However, you will see when the book comes out. I don't expect much from it: indeed I am weary of my own writing, & imagine other people are too by this time. (*Letters,* V6.359)

So, Hardy is now adopting Cockerell's "suggestions as to words here & there."

May O'Rourke, who found Hardy's household kind and good-humored, described him as pensive, and aside from his failing health,[29] he did indeed have much to sorrow over. Among the many recently departed dear ones, his beloved friend of 30 years, Florence Henniker, had died in 1923, barely a year after he had somberly shared with her his sense that they were both rapidly losing all their friends, leaving only "we who remain ... to 'close up'" (*Letters*, V6.120).

Human Shows is filled with loneliness, what one American contemporary, Isabelle Wentworth Lawrence, described as the "essential but terrible loneliness of the individual human soul" (*Boston Evening Transcript*, January 1926). The loneliness lingers at familiar thresholds, spiritually silenced: "And mute by the gate I stand again alone,/And nobody pulls up there" ("Nobody Comes").

The physical reality of everyday life was very different, exhaustingly so for the Grand Old Man of English Letters approaching his nineties. Max Gate overflowed with visitors from all walks of life (Hardy turned no one away if the visitor wrote ahead of time—aside from gossip-mongering journalists). Visitors included the Prince of Wales, later King Edward VIII—of brief and infamous reign (1936). Half a century after describing, in *The Mayor of Casterbridge*, the ceremonious arrival in town of the reigning monarch—who is beset by an inebriated Henchard desperately bidding for attention—Hardy sits down to tea with his real-life princely heir. If a flustered Florence had to manage the facilities—"He will want to wash his hands ... terrible. You know what our house is like"—Hardy had to manage the royal intellect: "My mother," said the Prince, "tells me you have written a book called *Tess of the d'Urbervillles*. I must try to read it some time."[30]

Entertaining was arduous, and Hardy was clearly feeling his own mortality: "Walked to the top of High Stoy," he notes, adding, "probably for the last time" (*LW*, 450). Many of the poems in *Human Shows* reflect this quiet mode of acceptance and detachment, and many others transcend all sense of "mortal coil" altogether. Yet others explore situations of farce, satire, humor, and the absurdity of the human condition conveying, as ever, that true spirit of Hardyan iconoclasm and antiestablishment mischief.

If Hardy had feared his readers were wearying of him, his critics proved him wrong. He was faced with a stunning array of reviews. True, Edmund Gosse, given to frowning even as he delivered praises, couldn't get beyond pessimism: *Human Shows*, he writes, reveals "a brooding and dejected temperament left during extreme old age in possession of a cerebral acuity rarely equaled" (*Sunday Times*, December 1925). And while the *Times Literary Supplement* agrees with Gosse, the *Saturday* (December 1925) extols Hardy's love of life even though he sees death behind it: *Human Shows*, says the reviewer, is "much more exuberant and tonic in its nature than one expects from a settled pessimism." Hardy is "the most fertile inventor of stanza-forms in all English literature." The *Observer* goes further and claims that Hardy's new collection disproves all notions that only younger poets can produce great lyrics, while the most surprising aspect of *Human Shows*, for *The Literary Review*, is that Hardy, in old age, possesses the same intellectual vigor, spareness of language, and delicacy of description that characterizes his early poetry. Hervey Allen reinforces this view in the *North American Review*, waxing eloquent about Hardy's themes, that each one completes an entire life history from swaddling clothes to shroud.

Meanwhile, braving the wrath of the establishment, *The New Statesman* is "conscious of an intense relief" that there is a voice in the land that refuses to suppress the truth: Hardy "never flatters or falters with the truth." Echoing this salutation, *The Saturday Review of Literature* praises Hardy for not capitulating to the "escape poetry of other contemporaries." Finally, the most famous of all these notable critics, Leonard Woolf (Virginia Woolf's husband), is the most prophetic. Hardy, he declares, is one of the spiritual parents of modern poetry.

Hardy must have been deeply gratified. Weak and weary as he was and as pessimistic as he might have been about the reception of *Human Shows*—he was not to know it would be the last collection to be published in his lifetime—the critics lionized him. All but a handful acclaimed his achievement with strong, positive views. Most rewarding of all, perhaps, was the reception in America where Hardy had earlier felt he was underrepresented. For the novelist of 30 years who had returned to poetry at age 60, this was a triumph indeed—and Hardy did not stop here.

Grouping of Poems in *Human Shows, Far Phantasies, Songs and Trifles*

Poems of Tragedy and Sorrow

"Discover the tragedy that always underlies the Comedy if you only scratch it deeply enough," Hardy wrote in his pseudonymous autobiography (*LW*, 474). Scratching deeply, many critics find that he keeps close to tragic patterns in his pastoral poems. Certainly the rustic scenes and events of many poems in *Human Shows*, most notably "A Hurried Meeting" and "The Turnip-Hoer"—which follow one of his well-explored themes of sexual obsession—have tragic outcomes. The full patterning of sorrow customarily takes the form of time passing or of a vanishing past, as in "The Later Autumn." Here, a sense of loss is established at the outset. Stanza one begins without ado, almost crashingly, with "Gone." Thereafter, this word resonates throughout the poem (stanza two beats it out in off rhymes and strung measures, "soon to end"), picking up motion and color in "Spinning leaves join … shrunk and brown" and dropping finally to the softly lipped "A robin looks on." So, a curious thing has happened, phantasmal almost. From the moment of "Gone" to the moment of a robin looking on, a vanishing has occurred, which does not in fact occur but is perceptible only from the empty space left behind—the loneliness, the loss, is palpable.

There are many solitary birds in Hardy. From the renowned "Darkling Thrush" to the cruelly mutilated caged goldfinch birds are harbingers, signifiers, and oracles, the holders of earth's secrets. In modern science these powers come under close scrutiny—in nature they have been known since time began. Birds signal oncoming storms, changes in barometric pressure, flight patterns, and migration routes, just as, at a less mysterious level, their song tells of territorial boundaries, mating preferences, encroaching predators, and the lunch menu. In "Life and Death at Sunrise," birds embody nature's rhythmic patterns—"woodlarks, finches, sparrows, try to entune at one time," mirroring, in their dawn chorus of concerted activity, the night's pattern of events in the human world that "entune at one time" to one child born and one old soldier dead.

A lone sparrow in "Snow in the Suburbs" is overturned by a "snow-lump twice his own slight size." The poetic patterning here consists of rhyming couplets set against uneven metric rhythms of three to five beats—a structure that beautifully matches the regularity of seasonal weather changes (nature's rhythms) on the one hand, and the unbalancing of the bird on the other. The overturned bird, however, has its own rhythmic orientation, and as it drops to alight on a "nether twig," another oddity appears: a stray "black cat" "wide-eyed and thin" arrives on the scene, "And we take him in." There is less sorrow than pathos in "Snow in the Suburbs"—the "odd" moments are evened out, and the "stray" is taken care of by an act of human kindness, but quite by chance and only in the nick of time. Balance is precarious in this poem.

"Art," wrote Hardy, "is a disproportioning ... of realities, to show more clearly the features that matter in those realities" (*LW*, 239). The organization of this collection is purposefully unsettling, arranged under the odd juxtaposition of the external (in the title) *Human Shows* and the internal, *Phantasies*, of ephemeral *Trifles* and enduring *Songs*. It is significant, then, that the compassionate "Snow in the Suburbs" is juxtaposed with the dispassionate "A Sheep Fair"—a world also disarranged by weather, in this instance torrential rain—where "each mewed and meek" creature is "consigned to doom" under the auctioneer's hammer. "Horses Aboard," where the "horses of war" will eventually be itemized as "war waste," is likewise the more unsettling for its position close to a poem of ephemera, "The History of an Hour." As its title conveys, "Bags of Meat" also treats with the same distressing theme of animal slaughter.

"Unsettling" discordancy is part of Hardy's purpose, and if his pastoral poems frequently follow tragic patterns, this reflects the paradox of nature itself—the red-and-raw-in-tooth-and-claw idea that goes hand in hand with rhythmic balance, seasonal renewal, and nature's harmony (exemplified by "A Bird-Scene at a Rural Dwelling"). "A Winter Night in Woodland" exploits this paradox. "The bark of a fox rings" through the frosty night and the "quality" of the "sonorous" sound is "horn-like," a sound that comes home in the "rhythm of voices and strings" in the last stanza as the choir sings "worn carols." The notion is of man and nature in opposition—at best in juxtaposition, at worst in antagonism. The harsh reality is, of course, that the fox will steal the livestock and that "The hand of man is against him." And the "horn-like" sound of the fox calling in the night is also the call of the hunting horn by day. Harsh reality also afflicts the innocent game birds, roosting in the copse, who are about to be bludgeoned to death in their drowse by poachers with "swingels." Meanwhile, to complete the paradox, the choir will "call" forth the birth of a savior sweetly evoked in "worn carols" as sleeping in a cattle-manger with angels (not poachers) watching over. The sentiment is both ironic and inappropriate. Another poem, "The Paphian Ball," subtitled "Another Experience of the Mellstock Quire," details these carols: "Drowsy at length, in lieu of the dance/'*While Shepherds watched …*' they bowed by chance." And, later in the poem, "'*Rejoice, ye tenants of the earth,/And celebrate your Saviour's birth.*'" In Hardy's view, the "tenants of the earth" are foxes and birds no less than human beings.

A little boy cannot take the brutality in "The Bird-Catcher's Boy." He cries out to his father, "Larks bruise and bleed in jail./Trying to rise;/Every caged nightingale/Soon pines and dies." The "jingle" of the rhyme scheme enhances the tragic outcome. There is, in effect, one crude scheme for all. If a bird's life comes cheap, why not a boy's? Interestingly, the tragic "The Bird-Catcher's Boy" presents a more powerful outcry against cruelty to animals than Hardy's purpose-built poem "Compassion—An Ode," subtitled "In Celebration of the Centenary of the Royal Society for the Prevention of Cruelty to Animals." On the other hand, it is curious that "A Jingle on the Times," which embodies one of Hardy's most pervasive themes in *Human Shows*, is not published in this volume and remained uncollected in his lifetime. Designed to open eyes to "Life and its secrets," to unsettle fixed minds, and to raise awareness in readers by juxtaposing the wasting effects of time and nature upon culture and society, and vice versa, "A Jingle on the Times" hits at itself, advising all do-gooders from preachers to artists to quit thinking of plying their wares to make the world a better place. Human virtue, the poem implies, is not a commercial transaction.

In Memoriam

"In the Evening" is a tribute (Hardy says "hastily" written) to a long-standing family friend, Sir Frederick Treves (of Elephant Man fame), who had attended the same Dorchester school as his beloved sister Mary—her "immortality" is celebrated in another poem, titled "Paradox." "The Sea Fight" memorializes Captain Prowse, who went down with his ship, and "A Popular Personage at Home" celebrates Hardy's beloved dog, Wessex. A sad and troubling little poem, "When Dead" appears to be a tribute to Florence, but the dedication is left blank: "To—" "It will be much better when/I am under the bough," says the speaker, "No sign of querulousness/To wear you out." An unusually candid and somewhat backhanded "tribute" to Emma appears in "The Frozen Greenhouse," subtitled "St Juliot," where "she" grieves over her pretty plants, "Cold, iced, forgot" but, says the speaker, "Herself is colder,/And knows it not." "The Monument-Maker," dated 1916, more conventionally celebrates Emma's ghost—a happy ghost who laughs and jests with the speaker and leaves him regretful.

The Nature of Comedy and the Grotesque

The way *Human Shows and Far Phantasies* was printed in the first edition, in large capitals on consecutive lines is, in itself, comedic—reminiscent of freak shows or circus performances. "Songs" and "Trifles" embody, in turn, the spangles on the circus headgear or the grotesquerie of the performers. "A Song to an

Old Burden" encapsulates these elements as dancers no longer dance, the floor is "wormholed," the songsters have ceased to sing, and only "cobwebs stir." Maytime is now simply "tedious" and "Phantoms call the tune!"

Hardy's experimentalism is now a commonplace—not least in his balladic forms into which he inventively infuses narrative voices, folk memories, trivial anecdotes, and multiple focalization without losing that dreamlike quality peculiar to the genre. Many contemporaries were startled by his genre breaking; others were confused, but most were beguiled. For one critic *Human Shows* evinced "a strange, tangled mood … painful, yet thrilled; saddened, yet exhilarated." Much consists of "stringing together distant moments into a necklace of flashing irony."[31] The image is an apt one. Hardy's particular gift for depicting the minutiae of life and the tiny details of character, event, and setting, into which he infuses ideas and emotions, is well represented by a string of jewels, gemstones, and pearls reflecting the vibrance and the ever-changing light and color of his world in view. The variety of songs in *Human Shows* reflects just one melodic way of stringing together those distant moments encapsulated in reverie ("Lover to Mistress"), in desire ("Come Not; Yet Come!"), in nostalgia ("Let Me Believe"), in remorse ("Last Love-Word"), in secret love ("In the Street"), in jaunty cynicism ("What's There to Tell?")—and much more.

Some of these distant moments are made immediate and present in completely different poetic forms, as in "Why She Moved House (The Dog Muses)." This patterns the poetic form of "The Milestone by the Rabbit-Burrow" (*LL*), where the innocent unknowingness of the dumb animal throws human action into perspective. The grotesque is a feature of both poems, offering humorous representations of a world familiar to the reader.

Another moment occurs in "Inscriptions for a Peal of Eight Bells—After a Restoration," where the humor derives from seeing things from the bell's point of view: "I bang and bid/In commoner metal than I did,/Some of me being stolen and hid." Alternatively, "The Sundial on a Wet Day" presents the point of view of the sundial, and in "The Peace Peal" it is a jackdaw that speaks. In keeping with Hardy's penchant for the grotesque but in contrasting mood, "Lady Vi" presents a satiric view of religion, and with a touch of feminism, "A Beauty's Soliloquy during Her Honeymoon" conjoins regret to that "flashing irony."

From Old Manuscripts

"Discouragement" has the appended note, "Westbourne Park Villas, 1863–7 (From old MS.)" and has the feel of being forced back into life. On the other hand, "Retty's Phases"—"From an old draft of 1868"—abounds with that delightfully skittish female sexuality Hardy evokes so well: "Then she'd hot-up scarlet red" or, more seductively, "used to draw me down/To the turfy heaps" (one of the more erotic verses in this collection is "The Pat of Butter," which plays, suggestively, on the tasting of succulent buttery flavors). Of singular interest is the poem "A Poor Man and a Lady," which carries the note: "The foregoing was intended to preserve an episode in the story of 'The Poor Man and the Lady', written in 1868, and, like these lines, in the first person; but never printed, and ultimately destroyed."

Philosophical Reflections and Ironies

Many of the love poems (and there are happy ones) are also flashes of irony—to cite three, "The Echo Elf Answers," "He Inadvertently Cures His Love-Pains," "To a Sea-Cliff"—as are several philosophical verses. The collection opens on a philosophical note and with a deliberately naive conversation. "Waiting Both" reiterates the word "mean" (which simultaneously signifies intention and meaning) at the end of both stanzas: What do you mean?—What do you mean to do? The joke is on philosophy, which is first and foremost a convoluted discourse (never this simple) and which has never ceased, since time began, to debate the meaning of meaning and the intentionality of intention. Philosophy has never resolved these questions, yet the "star" in this poem resolves them—with simplicity and certitude. The philosophical resolution and certitude is, of course, a freak, a "far phantasy." Freakish, too, is the fact that the timeless debate is reduced to the simple tropes of nursery rhyme, as if to stress the primal forces at play in the cosmic discourse that is thrust far back into time with the biblical allusion to Job 14:14, "Till my change come." On the other hand, the broken rhythms of "Waiting Both" point to the loss of innocence among the rationalists and the emptiness of their rhetoric. Pure (unbroken) nursery rhyme with its singing rhythm and heartbeat meter would have resonated with too much sincerity for the poet's purposes.

A new look is given to traditional philosophical ideas in "Sine Prole," "The Aerolite," and "Genetrix Laesa" (the injured Earth-Mother): adopting the metric arrangement of twelfth-century Latin (Sarum) hymns thus employing a well-established form to which the topic (a damaged Nature) will provide "discordia," Hardy fulfills two purposes. First is that he has adopted classical form to which he now applies classical doctrine: the Renaissance doctrine of "*Concordia discors*" (that beauty and harmony are generated by contraries). This recovers the notion (discussed earlier) that Nature's brutal law (as Jude calls it), the red-in-tooth-and-claw idea, is but the Janus face of a Nature whose other countenance manifests harmony, renewal, and regeneration. Second, Hardy goes one step further in "Genitrix Laesa," mirroring the theme of his anti-God poems, and has Nature accused of malpractice. This plays cleverly on the *Concordia discors* doctrine insofar as classical and modern are drawn into the same orbit but are set in opposition to one another. Form and doctrine serve one another to provide rhythmic/philosophical substance to nontraditional ideas. Simultaneously this fulfills Hardy's own dictum that the business of the poet "is to show the sorriness underlying the grandest things, and the grandeur underlying the sorriest things. To find beauty in ugliness is the province of the poet" (*LW*, 178, 222).

Hardy evidently enjoyed the sheer cacophony in this collection. "Donaghadee"—a song—seems to have been created purely out of love of the sound of the name that rings throughout (5 times) as the speaker, unabashed, reveals nothing *whatsoever* about the village of this name and jauntily self-rebukes: "that is where I never shall be; —/And yet I sing of Donaghadee!" This air of modernism in which aspects of the world are fragmented, disassociated, or disintegrated from other forms, in which significance is given to what seems insignificant, pervades much of *Human Shows* and is often modified by a blithe existentialism as in "Donaghadee." The much-loved "Any Little Old Song" follows a similar course of playfulness and fine-tuning for its own sweet sake.

UNCOLLECTED POEMS

Bernard Jones compiled *Fifty-Seven Poems by Thomas Hardy* (Meldon House, 2002),[32] commonly known as the "baby poems." Several have been previously collected, and all were originally produced, with Florence Hardy, for a series of books—*Baby Birds, Baby Beasts, Baby Pets* (1911–15)—primarily to accompany the exquisite illustrations of Edward Julius Detmold.

Two recent standard editions of Hardy's poems (Gibson and Hynes) also feature approximately 30 uncollected poems, some dating back to the 1890s ("Thoughts from Sophocles"), some earlier—"To a Bridegroom," 1866, and "The Unplanted Primrose," 1865–67. Two scathing epitaphs—G. K. Chesterton and George Moore—testify to Hardy's unsuppressed rage at two of his detractors, and fragments on the novels include "Eunice" (*DR*), a 4-line "Epigraph to 'The Woodlanders,'" and a sizable collection from *The Dynasts*.

WINTER WORDS IN VARIOUS MOODS AND METRES (1928)

Hardy had prepared *Winter Words* for a birthday edition—probably his 90th, which would have been June 2, 1930.[33] There is no evidence in his correspondence with his publishers (Macmillan) that he had prepared this collection of 105 poems for an earlier publication—on his 88th birthday, as some scholars have surmised. Nor that he was "closing up" and driving toward "silence." On the contrary, the vigor of the collection is astonishing—the spirit was manifestly willing even if the flesh was weak.

As a rule, Hardy corresponded with his publishers well ahead of time to discuss details of book presentation (leather, cloth, paper quality) and other related issues, but not in this instance. In February 1927, he did, however, negotiate with Macmillan over the Golden Treasury volume called *Selected Poems* (1916). Consequently, a revised and expanded version with 41 poems added to the original 120 came out posthumously under a new title, *Chosen Poems*, in August 1929.

In an introductory note he was preparing for *Winter Words*, Hardy indicates, with unconcealed pride, something of a debut: "So far as I am aware, I happen to be the only English poet who has brought out a new volume of his verse on his … birthday." Evidently he hoped the ellipses would be filled in at some future point—at age 90 (?), had he lived to see the day (no doubt he felt the hubris, the tempting of fate, of affixing this auspicious date ahead of time). But this master of irony died on January 11, 1928, without even preparing a table of contents, let alone arranging those same contents with his customary skill and mischief—as, for example, in an earlier collection, sandwiching "God-Forgotten" between two innocuous and somewhat deceptive titles: "The Bullfinches" (which actually treats with birds awaiting a bird heaven) and "The Bedridden Peasant" (which is less about the peasant than about his being exploited by a callous God—*PPP*). Characteristically, "no harmonious philosophy," as Hardy puts it, is to be found in *Winter Words*, which was published posthumously (prepared by Cockerell with help from Florence), without the benefit of any Hardyan fine-tuning.

During the last four years of his life, following the publication of *Human Shows* in 1925, Hardy was extraordinarily productive despite his failing health (never going to London now) and the enormous strain on his weak eyes. He could no longer read for sustained periods of time and reserved his creative energies, in the main, for poetry. Daily dictating most of his letters, hosts of them—in response to distressed gentlewomen and animal activists, fund-raisers (including saviors of the pre-Reformation cracked church bell at Stinsford), plagiarists, the journalistic hordes plying excuses for getting into Max Gate (filtered out from the visitor list), and many, many more—he rarely had time or energy to write to those of his friends who were still alive. The poets Edward Clodd and Edmund Gosse were among the exceptions. Hardy had a deep affinity with Clodd, and his strong friendship with Sir Edmund Gosse (recently knighted) had survived several hurdles—the missed lunch appointments (on Hardy's part), the disagreements and misunderstandings, and, most difficult of all, Gosse's stern reviews of Hardy's work, which may have been rare and forgiven but not forgotten.

Hardy's last letter, as he lay dying, was written to Gosse and was, most aptly, concerned with poetry—specifically "Christmas in The Elgin Room." Gosse had read it in *The Times* on December 24 and had written to say how much he had enjoyed it. The poem voices the longing, on the part of the Elgin Marbles, to go home: "would I were still/Radiant as on Athenai's hill." It was subsequently collected in *Winter Words*.

The extent to which Hardy tended to dwell on negative criticism is revealed in his introductory note. There had been many sincere acclamations of *Human Shows* (see earlier section), yet Gosse's emphasis on the "pessimism" of the collection stands at the forefront of Hardy's mind as he gathers up his pieces for his eighth and final volume of verse. Looking back at *Human Shows*, he is preoccupied with this: "My last volume of poems," he writes, "was pronounced wholly gloomy and pessimistic by reviewers—even by some of the more able class" (*CP*, 834; this mild snipe at Gosse would never have reached the latter's ears; he died a few months after Hardy and was never to read *Winter Words*). "As labels stick," Hardy continues, "I foresee readily enough that the same perennial inscription will be set on the following pages" (*CP*, 834). He was right, the label stuck. But had he lived, and had he managed to overcome his sensitivity to the few pessimism hunters in favor of the many connoisseurs, he would have found it a tawdry label somewhat fraying at the edges.

Take, for example, *The Saturday Review* (November 1928), which speaks of his "omnivorous" love of life, or the *Spectator* (October 1928), for whom *Winter Words* evinces "a very subtle and very substantial delight in life." Hardy's "pose of despair" is but "a paradoxical expression of his delight in life," his pessimism but a "mask shielding his powerful and agonized sensibility." The *Spectator* reviewer goes further and sees *Winter Words* and Hardy's "dramatic genius" as expressing a "youthful lyricism controlled by sixty years of technical practice," and *John O'London's Weekly* (October 1928) endorses this view, lauding his "unbounded attachment to life"—*Winter Words* shows "a robust, powerful, and invigorating acceptance of the things that happen." For the *Dial*, Hardy is "A Tragedian of Sentience" (February 1929)—the poems of *Winter Words* show he is not a pessimist but rather that he experienced "life as an emotion." And under the evocative title "Hardy's Last Verses Are Gnarled and Powerful," the *New York Times Book Review* argues that Hardy can be compared only to Wordsworth as a lyricist, and that although *Winter Words* breaks all the rules of poetry, it still bears the stamp of greatness. Robert Frost, says the reviewer, learned from Hardy's example.

Severally, Hardy's reviewers applaud his ingeniousness. Observing that Hardy's only competitor for first place among twentieth-century British poets was William Butler Yeats, *The Nation* (February 1928) reasons that if Yeats may be sometimes more admirable, he is never as *interesting* as Hardy, whose background as a novelist and rare insights, along with his ways of seeing and describing things, infuse his poetry and make him unique among the greats.

Grouping of Poems in *Winter Words in Various Moods and Metres*

Love Songs

Hardy seems to have enjoyed a youth filled with romantic trysts in country lanes. "That Kiss in the Dark" has all the sexual urgency of young love, and "To Louisa in the Lane" (Louisa Harding) is filled with tender memories for the girl "Sweet of eyes" who possesses that lissome, willowy grace, "Your aspen form," Hardy admired so much (in "Lorna the Second" he prefers the mother). Other poems recollecting earlier phases from his life are "The Musing Maiden" (Eliza Bright Nicholls) and "A Countenance"—"Childhood Among the Ferns" and "Yuletide in a Younger World" evoke the Bockhampton birthplace. "The Love-Letters," dedicated to H. R. (unknown), dramatizes a hurtful moment in a broken relationship where his letters have been returned to him (the love letter itself speaks in "The Letter's Triumph"), and "Love Watches a Window" portrays a long-forsaken love—she, who once "drew delight," becomes a spectral gleam of glowing light at the window where she used to watch for him.

"Aristodemus the Messenian," set in "Dramatic Hendecasyllabics," is less a love poem than a grotesque romantic tragedy. An experiment in form, it treats, gruesomely, with the sacrifice of virgins and the lover's attempt to save his beloved from this appalling fate by claiming she's with child: her enraged father, the perpetrator of the sacrificial act, takes his sword and rips open her belly to prove the lover wrong.

A mood of dark regret pervades "The Dead Bastard," and "The Whaler's Wife" tells of a tragic misunderstanding generated by gossip when the whaler returns home. This theme is mirrored in "The War-Wife of Catknoll," where troubles arise for the lonely wife with an absentee husband. Yet more dire consequences ensue when a wife sews her drunken husband into his bed sheets to forfend unwanted sex ("Her Second Husband Hears Her Story")—less gruelingly, erotic fantasies sustain the lonely wife in "In the Marquee." The theme of crossed fidelities is continued in "The Son's Portrait."

Pastoral Poems

There is an enviable unknowingness about the birds that sing in "Proud Songsters" with no sense of destiny, "As if all Time were theirs." Likewise, the singing blackbird in "I Watched a Blackbird," for whom the "man who liked to notice such things" was standing by when he opened his "crocus-coloured bill" and trilled his song. The popular poem "An Unkindly May" also commends a kind of "unknowingness"—more precisely a consciousness so intently focused that "the sour spring wind" and the distinctly noncommendable May weather is of no account. Gesturing, in the intentness of close focus, at the spiritual strength of transcendence, these verses also exemplify Hardy's power of seeing into the life of the littlest things—transient, tiny, barely perceptible things. More prosaically, "We Field-Women" recalls the Flintcomb-Ash of the *Tess* story, yet with a joyful outcome: "To start at dairywork once more/In the laughing meads, with cows three-score,/and pails and song, and love—."

A strange little poem called "Burning the Holly" reiterates the choric line "O you are sad," "Yes: I am sad," "Why are you sad" at the opening of each stanza and the effect is of a sobbing or a mind crazed with shock. As the poem moves through rhythms that gasp and choke to the very end, repeating words that only a mind in deep distress repeats over and over in this way, the emotional disturbance is made palpable and real.

"Two hundred years' steady growth" is ended in "less than two hours" in the anguished poem "Throwing a Tree," which employs one of Hardy's favorite verse forms of mimicking the action in poetic rhythms—here, a sawing motion culminating in an overbalancing last line. "The Felled Elm and She" follows the same theme. By contrast, the speaker in "To a Tree in London" mourns a life never lived where the "air is sweet"—the discomfort of city life is encapsulated in short, truncated stanzas that stumble their way to the last fragmented phrase: "Never seen/Miles of green."

There is a surprising lack of morbidity in this collection, but "After the Burial" helps to fill the gap, as does "Silences," with its pretty, haunting phrases: "the wind sinks dumb," "the rapt silence of an empty house/Where oneself was born—".

Ironies and Satires

The trenchant satire "Unkept Good Fridays" celebrates all the "nameless Christs" who remain "unpenned" throughout history, the Christmas spirit of goodwill to all men is exemplified by a sodden tramp in "Christmastide" ("Whispered at the Church-Opening" follows a similar theme), and the experience of being "the single woman in the field" shapes the mood of irony in "Expectation and Experience." The unknowingness of the "lofty lovely woman" in "The Lady in the Furs" is not enviable but outrageous (a cry against the fur trade); utterly heartbreaking is "The Mongrel," who so trustingly allows his master to drown him. More pathetic than distressing, mad Nancy in "Henley Regatta" plays with toy paper boats: outside her window Regatta Day is ruined by teeming rain and inside "she sheds half-crazed tears."

"An Evening in Galilee," one of Hardy's wittily sacrilegious accounts of the life of Jesus (in Monty Python vein), has the Virgin Mary seriously concerned about her son's mental health, that he "knows not" his own mother, that he mixes with "the lowest folk," not to mention "That woman of no good character, ever following him." Two unusual poems of irony are "A Self-Glamourer," which is oddly life enhancing given that aging looms on the woman's horizon, and the tragicomic "Squire Hooper," where the 90-year-old squire puts the interests of his houseguests before his own (ill health)—"unusual" because Hardy is customarily tough on the upper classes in such situations of privilege.

Grotesquerie shapes both "The Gap in the White" and "Family Portraits," in which one candlelit night, "Three picture-drawn people stepped out of their frames" and set about "acting some drama, obscure." The chilling moment arises when the speaker realizes they are unraveling an "ancestral mystery," reliving past events—their "restless enghostings, it seemed, were to teach/Me in full." "Lying Awake" echoes this theme in which names start "creeping out everywhere" from the headstones in the graveyard.

"The New Dawn's Business" and Poems of Reflection

The collection opens with a conversation between a voice of quiet acceptance and an all-knowing dawn: "The New Dawn's Business." Tonally, there is gentle detachment commingled with a rather comforting banality as the rising sun is faced with several "odd jobs" such as lighting the way "for earthing a corpse or two," for births and deaths, for killing and paying "for board and bed" in equal measure. It is a poem of settlement rather than valediction. "A Wish for Unconsciousness" adopts a similar theme and "I Am the One" a similar tone, gently communing with nature—"I am the one whom ringdoves see": the verse is structured in aptly shaped stanzas creating a visual sense of inner and outer worlds reaching to the stars above, who are heard to say, "He is one with us/Beginning and end." Various irreconcilable moods are felt in "Thoughts at Midnight," which conjure a rant against mankind's "senselessness"—the verse moving at a suitably frantic pace. More examples of the amazing variety Hardy could produce within a single mood can be found in "So Various" and "Concerning His Old Home."

Hardy is delightful with children. The little boy in "Boys Then and Now" thinks that only one cuckoo exists, that it returns every year to herald the spring. Another little boy in "No Bell-Ringing" gets lost in the poem as it becomes obsessed with its own narrative; and in yet another, "The Boy's Dream," the child is lame and he dreams: "His face beautified by the theme" of having "A real green linnet—his very own." The bird will be himself, denied freedom and flight—trapped in a cage forever.

Tributes

"Liddell and Scott," subtitled "On the Completion of their Lexicon," celebrates, in lighter vein, the completion of the standard lexicographical work of ancient Greek in 1843 (the lexicon is now in its ninth revised edition). On a more personal note, "Concerning Agnes" offers a tribute to one of Hardy's dearest friends, the beautiful Lady Agnes Grove, beloved dancing partner of yesteryear.

Hardy does an unexpected thing in *Winter Words*. He writes a reflective self-tribute on his "Eighty-Sixth Birthday" called "He Never Expected Much." Far from maudlin, far from gloomy or pessimistic, it celebrates a life in which the world has kept faith with him—a simple goodwill pledge harking back to his childhood, to the days when "as a child I used to lie/Upon the leaze and watch the sky." The tone and tenor point to an easeful, pleasant life, quietly appreciated, which met all modest expectations of "neutral-tinted haps and such." This isn't quite the "glory and the dream," but shades of Wordsworth echo in such phrases as "In that mysterious voice you shed/From clouds and hill around." Indeed the poem could be said to be a tribute to a happy life except that that sounds alarmingly un-Hardyan.

The juxtaposition of poems here almost certainly has to be Hardy's although there is no evidence that he had time to arrange the contents of *Winter Words* before he died. For "He Never Expected Much" sits right across the page from "Standing by the Mantelpiece," subtitled "H.M.M., 1873." Now, where the former poem has every appearance of a tribute to the happiness of existence—an uncommon thing for a poet, and most surprising coming from Hardy—the latter memorializes one of the most tragic, if not the most traumatic, events in his life. Writer and Cambridge scholar Horace Moule, a youthful friend from Dorset turned mentor and kindred spirit, killed himself in his college room in 1873. He slit his throat. They were young men then, and Moule never lived long enough to see his fondest protégé become a famous man.

Hardy must have known of Moule's depression, his alcoholism, and more besides. That "Standing by the Mantelpiece" did not surface in his oeuvre until the year of his own death, or rather, was not prepared for publication until his own death was imminent suggests its dark burial in his mind—repressed memory perhaps. Fifty years is a long time. And nowhere an accounting. The poem, portraying a premonition (the candle wax is shaping to a shroud—to touch it means death will come), is set in the present tense. It is ambiguously phrased so that the reader can never be completely sure that the voice is Moule's, ventriloquized (although most scholars seem to assume it). The subtle nuances of the poem blur the edges of identity, and given the deep affinity between these two men, such a blurring is apt. What one thinks the other speaks, and vice versa. In the haze of ambiguity, the question arises, if the speaker is the "claimant" of the curse or omen or premonition, is the claimant himself, or the other? "One of us dies," he says, but which one? If we didn't know of Moule's suicide, would this alter our reading?

The most chilling moment occurs when the speaker himself shapes the wax: "it's I who press my finger—so." Hence, he is implicated in the subsequent tragedy, whether his own or that of his listener. One thing is plain. The two souls involved are caught in a terrible secret, and the premonition of disaster came true. The auto-suggestion (if that is what it is) worked. And, for Hardy, the legacy remained forever, until his dying day.

If this can be called a bereavement poem, it is a rare one for Hardy insofar as it looks forward to a meeting beyond the grave: "The rest must wait till we/Are face to face again, yonside the tomb." No poem to Emma ever prophesied a supernatural destiny.

Toward the end of the collection, "Dead 'Wessex' the Dog to the Household" memorializes, in delightfully bounding meters, the beloved Max Gate pet. Speaking to his master in line-ending rhymes as if to effect an ear-pricking, doglike intensity coupled with protective reassurances (if you say it enough times your master will hear you), Wessex cautions that when walking time comes or when stairways creak, he will not be there.

A few poems later, "He Resolves to Say No More" draws the curtain down on Hardy's last volume. Opening with a line from the Greek epigrammatist Agathias, the verse employs a rhyme scheme rare in Hardy's corpus. The poem is retentive and quiet, implying that there is more to come but that it will remain unknown.

Some scholars have read this as a valediction, but it is not quite that simple. That "none shall gather what I hide" is a withholding but also an indication that the poet has a good deal more to convey—planted but not reaped (alternatively, some critics hold the visionary, thematically waning "Seeing the Moon Rise," dated August 1927, to be Hardy's last, but it's unlikely he spent his last four months without penning lines). "He Resolves to Say No More" is coupled on the page with "We Are Getting to the End," which pleads for an awareness of the "demonic force" of nations at war and cautions that "We are getting to the end of dreams," reaffirming Hardy's original claim that the collection bears "no harmonious philosophy." However, the apocalyptic imagery in both verses heralds a departure that is less than quietly accepting. The poet will quit on his own terms.

NOTES

1. "Domicilium" opens *Thomas Hardy: The Complete Poems*, edited by James Gibson (London: Macmillan, 1976), hereafter referred to as CP.

2. Hardy loved drama. In addition to *The Dynasts,* he also wrote a tragedy called *The Queen of Cornwall;* a dramatic version of "The Three Strangers," titled *The Three Wayfarers* (1893), which was frequently acted in his lifetime; a dramatization of *Tess of the d'Urbervilles* (1894–95); a recension of an old Wessex version of the mumming play of Saint George (1920); and a little operatic piece he had heard in childhood, known locally as "O Jan, O Jan, O Jan" (1923).

3. Published by Harper & Brothers, December 1898, in an edition of only 500 copies. An American edition followed a month later. The manuscript is held by Birmingham City Museum and Art Gallery.

4. Hardy's original title had been *Wessex Poems: with Sketches of their Scenes by the Author.* He describes the illustrations to Florence Henniker as "a mysterious occupation" he is engaged in (*Letters,* V2.199).

5. Although dated 1902, 1,000 copies were published by Harper & Brothers in November 1901.

6. The holograph manuscript is in the Bodleian Library, Oxford.

7. These poems are a response to the Boer Wars of 1880–81, 1899–1902 between the British Empire and the Dutch settlers (Boers) in Southern Africa. Five hundred thousand British troops engaged in what was basically a war of attrition; 40,000 of these troops died.

8. There is a similar reference to Gibbon in *Jude the Obscure.*

9. Iconoclastic: one who attacks cherished beliefs.

10. The doctrine that the world will be made better by human effort.

11. *Time's Laughingstocks* was published in an edition of 2,000 copies followed by a second impression the following year.

12. The phrase is Tennyson's: "laughing-stocks of Time," from *The Princess* (IV.496). Hardy titled the first poem in this collection "Time's Laughingstocks," but later renamed it "The Revisitation"—first published in the *Fortnightly Review,* August 1, 1904.

13. This is Jude's phrase describing himself as he approaches Christminster.

14. The full translation by Elena Carp can be found on the Thomas Hardy Association's Web site, at http://www.yale.edu/hardysoc/VPBOX/elena.htm.

15. In 1802, William Paley, natural theologist, argued that the nature of God could be understood by reference to a metaphor (in the philosophy of science), which is that of the image of the watchmaker: the nature of the universe is analogous to the action of the watchmaker who creates all things to run like clockwork.

16. The manuscript is held by the Dorset County Museum.

17. There is some doubt about this poem's dating. If it was, in truth, composed in the 1870s, the question arises, why did Emma never set eyes on it? It is surely the most loving of testaments an overly anxious bride could wish for. Then, also, why was it not published earlier if it is, indeed, an early poem? Alternatively, if it was an unfinished fragment of an early verse, when did Hardy rework it for publication—after Emma's death to balance out the present group?

18. In the manuscript this reads "O woman weird," and "air-blue gown" (an inspired phrase) was originally "hat and gown."

19. Published in an edition of 3,000 copies in November 1917. The manuscript is held by Magdalene College, Cambridge. These were, of course, the catastrophic years of World War I, so inevitably *Moments of Vision* didn't go into more than one printing, and only six of the poems had been previously published in periodicals. Of the remainder, nearly all, bar five from earlier phases of his life (with dates varying from 1871–98), were written between 1913 and 1916.

20. *Selected Poems* (2,000 copies) is divided into categories of poems chiefly lyrical, poems narrative and reflective, and war poems and includes lyrics from *The Dynasts*. Later Hardy revised *Selected Poems* and published an expanded version (posthumously) as *Chosen Poems* (1929). This comprises 169 poems: 8 of the earlier poems are dropped, 4 are added, and 45 extra poems are taken from collections published after *Moments of Vision*. Thus, there is no sense of a "definitive" collection of choice on Hardy's part, although the selections and their various changes provide a fascinating study.

21. Michael Millgate, *Thomas Hardy: A Biography Revisited* (Oxford: Oxford University Press, 2004), 458.

22. There are no subdivisions in *Moments of Vision* aside from poems of war, so I have arbitrarily supplied them.

23. Cockerell had persuaded Hardy in September 1911 to let him distribute his manuscripts to various museums and had, over time, become a regular visitor at Max Gate.

24. "Though I am by no means anxious to rush into print again—quite the reverse, indeed—the question arises whether it would not be advisable to bring them out—say early next year, or whenever you think convenient—and not leave them to the mercy of curious collectors, and people who print things privately and then coolly sell them" (Letter to Sir Frederick Macmillan, *Letters*, V6.104).

25. An edition of 3,200 copies was issued in May 1922, followed by two reprints before the year was out. The manuscript is held by Dorset County Museum. Several poems, including "Haunting Fingers," "Voices From Things Growing," and "The Fiddler's Story," were previously selected by Florence Emily Hardy for publication in limited private editions.

26. See Hewlett's review of *Late Lyrics* in the *Times*, 8 June 1922, where he speaks of being "fairly revolted" by some of Hardy's poems: "The Wood Fire" would "offend many, and gratuitously ... I think that you shall as well scoff at a man's mother as at his religion."

27. There are no subdivisions in *Late Lyrics*. I have arbitrarily supplied them.

28. The 5,000 copies of the first printing of *Human Shows* sold out within the month. This seventh volume of verse includes the 25 poems currently printed in magazines, some 19 others dating back to the 1860s, and yet more of the war period. The collection went into several printings and a reset American edition was published by Macmillan in New York in December 1925. Hardy provides no preface and no subdivisions. I have supplied the latter.

29. When laid up in bed, he relied on generous quantities of champagne as a cure.

30. This is Siegfried Sassoon's anecdote. See Millgate, *Revisited*, 506.

31. Frank Lucas, "The Triumph of Time," *The New Statesman* 26, 23 January 1926, 448–49.

32. Several of these poems are published in *The Hardy Review*, V, edited by Rosemarie Morgan (New Haven, CT: The Hardy Association Press, 2000).

33. The manuscript is held by Queens' College, Oxford, of which Hardy was an honorary fellow.

8

Afterword: Hardy's Last Novel

Two life-altering events happened to Hardy between the publication of *Tess* in 1891 and the publication of *Jude* four years later. The first was that in 1892 Thomas Hardy Sr. died. Hardy had visited his father every weekend, as regular as clockwork, and the loss was felt by all, for Hardy Sr. had also been an invaluable buffer to the strained relations between Jemima, Hardy's mother, and Emma, his wife. Thomas Hardy Sr.'s death also signaled the end, for his son, of many recounted memories of early-nineteenth-century rural life and many anecdotes associated with local people, places, and traditions. It had been Hardy's father's background in church music—singing and playing among the viols, fiddles, and cellos in the church gallery—that provided much of the inspiration for one of Hardy's best-loved novels, *Under the Greenwood Tree*, published exactly 20 years before *Jude* in 1872. It had also been his father who had introduced him to life in the great country houses of the aristocracy where father and son would add their skills to the band—playing the fiddle to jigs and reels into the wee hours of the morning. It was on such occasions that the boy Hardy developed his passion for dancing.

Ultimately, it was his father who mediated the mean-minded snobbery that Emma Hardy was not averse to generating about her husband's family. For when Thomas Hardy Sr.'s will and testament came to light, it became apparent that the Hardys were not at all the lowly country laborers so fondly patronized by critics. The will revealed that they owned several cottages, substantial freehold land, and small commercial premises in the village of West Knighton. Like the best of legacies, Hardy Sr.'s made a difference. But there was more, a kind of inspirational legacy. For at this time, Hardy started on the composition of *Jude*, and with it the creation of an odd fictional merge of father and son: Jude, the young dreamer and aspirant scholar, is not only fatherless—an orphan—but a stonemason, as Hardy's own father had been.

The second life-altering event occurred the following year. On a visit with Emma to Lord Houghton's Viceregal Lodge in Ireland, the door was opened to Hardy by a remarkably handsome woman—Lord Houghton's sister. This "charming *intuitive* woman" (as Hardy described her on first meeting) was Florence Henniker, and she was to become his most cherished lifelong friend. Henniker was already the author of three novels, and later she and Hardy would collaborate as authors, on another— *The Spectre of the Real.*

Hardy's friendship with Florence Henniker, wife of Major Henniker, started on that auspicious day in Ireland and continued on throughout his lifetime, until the day she died—just five years before he did. It was undoubtedly the deepest, most sustaining friendship he would ever know. Whether they ever became lovers is not known.[1] Certainly they were deeply intimate. What is known (from their letters) is Henniker's dependence on him. She had an ability to draw from him a fervent intellectual interest, a warm responsiveness, and what another writer described as "his smile of remarkable sweetness … and still intensity of observation."[2]

For sure, Henniker drew from Hardy an affection that extended beyond what most Victorian wives might consider decorous. She frequently entertained him alone at her home, went on outings, dinners, theatrical events, and parties with him, and, after knowing him just a few weeks, gave him her photograph together with a silver inkstand engraved "T.H. FROM F.H. | 1893." They talked about everything. And when they were not together, they were writing notes and letters to each other, often the very same day of meeting. They filled each other's intellectual lives, providing constant companionship, mutual literary support, and considerable emotional understanding—and this at a time when she was playing "grass widow" to a military husband and Hardy was suffering increasing domestic unhappiness with a mentally unstable wife.

Hardy was lonely at his Max Gate home. He found it isolated and isolating. Migrating to London and the life of the literati was thus doubly rewarding after meeting Henniker, who was eager to introduce him to new friends and acquaintances among the social elite. She was high-born, beautiful, clever, and wealthy—and she greatly admired the astute, mild-mannered, intense, and gentle 53-year-old Hardy.

Henniker, some critics say, provided the model for Sue Bridehead in *Jude*. It would be hard to deny her influence given that Hardy was constantly in her company at the time, but "model" is an oversimplification. Writing to his close friend Sir Edmund Gosse (poet, writer, and librarian of the House of Lords) about Sue's perverse and somewhat fastidious sexuality, Hardy observes that the

abnormalism consists in disproportion: not in inversion, her sexual instinct being healthy so far as it goes, but unusually weak & fastidious; her sensibilities remain painfully alert notwithstanding, (as they do in nature with such women). One point illustrating this I cd not dwell upon: that, though she has children, her intimacies with Jude have never been more than occasional, even while they were living together (I mention that they occupy separate rooms, except towards the end), & one of her reasons for fearing the marriage ceremony is that she fears it wd be breaking faith with Jude to withhold herself at pleasure, or altogether, after it; though while uncontracted she feels at liberty to yield herself as seldom as she chooses. This has tended to keep his passion as hot at the end as at the beginning, & helps to break his heart. He has never really possessed her as freely as he desired.

Sue is a type of woman which has always had an attraction for me—but the difficulty of drawing the type has kept me from attempting it till now. (*Letters*, V2.99)

Was the difficulty of the typology ("type of woman") resolved then by knowing Henniker? This is extremely doubtful. A living person is not a type except at the most superficial level. Hardy would scarcely, in all seriousness (jest or irritation aside), reduce a close friend to a type. Moreover, given that he discussed the novel with Henniker while writing it (to the point where he thought he had bored her), he would scarcely represent her sexuality to her own face as it were, as a topic to be analyzed and criticized by thousands of readers. How awkward, embarrassing, even alienating that would have been—to have emblazoned in public the private and intimate details of a woman he loved dearly. Henniker would never have spoken to him again!

As it was, she exchanged letters with Hardy back and forth every week while she was taking the waters in Marienbad and he was putting the revising touches to the volume edition of *Jude*. And as soon as she returned to London, they resumed their meetings again as before. However, despite her levity with Hardy, she was not a "free love" advocate and he was rather hurt when she used the term pejoratively to describe his novel. It is certainly rather reductive—the complicated relations between Jude and Sue are by no means that simple—although it does show that Henniker identified with Sue's sexuality not at all.

It has to be said, at this point, that a fictional character rarely relies on a real-life model without considerable mutation and assimilation of alternative sources. Psychoanalytical studies of aesthetics stress the act of projection, that a type, a fictional character, emerges from the author's storehouse of images, ideas, and recollections after undergoing a variety of processes of selection and modification ultimately to be projected onto the created form. This process includes projections of the self. For example, there is no reason why Hardy's own projection of sexual fastidiousness onto a fictional character should be ruled out. As a man not only of extraordinary empathy but of thin-skinned sensitivity and wide-ranging emotions, he would surely have experienced moments of disdain, distaste, and disgust—not solely the breathless ecstasies of desire and ardour. It needs only a single moment. One moment would suffice, to be enlisted in the creation of characters as contrasting as the sexually fastidious Henry Knight in *A Pair of Blue Eyes* and the nervously repressed Sue Bridehead in *Jude*.

Inevitably, a fictional character has to draw on the author's life experiences, but imagination is a transcending of life, it reinvents the world: it is the birth of art. Having said that, of the various models for Sue, Hardy's beloved tomboy sister

Mary bears a far closer resemblance to her fictional counterpart than does Henniker and not simply because she was kin, as Sue is kin to Jude. And yes, there is an element of incestuousness in the Jude-Sue relationship. "One person split in two," observes Phillotson. The brother-sister, or cousin to cousin, affinity was always attractive to Hardy—a perennial in his fiction.

Gazing with deep tenderness on the sleeping Sue, curled up in his Sunday clothes while her own garments dry by the fire, Jude sees "the rough material called himself done into another sex—idealised, softened, & purified." That is the manuscript version. Did Hardy feel this to be too close to the mark? We may never know, but at any rate he altered it. Jude still sees her as if seeing himself, but now "a slim and fragile being masquerading as himself on a Sunday, so pathetic in her defencelessness that his heart felt big with the sense of it" (first edition: III.iii).

Henniker was never the "epicene" (boyish), nervous, vivacious, impetuous, and often rebellious wild thing that Mary was and Sue is. Nor did she ever attend teacher training school or possess the graphic-arts skills that both Mary and Sue possess. These were all qualities Mary owned and Hardy loved and admired. Indeed, he mourned the fact that his sister's teaching career so ill-fitted her nature, much as Sue is constrained by the conventions of her training college.[3] But career opportunities for women were limited in Hardy's day—this, too, enters Sue's consciousness as she struggles to live as an equal with men in the male-dominated, class-riven world of *Jude the Obscure*.

In contrast to his preparation for *Tess*, Hardy seems to have thoroughly enjoyed his research and composition of *Jude* as he traveled around the region and contemplated settings for various scenes. No doubt having Henniker at his elbow, at it were, made him feel all the more confident and encouraged, although he would have liked to have enjoined her to his activities even more than he did. He appears to have relied on her insights from the outset. Within a month of entering into an agreement to serialize *Jude* with *Harpers* (December 1893), he had asked Florence Henniker what name he should give to his new heroine, who, he says (shortly afterward), is "beginning to get interest[ing]——as she takes shape & reality: though she is very nebulous at present" (*Letters*, V2.48). Who, I wonder, came up with the name Susanna *Florence* Mary Bridehead?

NOTES

1. There was clearly an immediate attraction between them. A month or so after meeting her, when she had evidently asked him to chronicle his "doings" for her, he wrote, "You seem quite like an old friend to me, and I only hope that Time will bear out the seeming. Indeed, but for an adverse stroke of fate, you would be --a friend" (*Letters*, V2.23). The ellipsis does not require much imagination to complete.

2. See also Michael Millgate, *Thomas Hardy, A Biography Revisited* (Oxford: Oxford University Press, 2004), 295–96.

3. According to Michael Millgate, Melchester Training College, in *Jude*, is modeled on the Salisbury training school where Hardy's two sisters studied to become teachers.

Appendix

The Evolution of Wessex

Nearly two decades after Hardy had written his last novel, *Jude the Obscure* (1895), his publishers (Macmillan) decided to bring out a uniform edition of all 14 novels under the general heading of the Wessex Edition (1912).[1]

The most important task now confronting Hardy was to piece together the topographical jigsaw of highways, towns, hillsides, valleys, meadows, villages, plantations, heathlands, hamlets, rivers, and streams that had come into being over 25 years and to shape them all into a coherent Wessex. This proved to be a difficult task because there were many ill-fitting pieces, and, inevitably, in trying to coordinate mileages and distances, Hardy accidentally created a number of anomalies. A good example occurs with the resituating of Weatherbury Church (*Far From the Madding Crowd*) to accord with its real-life model some distance from the manor house (Bathsheba's house). Hardy evidently forgot that, at one point, Bathsheba gazes out of her bedroom window on the children playing in the churchyard below. In the Wessex Edition she would need a telescope. Unfortunately, anomalies were probably inevitable not only because at the outset of his novel-writing career, in the 1870s, Hardy hadn't even conceived of a "Wessex," coherently designed or otherwise, but also because many years had elapsed between first composition and final revision.

As Wessex began to emerge from the novels of the 1870s, readers went in search of the enchanted dream country, trying to trace its shape and meaning in the real world. *Far From the Madding Crowd* had initiated this quest. The pastoral world of Weatherbury, so vividly evoked month by month in the *Cornhill*, bringing fresh breezes, fields of clover, and the soft hum of bees into a stuffy London drawing room had, somewhat late in the day (in one of the last installments), been given a regional name. It was dubbed Wessex. Immediately, Victorian nostalgia seized upon it. Harboring dreams of the ancestral village—the ancient, lost world of old England—enthusiasts went off (on the bright new railway system) in search of it.

Over the next decade, in making forays into Dorset (the real-life model, central to the fictional Wessex), writing articles about it, drawing maps of "Hardy country," evaluating the social conditions, bemoaning the poverty, romanticizing the rusticity, counting the miles, and walking the routes taken by Hardy's characters, Victorian readers unwittingly assisted in the creation of Wessex. Along the way Hardy was criticized for this and praised for that: his laborers were too articulate; no! they were too boorish; no! they were too quaint—rather, they were not sufficiently politicized.[2] It was as if readers were unearthing an ancient culture, ruins and all, rather than engaging in a work of imaginative fiction. Indeed, so vividly did Hardy's characters live in the real world that arguments would break out in the press about their behavior and attitudes, much as the lives of Hollywood stars are gossiped about today.

Literary fiction presents a version of the world, not the way the world is or should be but aspects, dimensions, and representations of the existing world re-created and reinvented by the visionary writer. Hardy's Wessex is one such world—it is termed a microcosm, a representative world in miniature, an entity complete and entire unto itself. But as a consequence of all the questing and intense curiosity about the real behind the dream, Wessex has become, in turn, an artifact in its own right. It is now a region where tours operate as if in exploration of a historical reality. The word has become flesh.

At various points in his career, Hardy picked up on the growing public enthusiasm for authenticating his locations and characters while, at the same time, recoiling for aesthetic reasons from precise verification. In a postscript to his 1895 preface to *The Return of the Native*, he is keen to point out:

> To prevent disappointment to searchers for scenery it should be added that though the action of the narrative is supposed to proceed in the central and most secluded part of the heaths united into one whole ... certain topographical features resembling those delineated really lie on the margin of the waste, several miles to the westward of the centre. In some other respects also there has been a bringing together of scattered characteristics.

Works of art yield unlimited interpretations and epiphanies, but reduced to the literal and the unambiguous, they lose not only their inspirational force but also their cultural potency. The mystique of a lost world is one thing; searching through ancient artifacts stirs the imagination and yields bountiful interpretations. But fixing boundaries to that world and its people is quite another, and Hardy resisted that literalness, that fixity. He tried to steer a middle course between the commodification of his Wessex and the artistic principles by which it exists. To one visitor he might offer a tour of model locales, but to another he might blur all boundaries. Either way, and in common with many great artists, he was caught, whether he liked it or not, between life and art. And although he disliked the commercialism, the benefits to be gained by providing maps and feeding the public imagination were all to his advantage.

There was, though, little media interest in his disclaimers about rough approximations or imaginative leaps. The public appetite is almost insatiable when it comes down to seeking and defining the recognizable and the familiar; certainty and intelligibility seem to be paramount, even to the point of gainsaying the literary imagination and pinning an author down to facts and "real life"—including biographical sources. It is something of a paradox that whereas works of the imagination open up new worlds, new truths and understandings, and new insights and experiences for free-thinking readers, some of those selfsame readers may, in a second breath, close their minds to the novel's inner reality and accuse the author of deception and misrepresentation of the facts. Hardy has had his fair share of this.

Recently, a critic claimed that Hardy had got it all wrong—rural life was never like that. Others, mainly contemporaries, would accuse him of misrepresenting women. Even biographers fall into the trap—trying (in one case) to persuade readers that Hardy's wish not to be pinned down to specific internal dates or locations reveals a curious deception on his part. The argument goes that he is discharging a victimized sense of his own anxiety and guilt (filial, sexual, relational) and thus uses his fiction to conceal or rewrite his past. Suffice it to say that these lobbyists reveal more about their own aesthetic limitations than about Hardy's.

Once a purely imaginative construct and now a cultural icon, Wessex lives. In common with Homer's Ionia and Shakespeare's Illyria, it takes life from as many myths as it now gathers.

NOTES

1. This is the so-called definitive edition—theoretically, the most nearly accurate and complete. In actuality, accuracy and completeness are indefinable, and the concept of a definitive edition remains questionable. An author might apply a hindsight evaluation to texts composed at an earlier historical time, but cannot recover the vision, mood, or sensibility of that time. Thus, first editions (and, of course, the manuscript versions) are frequently regarded as the authentic text. They remain untouched by the various editorial interventions that accrue to published editions over the years, and they are not marked by the author's hindsight evaluation, which may be affected by received public opinion. Insofar as this is verifiable, first editions constitute the author's own work, solely.

2. This was the region famous for the TolPuddle Martyrs. In 1834 six agricultural laborers in Dorset rebelled against wage cuts by forming a union. Arrested and condemned for illegal oath taking, they were transported, as convicts, to Australia. In 1838, one convict, George Loveless, returned to agitate as delegate to the Chartist Convention for Parliamentary reform in 1839.

Bibliography

All page references for novels in the text are to the Penguin World Classics First Editions of 1871–97 with the exception of *Far From the Madding Crowd*, which follows the Penguin World Classics edition of Hardy's holograph manuscript of 1874. With the exception of the *Far From the Madding Crowd* manuscript, which was bowdlerized by the editor and subsequently revised by Hardy for the first edition, these are the texts his readers first encountered. Unlike the 1912 Wessex edition, these editions remain pristine. They were not tampered with or amended as follows:

1. They were not subjected to Hardy's comprehensive revisions made in preparation for the Wessex Edition of 1912 with the intention of rendering the inner world of his novels uniform.
2. They remain free of the editorial alterations and errors that accrued in versions published between the first edition and all later editions.
3. They represent the original unbowdlerized versions of Hardy's serialized novels based on the first volume edition as it was presented to the British reader, and remain untouched by current critical opinion insofar as this shaped Hardy's 1912 revisions.
4. They are works created at a unique moment in the historical process—each a product of its own period.

The Penguin Classics First Editions carry detailed analyses of Hardy's late revisions for the Wessex Edition of 1912 and all subsequent editions. Readers are advised to consult the Wessex Edition for a full appreciation of the historical process of production.

NOVELS BY THOMAS HARDY

Desperate Remedies (Penguin Classics, 1998). First published 1871.
Far From the Madding Crowd (Penguin Classics, 2000). First published 1874.
The Hand of Ethelberta (Penguin Classics, 1996). First published 1876.
Jude the Obscure (Penguin Classics, 1998). First published 1895.
A Laodicean (Penguin Classics, 1997). First published 1881.
The Mayor of Casterbridge (Penguin Classics, 1997). First published 1886.
A Pair of Blue Eyes (Penguin Classics, 1998). First published 1872–73.
The Return of the Native (Penguin Classics, 1999). First published 1878.
Tess of the d'Urbervilles (Penguin Classics, 1998). First published 1891.
The Trumpet-Major (Penguin Classics, 1997). First published 1880.
Two on a Tower (Penguin Classics, 1999). First published 1882.
Under the Greenwood Tree (Penguin Classics, 1998). First published 1872.
The Well Beloved (Penguin World Classics, 1998). First published 1892, rewritten 1897.
The Woodlanders (Penguin Classics, 1998). First published 1887.

SHORT STORIES BY THOMAS HARDY

A Changed Man (1913)
A Group of Noble Dames (1891)
Life's Little Ironies (1894)
Thomas Hardy: The Excluded and Collaborative Stories (1992), edited by Pamela Dalziel.
Wessex Tales: Strange, Lively and Commonplace (1888)

POEMS BY THOMAS HARDY

All references to poems in the text are to *The Complete Poems of Thomas Hardy* (Macmillan, 1976), edited by James Gibson. Gibson includes a section of previously uncollected poems and fragments. For textual information see *The Variorum Edition of the Complete Poems of Thomas Hardy* (1979), edited by James Gibson.

Human Shows, Far Phantasies, Songs and Trifles (1925)
Late Lyrics and Earlier (1922)
Moments of Vision and Miscellaneous Verses (1917)
Poems of the Past and the Present (1901)
Satires of Circumstance: Lyrics and Reveries with Miscellaneous Pieces (1914)
Time's Laughingstocks and Other Verses (1909)
Wessex Poems and Other Verses (1898)
Winter Words in Various Moods and Metres (1928)

DRAMA BY THOMAS HARDY

The Dynasts (originally published in three parts, 1904, 1906, 1908)
The Famous Tragedy of the Queen of Cornwall (1923)

MISCELLANEOUS PROSE OF THOMAS HARDY

The Architectural Notebook of Thomas Hardy, edited by C.J.P Beatty (1966).

Hardy, Florence. *The Life of Thomas Hardy 1840–1928* (1962—dictated by Thomas Hardy).

Hardy, Thomas. *The Life and Work of Thomas Hardy*, edited by Michael Millgate (1984, originally published in two volumes under Florence Hardy's name in an abridged version as *The Life of Thomas Hardy*).

The Literary Notebooks of Thomas Hardy, edited by Lennark Björk, 2 vols. (1985).

The Personal Notebooks of Thomas Hardy, edited by Richard H. Taylor (1979).

Thomas Hardy's "Facts" Notebook: A Critical Edition, edited by William Greenslade (2004).

Thomas Hardy's Personal Writings, edited by Harold Orel (1966).

Thomas Hardy's Public Voice: The Essays, Speeches, and Miscellaneous Prose, edited by Michael Millgate (2001).

Thomas Hardy's 'Studies and Specimens etc.' Notebook, edited by Pamela Dalziel and Michael Millgate (1994).

THE LETTERS OF THOMAS HARDY

The Collected Letters of Thomas Hardy, edited by Richard Little Purdy and Michael Millgate, 7 vols. (1978–88).

The Collected Letters of Thomas Hardy, CD-ROM. Past Masters, Humanities Databases, Intelex Corporation (1992).

One Rare Fair Woman: Thomas Hardy's Letters to Florence Henniker 1893–1922, edited by Evelyn Hardy and F. B. Pinion (1972).

BIBLIOGRAPHIES

Davis, W. Eugene, and Helmut Gerber. *Thomas Hardy: An Annotated Bibliography of Writings About Him II 1970–1978, and Supplement for 1871–1969* (1983).

Draper, Ronald P., and Martin Ray. *An Annotated Critical Bibliography of Thomas Hardy* (1989).

Gerber-Davis Annotated Bibliography: TTHA. yale.edu/hardysoc/Members/MRRHome.htm.

Purdy, Richard L. *Thomas Hardy: A Bibliographical Study*, edited by Charles P. C. Pettit (2002).

Taylor, Richard H. "Thomas Hardy: A Reader's Guide," in Norman Page, editor, *Thomas Hardy: The Writer and His Background* (1980).

REFERENCE WORKS

Bailey, J. O. *The Poetry of Thomas Hardy: A Handbook and Commentary* (1970).

Lea, Hermann. *The Hardy Guides*, 2 vols. (1986).

Millgate, Michael. "Searching for Saxelby: A Hardy Item Lost and Found," *The Thomas Hardy Journal* 19.1 (2003).

Pinion, F. B. *A Hardy Companion* (1968).

————. *A Thomas Hardy Dictionary* (1989).

Wright, Sarah Bird. *Thomas Hardy: A–Z : The Essential Reference to His Life and Work* (2002).

TEXTUAL STUDIES

Chase, Mary Ellen. *Thomas Hardy from Serial to Novel* (1927).

Fischer, Jeffrey. "Killing at Close Range: A Study in Intertextuality," *English Journal* 95.3 (2006).

Laird, J. T. *The Shaping of* Tess of the d'Urbervilles (1975).

Lu, Jie. "Similar Phenomena, Different Experiments? A Study of Thomas Hardy's Literary Influence on Theodore Dreiser," *The Midwest Quarterly* 45.4 (2004).

Nishimura, Satoshi. "Thomas Hardy and the Language of the Inanimate," *SEL: Studies in English Literature 1500–1900* 43.4 (2003).

Patey, Caroline. "Lost in the Luminiferous Ether: Thomas Hardy and the Epistemology of His Age," *Textus: English Studies in Italy* 16.2 (2003).

Ray, Martin. *Thomas Hardy: A Textual Study of the Short Stories* (1997).

Rosenbaum, Barbara. *Index of English Literary Manuscripts*, Vol. 4, 1800–1900: Part 2, Hardy-Lamb (1990).

BIOGRAPHICAL WORKS

Archer, William. *Real Conversations* (1904).

Collins, Vere. *Talks with Thomas Hardy at Max Gate 1920–1922* (1928).

Cox, J. Stevens, ed. *Thomas Hardy: Materials for a Study of His Life, Times and Works*, Vols. 1 (1968) and 2 (1971) (originally published as series of monographs).

Deacon, Lois, and Terry Coleman. *Providence and Mr Hardy* (1966).

Gibson, James. *Thomas Hardy: A Literary Life* (1996).

————, ed. *Thomas Hardy: Interviews and Recollections* (1999).

Gittings, Robert. *The Older Hardy* (1978).

————. *Young Thomas Hardy* (1975).

Halliday, E. F. *Thomas Hardy: His Life and Work* (1972).

Hardy, Emma Lavinia. *Diaries*, edited by Richard H. Taylor (1985).

————. *Some Recollections*, edited by Evelyn Hardy and Robert Gittings (1961, 1979 revised).

Hardy, Evelyn. *Thomas Hardy: A Critical Biography* (1954).

Hardy, Florence Emily. *The Early Life of Thomas Hardy 1840–1891* (1928).

————. *The Later Years of Thomas Hardy 1892–1928* (1930).

Millgate, Michael, ed. *Letters of Emma and Florence Hardy* (1996).

————, ed. *The Life and Work of Thomas Hardy by Thomas Hardy* (1984).

————, *Thomas Hardy—A Biography Revisited* (2004).

Norman, Andrew. *Thomas Hardy: Behind the Inscrutable Smile* (2004).

Orel, Harold. *The Final Years of Thomas Hardy* (1976).

————. *The Unknown Thomas Hardy* (1987).

O'Sullivan, Timothy. *Thomas Hardy: An Illustrated Biography* (1975).

Pinion, F. B. *Thomas Hardy: His Life and Friends* (1992).

Pite, Ralph. *Thomas Hardy: The Guarded Life* (2006).

Ray, Martin, ed. *Thomas Hardy Remembered* (2006).

Seymour-Smith, Martin. *Hardy* (1994).

Stewart, J.I.M. *Thomas Hardy: A Critical Biography* (1971).

Tomalin, Claire. *Thomas Hardy: The Time–Torn Man* (2006).

Turner, Paul. *The Life of Thomas Hardy: A Critical Biography* (2000).

Weber, Carl. *Hardy and the Lady from Madison Square* (1954).

———. *Hardy of Wessex: His Life and Literary Career* (1940, 1965 revised).

CRITICAL WORKS

General

Abercrombie, Lascelles. *Thomas Hardy: A Critical Study* (1912).

Armstrong, Tim. *Haunted Hardy: Poetry, History, Memory* (2000).

Asquith, Mark. *Thomas Hardy, Metaphysics and Music* (2005).

Bäckman, Sven. *The Manners of Ghosts: A Study of the Supernatural in Thomas Hardy's Short Poems* (2001).

Bayley, John. *An Essay on Hardy* (1978).

Beach, Joseph Warren. *The Technique of Thomas Hardy* (1922).

Berger, Sheila. *Thomas Hardy and Visual Structures* (1990).

Björk, Lennart. *A Psychological Vision and Social Criticism in the Novels of Thomas Hardy* (1987).

Bloom, Harold, ed. *Thomas Hardy* (2004).

Blunden, Edmund. *Thomas Hardy* (2003, first published in 1942).

Boumelha, Penny. *Thomas Hardy and Women: Sexual Ideology and Narrative Form* (1982).

Brennecke, Ernest. *Thomas Hardy's Universe: A Study of a Poet's Mind* (1924).

Brooks, Jean. *Thomas Hardy: The Poetic Structure* (1971).

Bullen, J. B. *The Expressive Eye: Fiction and Perception in the Work of Thomas Hardy* (1986).

Butler, Lance St. John. *Thomas Hardy* (1976).

Carpenter, Richard. *Thomas Hardy* (1964).

Cecil, Lord David. *Hardy the Novelist* (1943).

Chew, Samuel C. *Thomas Hardy: Poet and Novelist* (1921, 1928).

Child, Harold. *Thomas Hardy* (1916).

Cox, R. G., ed. *Thomas Hardy: The Critical Heritage* (1970).

Cullen Brown, Joanna. *Let Me Enjoy the Earth: Thomas Hardy and Nature* (1990).

Daleski, H. M. *Thomas Hardy and the Paradoxes of Love* (1997).

Dave, Jagdish Chandra. *The Human Predicament in Hardy's Novels* (1985).

Davis, William. *Thomas Hardy and the Law: Legal Presences in Hardy's Life and Fiction* (2002).

Drabble, Margaret, ed. *The Genius of Thomas Hardy* (1976).

Duffin, H. C. *Thomas Hardy: A Study of the Wessex Novels* (1916).

Dutta, Shanta. *Ambivalence in Hardy: A Study of His Attitude to Women* (2000).

Ebbatson, Roger. *Hardy: The Margin of the Unexpressed* (1993).

Enstice, Andrew. *Landscapes of the Mind* (1979).

Fisher, Jo. *The Hidden Hardy* (1992).

Garson, Marjorie. *Hardy's Fables of Integrity: Woman, Body, Text* (1991).

Gatrell, Simon. *Thomas Hardy and the Proper Study of Mankind* (1993).

Giordano, Frank. *"I'd Have My Life Unbe": Thomas Hardy's Self-Destructive Characters* (1984).

Goode, John. *The Offensive Truth* (1988).

Gossin, Pamela. *Thomas Hardy's Novel Universe: Astronomy and the Cosmic Heroines of His Minor and Major Novels* (2002).

Gregor, Ian. *The Great Web: The Form of Hardy's Major Fiction* (1974).

Grimsditch, Herbert Borthwick. *Character and Environment in the Novels of Thomas Hardy* (2003).

Grundy, Joan. *Hardy and the Sister Arts* (1979).

Guerard, Albert. *Thomas Hardy: The Novels and the Stories* (1949, 1964).

Haldane, Sean. *Thomas Hardy* (2002).

Hands, Timothy. *Thomas Hardy* (1995).

Hardy, Barbara. *Thomas Hardy: Imagining Imagination in Hardy's Poetry and Fiction* (2002).

Hasan, Noorul. *Thomas Hardy: The Sociological Imagination* (1982).

Holloway, John. *The Victorian Sage* (1953).

Howe, Irving. *Thomas Hardy* (1967).

Hughes, John. *Thomas Hardy's Uses of Music* (2001).

Hyman, Virginia. *Ethical Perspective in the Novels of Thomas Hardy* (1975).

Ingham, Patricia. *Thomas Hardy* (2003).

Jackson, Arlene. *Illustration and the Novels of Thomas Hardy* (1981).

Jekel, Pamela. *Thomas Hardy's Heroines: A Chorus of Priorities* (1986).

Johnson, Bruce. *True Correspondence: A Phenomenology of Thomas Hardy's Novels* (1983).

Johnson, Lionel. *The Art of Thomas Hardy* (1894, 1923).

Johnson, Trevor. *Thomas Hardy* (1968).

Kajihara, Kimie. *A Life of Eternity* (2000).

Kettle, Arnold. *Hardy the Novelist* (1967).

Kramer, Dale. *Thomas Hardy: The Forms of Tragedy* (1975).

Langbaum, Robert. *Thomas Hardy in Our Time* (1995).

Lawrence, D. H. "A Study of Thomas Hardy," *Phoenix* (1936).

Lerner, Laurence, and John Holmstrom. *Thomas Hardy and His Readers* (1968).

Lock, Charles. *Thomas Hardy* (1992).

Meisel, Perry. *Thomas Hardy: The Return of the Repressed* (1972).

Milberg-Kaye, Anne. *Thomas Hardy: Myths of Sexuality* (1983).

Miller, J. Hillis. *Thomas Hardy: Distance ands Desire* (1970).

Millgate, Michael. *Thomas Hardy: His Career as a Novelist* (1971).

Moore, Kevin. *The Descent of the Imagination: Postromantic Culture in the Later Novels of Thomas Hardy* (1990).

Morgan, Rosemarie. *Cancelled Words: Rediscovering Thomas Hardy* (1992).

———. *Cancelled Words: Rediscovering Thomas Hardy*, Electronic book: Net Library (2002).

———, ed. *Editing Hardy* (2000).

———. *Women and Sexuality in the Novels of Thomas Hardy* (1988).

Morrell, Roy. *Thomas Hardy: The Will and the Way* (1965).

Musselwhite, David. *Social Transformations in Hardy's Tragic Novels: Megamachines and Phantasms* (2004).

Neill, Edward. *The Secret Life of Thomas Hardy: "Retaliatory Fiction"* (2004).

O'Toole, Tess. *Genealogy and Fiction in Hardy: Family Lineage and Narrative Line* (1997).

Page, Norman, ed. *Oxford Reader's Companion to Hardy* (2000).

———. *Thomas Hardy* (1977).

———. *Thomas Hardy: The Novels* (2001).

Pinion, Frank. *Thomas Hardy: Art and Thought* (1977).

Powys, John Cowper. *John Cowper Powys on Hardy*, edited by Kate Kavanagh (2006).

Radford, Andrew. *Thomas Hardy and the Survivals of Time* (2003).

Riesen, Beat. *Thomas Hardy's Minor Novels* (1990).

Rutland, William R. *Thomas Hardy: A Study of His Writings and Their Background* (1938).

Salter, C. H. *Good Little Thomas Hardy* (1981).

Schoenfeld, Lois. *Dysfunctional Families in the Wessex Novels of Thomas Hardy* (2005).

Sherman, G. W. *The Pessimism of Thomas Hardy* (1976).

Sprechman, Ellen Lew. *Seeing Women as Men: Role Reversal in the Novels of Thomas Hardy* (1995).

Springer, Marlene. *Hardy's Use of Allusion* (1983).

Sumner, Rosemary. *A Route to Modernism: Hardy, Lawrence, Woolf* (2000).

———. *Thomas Hardy: Psychological Novelist* (1981).

Taylor, Dennis. *Hardy's Literary Language and Victorian Philology* (1993).

Taylor, Richard H. *The Neglected Hardy, Thomas Hardy's Lesser Novels* (1982).

Thomas, Edward. *Edward Thomas on Thomas Hardy*, edited by Trevor Johnson (2002).

Thorne, Nicola. *In Search of Martha Brown: True Story of the Mysterious Woman Hardy Saw Hanged* (2000).

Thurley, Geoffrey. *The Psychology of Hardy's Novels: The Nervous and the Statuesque* (1975).

Tsuchiya, Shizuko. *Women and the Novels of Thomas Hardy* (2000).

Vigar, Penelope. *The Novels of Thomas Hardy: Illusion and Reality* (1974).

Weber, Carl. *Hardy Music at Colby* (2005, first published 1945).

White, R. J. *Thomas Hardy and History* (1974).

Widdowson, Peter. *Hardy in History: A Study in Literary Sociology* (1989).

———. *Thomas Hardy* (1996).

Williams, Merryn. *A Preface to Hardy* (1976).

———. *Thomas Hardy and Rural England* (1972).

Wooton, George. *Thomas Hardy: Towards a Materialist Criticism* (1985).

Wright, T. R. *Hardy and His Readers* (2003).

———. *Hardy and the Erotic* (1989).

Architecture

Anderson, Jordan. "'The Architecture of the Grave,'" *The Hardy Society Journal* 1.1 (2005).

Beatty, Claudius J. P. *Thomas Hardy: Conservation Architect. His Work for the Society for the Protection of Ancient Buildings* (1995).

Mink, JoAnna. "Some Dorset Church Restorations with Hardy Associations," *Dorset Life* (2002).

Film and Stage

Cardwell, Sarah. *Adaptation Revisited: Television and the Classic Novel* (2002).

Jays, David. "Hardier Than Thou," *Sight and Sound* 11.2 (2001).

Niemeyer, Paul J. *Seeing Hardy: Film and Television Adaptations of the Fiction of Thomas Hardy* (2002).

Selby, Keith. "Hardy, History and Hokum," in Robert Sheen and Erica Sheen, editors, *The Classic Novel: From Page to Screen* (2000).

Vineberg, Steve. "In Movie Adaptations, Changing Stories to Keep Their Essence," *The Chronicle of Higher Education* 47.22 (2001).

Wilson, Keith. *Thomas Hardy on Stage* (1994).

Wood, Anna, and David Jays. "Cruel Intentions," *Sight and Sound* 11.2 (2001).

Wright, Terry, ed. *Thomas Hardy on Screen* (2005).

Language and Style

Chapman, Raymond. *The Language of Thomas Hardy* (1990).

Elliott, Ralph W. V. *Thomas Hardy's English* (1984).

Philipps, K.C. *Language and Class in Victorian England* (1984).

Smith, J. B. "Dialect in Hardy's Short Stories." *THA* 3 (1985).

Taylor, Dennis. *Hardy's Literary Language and Victorian Philology* (1993).

Poetry

Banerjee, Amitav, ed. *An Historical Evaluation of Thomas Hardy's Poetry* (2000).

Bayley, John. *The Power of Delight: Essays 1962–2002* (2005).

Blain, Virginia. "Thomas Hardy and Charlotte Mew: Queering the Ballad/Issues of Poetic Identity," *Australasian Victorian Studies Journal* 9 (2003).

Bloom, Harold, ed. *Thomas Hardy: Comprehensive Research and Study Guide* (2004).

Blyth, Caroline. "Language and Subjectivity: 'The Darkling Thrush and the Golden Bird,'" *The Critical Quarterly* 45.3 (2003).

Brooks, Jean. *Thomas Hardy: The Poetic Structure* (1971).

Buckler, William. *The Poetry of Thomas Hardy: A Study in Art and Ideas* (1983).

Christie, Tara. "Seamus Heaney's Hardy," *Recorder: The Journal of the American Irish Historical Society* 17.1 (2004).

Clements, Patricia, and Juliet Grindle, eds. *The Poetry of Thomas Hardy* (1980).

Cooper, Rand Richards. "The Man He Killed," *Commonweal* 130.9 (May 9, 2003).

Cullen Brown, Joanna. *A Journey into Thomas Hardy's Poetry* (1990).

Davie, Donald. *Thomas Hardy and British Poetry* (1973).

Everett, Barbara. "Larkin and the Doomsters: Walking 'down life's sunless hill' with Hardy and Barbara Pym," *TLS* No. 5331 (2005).

Eymigan, William. "Essays—'An Ancient to Ancients': Thomas Hardy," *The Sewanee Review* 111.3 (2003).

Fuss, Diana. "Corpse Poem," *Critical Inquiry* 30.1 (2003).

Gervais, D. "'Cock Crow': Why Edward Thomas Isn't Thomas Hardy," *Pn Review* 30.2 (2003).

Hardy, Thomas. *Thomas Hardy: Fifty Poems*. Edited with Introduction and Commentaries by Norman Page, and edited and annotated in Japanese by Itsuyo (2000).

Harmon, William. "A Note on Hardy and Hulme," *The Thomas Hardy Journal* 19.2 (2003).

Harrison, DeSales. *The End of the Mind: The Edge of the Intelligible in Hardy, Stevens, Larkin, Plath, and Glück* (2005).

Hawkins, Desmond. *Hardy: Novelist and Poet* (1976, 1988).

Heaney, Seamus. "Something to Protect," *Parnassus: Poetry in Review* 25.1/2 (2001).

Hickson, E. C. *The Versification of Thomas Hardy* (1931).

Hoffpauir, Richard. "'Putting by the Claims of the World': Negations in the Poetry of Thomas Hardy and Yvor Winters," *New Compass: A Critical Review* 3 (2004).

Holste, Gayle. "Hardy's 'Christmas in the Elgin Room,'" *The Explicator* 59.4 (2001).

Hynes, Samuel. *The Pattern of Hardy's Poetry* (1961).

Ingelbein, R. "From Hardy to Yeats? Larkin's Poetry of Ageing," *Essays in Criticism* 53.3 (2003).

Jackson, Richard D. "Seen from High Windows" *TLS* 5326 (2005).

Joh, Byunghwa. *Thomas Hardy's Poetry: A Jungian Perspective* (2001).

Johnson, Trevor. *A Critical Introduction to the Poems of Thomas Hardy* (1991).

Kalra, Kamlesh. *The Poetic Element in Hardy's Major Novels* (2005).

Keery, James. "Inspired Triangulation: Thomas Hardy and British Poetry," *PN Review* 26.5 (2000).

Kerrigan, William. "'An Ancient to Ancients': Thomas Hardy Disciplines Nostalgia," *Sewanee Review* 111.3 (2003).

———. "Eight Great Hardys," *Raritan* 21.3 (2002).

Levi, Peter. *John Clare and Thomas Hardy* (1975).

Lucas, John. "Plain Speaking and the Language of the Heart," *PN Review* 30.6 (2004).

Maillikarjun, Patil. *Thomas Hardy's Poetry and Existentialism* (2000).

Manajita, Kaura. *The Feminist Sensibility in the Novels of Thomas Hardy* (2005).

Marsden, Kenneth. *The Poems of Thomas Hardy: A Critical Introduction* (1969).

Maynard, Katherine Kearney. *Thomas Hardy's Tragic Poetry: The Lyrics and The Dynasts* (1991).

Mellers, J. "Sad Tales for Winter," *Musical Times* 142.1887 (2001).

Meyers, Jeffrey. "Thomas Hardy and the Warriors," *New Criterion* 21.1 (September 2002).

Morgan, Rosemarie, and William W. Morgan, eds. *Thomas Hardy's Emma Poems* (2001).

Morimatsu, Kensuke. *Nineteenth-Century British Poets and Thomas Hardy—With Japanese Translations of The Famous Tragedy of the Queen of Cornwall and All the 'Hitherto Uncollected poems'* (2003).

Paulin, Tom. *Thomas Hardy: The Poetry of Perception* (1975).

Persoon, James. *Hardy's Early Poetry: Romanticism Through a "Dark Bilberry Eye"* (2000).

———. "Hardy's 'The Impercipient," *Explicator* 61.2 (2003).

Pritchard, W. H. "Hardy's Poetry of Old Age," *Literary Imagination: The Review of the Association of Literary Scholars and Critics* 6.1 (2004).

Ray, Martin, ed. *Poetry of Thomas Hardy: Contemporary Reviews* (2004).

Richardson, D. E. "Donald Davie and the Changing Shape of Poetry," *Sewanee Review* 108.1 (2000).

Richardson, James. *Thomas Hardy: The Poetry of Necessity* (1977).

Shelston, Alan. "Echoes of Hardy," *TLS* 5375 (2006).

Taylor, Dennis. "The Chronology of Hardy's Poetry," *The Thomas Hardy Journal* (2001–2).

———. *Hardy's Poetry, 1860–1928* (1981, 1989).

Thomas, Edward. *Edward Thomas on Thomas Hardy*, edited by Trevor Johnson (2002).

Thompson, L. A. "Darkling and Visible: Hardy's Repudiation of Romanticism in 'The Darkling Thrush,'" *Lamar Journal of the Humanities* 26.2 (2001).

Volsik, Paul. "'A Phantom of His Own Figuring': The Poetry of Thomas Hardy," *Études Anglaises* 57.1 (2004).

Ward, John Powell. *Thomas Hardy's Poetry* (1992).

Weissbort, Daniel. "Staying Afloat: Thomas Hardy and Joseph Brodsky," *Russian Literature* 47.3/4 (2000).

Wiman, Christian. "The Druid Stone: Thomas Hardy," *The Sewanee Review* 108.1 (2000).

Yezzi, David. "Thomas Hardy and American Poetry," *PN Review* 26.3 (2000).

Zietlow, Paul. *Moments of Vision: The Poetry of Thomas Hardy* (1974).

Religion

Collins, Deborah L. *Thomas Hardy and His God: A Liturgy of Unbelief* (1990).

Dalziel, Pamela. "Strange Sermon: The Gospel According to Thomas Hardy," *TLS* No. 5372 (2006).

Hands, Timothy. *Thomas Hardy: Distracted Preacher* (1989).

Jedrzejewski, Jan. *Thomas Hardy and the Church* (1996).

Laszlo, Noemi. "Unorthodox Theists: Thomas Hardy and Percy Bysshe Shelley," *Anachronist* (2000).

Newby, Mark. "He Hath Wrought Folly in Wessex: Hardy's Use of Biblical Narrative in Tess of the d'Urbervilles," *English* 54.209 (2005).

Roberts, Jon. "Mortal Projections: Thomas Hardy's Dissolving Views of God," *Victorian Literature and Culture* 31.1 (2003).

Short Stories

Ray, Martin. *Thomas Hardy: A Textual Study of the Short Stories* (1997).

Smith, J. B. "Dialect in Hardy's Short Stories," *THA* 3 (1985).

Topography and Folklore

Cornelius, David. "Hardy's 'A Tradition of Eighteen Hundred and Four' and the Nature of Urban Myths," *Australian Folklore: A Yearly Journal of Folklore Studies* 18 (2003).

Daiches, David, and John Flower. "Thomas Hardy's Wessex," *Literary Landscapes of the British Isles: A Narrative Atlas* (1979).

Edwards, Anne-Marie. *In the Steps of Hardy* (2003).

Firor, Ruth. *Folkways in Thomas Hardy* (1931).

Fowles, John, and Jo Draper. *Thomas Hardy's England* (1984).

Gatrell, Simon. *Hardy's Vision of Wessex* (2003).

Howard, Tom. *Hardy Country* (2002).

Irwin, Michael. *Reading Hardy's Landscapes* (2000).

Kay-Robinson, Denis. *Hardy's Wessex Reappraised* (1971).

———. *The Landscape of Thomas Hardy* (1984).

Lea, Hermann. *Thomas Hardy's Wessex* (1913).

Legg, Rodney. *Discover Dorset's Hardy Country* (2003).

Lowman, Roger. *Thomas Hardy's 'The Dorsetshire Labourer' and Wessex* (2005).

Pite, Ralph. *Hardy's Geography: Wessex and the Regional Novel* (2002).

Pitfield, F. P. *Hardy's Wessex Locations* (1992).

Rode, Scott. *Reading and Mapping Hardy's Roads* (2006).

Steel, Gayla R. *Sexual Tyranny in Wessex: Hardy's Witches and Demons of Folklore* (1993).

Udal, J. S. *Dorsetshire Folk-Lore* (1922).

Visual Arts

Andres, Sophia. "Beyond Gender Boundaries: Edward Burne-Jones and Thomas Hardy," *The Pre-Raphaelite Art of the Victorian Novel* (2005).

Bullen, J. B. *The Expressive Eye: Fiction and Perception in the Work of Thomas Hardy* (1986).

Durden, Mark. "Ritual and Deception: Photography and Thomas Hardy," *Journal of European Studies* 30.1 (2000).

Fernando, Lloyd. "Thomas Hardy's Rhetoric of Painting," *A Review of English Literature* 6 (1965).

Grundy, Joan. *Hardy and the Sister Arts* (1979).

Page, Norman. "Hardy's Pictorial Art in The Mayor of Casterbridge," *Études Anglaises* 25 (1972).

Smart, Alastair. "Pictorial Imagery in the Novels of Thomas Hardy," *Review of English Studies* 12 (1961).

Specific Texts

The Dynasts

Bailey, J. O. *Thomas Hardy and the Cosmic Mind: A New Reading of The Dynasts* (2003, first published in 1956).

Clifford, Emma. *The Trumpet-Major* Notebook: and "The Dynasts," *Review of English Studies* NS 8 (1957).

Dean, Susan. *Hardy's Poetic Vision in The Dynasts* (1977).

Orel, Harold. *Thomas Hardy's Epic-Drama: A Study of The Dynasts* (1963).

Wickens, Glen. *Thomas Hardy, Monism and the Carnival Tradition: The One and the Many in The Dynasts* (2002).

Wilson, Keith. "'Flower of Man's Intelligence': World and Overworld in *The Dynasts*," *Victorian Poetry* 17 (1979).

Wright, Walter F. "The Shaping of 'The Dynasts'" *A Study in Thomas Hardy* (1967).

Desperate Remedies

Jones, Lawrence O. "*Desperate Remedies* and the Victorian Sensation Novel," *Nineteenth-Century Fiction* 20 (1965).

Neale, Catherine. "*Desperate Remedies*: The Merits and Demerits of Popular Fiction," *Critical Survey* 5 (1993).

Page, Norman. "Visual Techniques in Hardy's *Desperate Remedies*," *Ariel* 4 (1973).

Far From the Madding Crowd

Chang, Jung-hee. "Victorian Novel and Women of Property: Thomas Hardy's *Far from the Madding Crowd* and *The Woodlanders*," *Nineteenth Century Literature in English* 8.1 (2004).

Giordano, Frank. "Farmer Boldwood: Hardy's Portrait of a Suicide," *English Literature in Transition* 21 (1978).

Jones, Lawrence. "'A Good Hand at a Serial': Thomas Hardy and the Serialisation of *Far From the Madding Crowd*," *Studies in Philology* 77 (1980).

Petit, Susan. "Proper Names and Improper Meanings in Thomas Hardy's *Far from the Madding Crowd*," *Names* (Journal of the American Name Society) 51.1 (2003).

Reid, Fred. "Art and Ideology in *Far From the Madding Crowd*," *THA* 4 (1986).

Schapiro, Barbara. "Psychoanalysis and Romantic Idealization: The Dialectics of Love in Hardy's *Far from the Madding Crowd*," *American Imago* 59.1 (2002).

The Hand of Ethelberta

Davies, Sarah. "*The Hand of Ethelberta*: De-Mythologising 'Woman'" *Critical Survey* 5 (1993).

Schweik, Robert. "Hardy's 'Plunge in a New and Untried Direction': Comic Detachment in *The Hand of Ethelberta*," *English Studies* 83.3 (2002).

Short, Clarice. "In Defence of *Ethelberta*," *Nineteenth-Century Fiction* 13 (1958).

Ward, Paul. "*The Hand of Ethelberta*," *THYB* (1971).

Wing, George. "'Forbear, Hostler, Forbear!' Social Satire in *The Hand of Ethelberta*," *Studies in the Novel* 15 (1972).

Jude the Obscure

Archimedes, Sondra. "Shapes Like Our Own Selves Hideously Multiplied: Sue Bridehead, Reproduction, and the Disease of Modern Civilization," *Gendered Pathologies: The Female Body and Biomedical Discourse in the Nineteenth-Century English Novel* (2005).

Camp, Mechel. "Novel, Tract, Biography: Why New Women Novels Don't Play by the Rules," *Tennessee Philological Bulletin: Proceedings of the Annual Meeting of the Tennessee Philological Association* 39 (2002).

Cunningham, A. R. "The 'New Woman' Fiction of the 1890s," *Victorian Studies* 17 (1973).

Elvy, Margaret. *Thomas Hardy's "Jude the Obscure": A Critical Study* (2000).

Faubert, Michelle. "Hardy's *Jude the Obscure*," *The Explicator* 60.2 (2002).

Fernando, Lloyd. *"New Women" in the Late Victorian Novel* (1977).

Fujita, Machiko. "The Changing Distance between Jude and Sue: Cousinship and Hardy in *Jude the Obscure*," *Shiron* 41 (July 2003).

Jenkins, Alice, and Juliet John, eds. Foreword by John Sutherland. *Rereading Victorian Fiction* (2000).

O'Malley, Patrick R. "Oxford's Ghosts: *Jude the Obscure* and the End of the Gothic," *Modern Fiction Studies* 46.3 (2000).

Reed, John R. "Jude's Music: Music as Theme and Structure in Hardy's *Jude the Obscure*," *Victorian Institute Journal* 29 (2001).

Rhee, Suk-Koo. "Social Criticism and Gender Discourse in *Jude the Obscure*," *Journal of English Language and Literature/Yongo Yongmunhak* 46.3 (2000).

Richardson, R. "*Jude the Obscure*? How the Idea Evolved for an Oxford College for Mature Students," *Oxford Magazine* 216 (2003).

Riquelme, John Paul. "Toward a History of Gothic and Modernism: Dark Modernity from Bram Stoker to Samuel Beckett," *Modern Fiction Studies* 46.3 (2000).

Sutherland, John. "A Note on the Teasing Narrator in *Jude the Obscure*," *English Literature in Transition* 17 (1974).

Taylor, Dennis. "The Chronology of *Jude the Obscure*," *THJ* 12 (1996).

Vance, N. "Secular Apocalyptic and Thomas Hardy," *History of European Ideas* 26.3–4 (2000).

Wright, Janet B. "Hardy and His Contemporaries: The Literary Context of *Jude the Obscure*," *Inscape* 14 (1980).

A Laodicean

Drake, Robert Y. "*A Laodicean*: A Note on a Minor Novel," *Philological Quarterly* 40 (1961).

Hochstadt, Pearl R. "Hardy's Romantic Diptych: A Reading of *A Laodicean* and *Two on a Tower*," *ELT* 26 (1983).

Wing, George. "Middle-Class Outcasts in Hardy's *A Laodicean*," *Humanities Association Review* 27 (1976).

The Mayor of Casterbridge

Asquith, Mark. "Caged Birds: The *Mayor of Casterbridge*," *The English Review* 14.4 (2004).

Brown, Douglas. *The Mayor of Casterbridge* (1962).

Draper, R. P. "The Mayor of Casterbridge," *Critical Quarterly* 25 (1983).

Heilman, Robert B. "Hardy's 'Mayor' and the Problem of Intention," *Criticism* 5 (1963).

————. "Hardy's Mayor: Notes on Style," *Nineteenth-Century Fiction* 18 (1964).

Karl, Frederick R. "*The Mayor of Casterbridge*: A New Fiction Defined," *Modern Fiction Studies* 6 (1960).

Tandon, Bharat. "'… among the Ruins': Narrative Archaeology in *The Mayor of Casterbridge*," *Studies in the Novel* 35.4 (2003).

Thompson, J. B. "Hardy's *The Mayor of Casterbridge*," *The Explicator* 59.2 (2001).

Winfield, Christine. "Factual Sources of Two Episodes in *The Mayor of Casterbridge*," *Nineteenth-Century Fiction* 25 (1970).

A Pair of Blue Eyes

Amos, Arthur K. "Accident and Fate: The Possibility for Action in *A Pair of Blue Eyes*," *ELT* 15 (1972).

Devereux, Jo. "Thomas Hardy's *A Pair of Blue Eyes*: The Heroine as Text." *Victorian Newsletter* (1992).

Fortey, Richard. *Trilobite! Eyewitness to Evolution* (2000).

Jacobus, Mary. "Hardy's Magian Retrospect," *Essays in Criticism* (1982).

Wittenberg, Judith Bryant. "Early Hardy Novels and the Fictional Eye," *Novel* (1983).

The Return of the Native

Cohen, William A. "Faciality and Sensation in Hardy's *The Return of the Native*," *PMLA* 121.2 (2006).

Fludernik, Monica. "The Diachronization of Narratology," *Narrative* 11.3 (October, 2003).

Ford, Ed. "The Influence of Thomas Hardy's *The Return of the Native* on Alain-Fournier's *Le Grand Meaulnes*," *Dalhousie French Studies* 71 (2005).

Loomis, Roger. *The Play of Saint George* (1928).

Qun, Z. "Eustacia—Victim of Fate—On Thomas Hardy's *The Return of the Native*," *Journal—China Textile University* 17.4 (2000).

Radford, Andrew. "Hardy's *The Return of the Native*," *The Explicator* 63.1 (2004).

Shead, Jackie. "*The Return of the Native*" and Greek Tragedy. *The English Review* 16.2 (2005).

Stallman, R. W. "Hardy's Hour-Glass Novel," *Sewanee Review* 55 (1947).

Thomas, Brian. *The Return of the Native: Saint George Defeated* (1995).

Weber, Carl J. "Hardy's Chronology in *The Return of the Native*," *PMLA* 53 (1938).

Tess of the d'Urbervilles

Asquith, Mark. "Hardy's Tess: A Pure Woman?" *The English Review* 14.3 (2004).

Brady, Kristin. "Tess and Alec: Rape or Seduction?" *THA* 4 (1986).

Carroll, A. "Human Milk in the Modern World: Breastfeeding and the Cult of the Dairy in *Adam Bede* and *Tess of the d'Urbervilles*," *Womens Studies* 31.2 (2002).

Clarke, J. S., and G. Law. "More Light on the Serial Publication of *Tess of the d'Urbervilles*," *Review of English Studies* 54.203 (2003).

De Laura, David J. "'The Ache of Modernism' in Hardy's Later Novels," *Journal of English Literary History* 34 (1967).

Efron, Arthur. *Experiencing Tess of the d'Urbervilles: A Deweyan Account* (2005).

Elvy, Margaret. *Thomas Hardy's "Tess of the d'Urbervilles": A Critical Study* (2000).

Fairhurst, Douglas R. "Making Sense of Victorian Endings: *Tess of the d'Urbervilles* and *Middlemarch*," *Use of English* 54.3 (2003).

Harbinson, Christopher. "Echoes of Keats' 'Lamia' in Hardy's *Tess of the d'Urbervilles*," *Notes and Queries* 49.1 (2002).

Harvey, Geoffrey. *Thomas Hardy—"Tess of the d'Urbervilles"* (2003).

Jacobus, Mary. "Tess's Purity," *Essays in Criticism* 26 (1976).

Laird, J. T. *The Shaping of "Tess of the d'Urbervilles"* (1975).

Lovesey, Oliver. "Reconstructing Tess," *SEL: Studies in English Literature 1500–1900* 43.4 (2003).

Malton, Sara. "'The Woman Shall Bear Her Iniquity': Death as Social Discipline in Thomas Hardy's *The Return of the Native*," *Studies in the Novel* 32.2 (2000).

McEathron, Scott, ed. *Thomas Hardy's Tess of the d'Urbervilles: A Sourcebook* (2004).

Michie, Elsie B. "Dressing Up: Hardy's *Tess of the d'Urbervilles* and Oliphant's *Phoebe Junior*," *Victorian Literature and Culture* 30.1 (2002).

Musselwhite, D. E. "*Tess of the d'Urbervilles*: 'A Becoming Woman'; or, Deleuze and Guattari Go to Wessex," *Textual Practice* 14.3 (2000).

Nicholson, Sarah. "The Woman Pays: Death and the Ambivalence of Providence in Hardy's Novels," *Literature and Theology* 16.1 (2002).

Nishimura, Satoshi. "Language, Violence, and Irrevocability: Speech Acts in *Tess of the d'Urbervilles*," *Studies in the Novel* 37.2 (2005).

Rode, Scott. "Sexual Identity on the Road in *Tess of the D'Urbervilles* [sic]," *Nineteenth-Century Gender Studies* 1 (2005).

Sternlieb, Lisa. "'Three Leahs to Get One Rachel': Redundant Women in *Tess of the d'Urbervilles*," *Dickens Studies Annual* 29 (2000).

Tague, Gregory. "Thomas Hardy: *Tess of the d'Urbervilles, Jude the Obscure*, and Character in Nature," *Character and Consciousness: George Eliot, Thomas Hardy, E.M. Forster, D.H. Lawrence* (2005).

Tanner, Tony. "Colour and Movement in Hardy's *Tess of the d'Urbervilles*," *Critical Quarterly* 19 (1968).

Ui Rak, Kim. "[Marxist Criticism, A Working Class, and Alienation in Thomas Hardy's *Tess of the d'Urbervilles*.]" *Journal of English Language and Literature* (2000).

Zhang, X. "On Hardy's Philosophical Thinking and Aesthetic Consciousness in *Tess of the d'Urbervilles*," *Journal of the Shangqui Teachers College* 21.6 (2005).

The Trumpet-Major

Bebington, W. G. *The Original Manuscript of The Trumpet Major* (1948).

Collister, Peter. "'Past Things Retold': A Study of Thomas Hardy's Under the Greenwood Tree and The Trumpet-Major," *Durham University Journal* 36, (1974–75).

Thomson, George H. "The Trumpet-Major Chronicle," *Nineteenth-Century Fiction* 17 (1962).

Two on a Tower

Bayley, John. "The Love Story in *Two on a Tower*," *THA* 1 (1982).

Irvin, Glenn. "High Passion and High Church in Hardy's *Two on a Tower*," *ELT* 28 (1985).

Sumner, Rosemary. "The Experimental and the Absurd in *Two on a Tower*," *THA* 1 (1982).

Ward, Paul. "*Two on a Tower*: A Critical Appreciation," *THYB* 8 (1978).

Wing, George. "Hardy's Star-Cross'd Lovers in *Two on a Tower*," *THYB* 14 (1987).

Under the Greenwood Tree

Danby, John F. "Under the Greenwood Tree," *Critical Quarterly* 1 (1959).

Draffan, Robert A. "Hardy's Under the Greenwood Tree," *English* 22 (1973).

Howard, Jeanne. "Thomas Hardy's 'Mellstock' and the Registrar General's Stinsford," *Literature and History* 6 (1977).

Tolliver, H. E. "The Dance under the Greenwood Tree: Hardy's Bucolics," *Nineteenth-Century Fiction* 17 (1962).

The Well-Beloved

Deangelis, Rose. "Triangulated Passions: Love, Self-Love, and the Other in Thomas Hardy's The Well-Beloved," *Studies in the Novel* 34.4 (2002).

Gerber, Helmut E. "Hardy's The Well-Beloved as a Comment on the Well-Despised," *English Language Notes* 1 (1963).

Neill, Edward. "'Genetically Unmodified': The Well-Beloved." *English* 53.207 (2004).

Priestley, Alma. "Hardy's The Well-Beloved: A Study in Failure," *Thomas Hardy Society Review* 2 (1976).

The Woodlanders

Bayley, John. "A Social Comedy? On Re-Reading *The Woodlanders*," THA 5 (1987).

Fayen, G. S. "Hardy's *The Woodlanders*: Inwardness and Memory," *Studies in English Literature* 1 (1961).

Pinion, F. B. "The Country and Period of *The Woodlanders*," THYB 2 (1971).

Radford, Andrew. "Hardy's *The Woodlanders*," *The Explicator* 58.3 (2000).

———. "The Unmanned Fertility Figure in Hardy's *The Woodlanders*," *Victorian Newsletter* No. 99 (2001).

Schweik, Robert C. "The Ethical Structure of Hardy's *The Woodlanders*," *Archive* 211 (1974).

Simpson, Charles. *The Country of the Woodlanders: An Account of a Year's Farming, 1943–1943, in That Part of Dorset Described by Thomas Hardy in His Novel The Woodlanders* (2005).

Steig, Michael. "Art versus Philosophy in Hardy's *The Woodlanders*," *Mosaic* 4 (1971).

COLLECTIONS OF ESSAYS

Dolin, Tim, and Peter Widdowson. *Thomas Hardy and Contemporary Literary Studies* (2004).

Hardy, Evelyn. *The Countryman's Ear and Other Essays on Thomas Hardy* (1982).

Higonnet, Margaret, ed. *The Sense of Sex: Feminist Perspectives on Hardy* (1993).

Ingham, Patricia, ed. *Thomas Hardy: Feminist Readings* (1989).

Kramer, Dale, ed. *Critical Approaches to the Fiction of Thomas Hardy* (1979).

Mallett, Phillip, ed. *The Achievement of Thomas Hardy* (2000).

———, ed. *Palgrave Advances in Thomas Hardy Studies* (2004).

———, ed. *Thomas Hardy: Texts and Contexts* (2002).

Mallett, Phillip, and Ronald Draper, eds. *A Spacious Vision: Essays on Hardy* (1994).

Morgan, Rosemarie, ed. *Days to Recollect: Essays in Honour of Robert Schweik* (2000).

Morgan, Rosemarie, and Richard Nemesvari, eds. *Human Shows: Essays in Honour of Michael Millgate* (2000).

Page, Norman, ed. *Thomas Hardy: The Writer and His Background* (1980).

———, ed. *Thomas Hardy Annual* (1982–87).

Pettit, Charles, ed. *Celebrating Thomas Hardy: Insights and Appreciations* (1996).

———, ed. *New Perspectives on Thomas Hardy* (1994).

———, ed. *Reading Thomas Hardy* (1998).

Pinion, Frank, ed. *Budmouth Essays on Thomas Hardy* (1974).

———, ed. *Thomas Hardy and the Modern World* (1976).

Southworth, J. G. *The Poetry of Thomas Hardy* (1947).

Szumzki, Bonnie, ed. *Readings on Tess of the d'Urbervilles* (2000).

Wilson, Keith, ed. *Thomas Hardy Reappraised: Essays in Honour of Michael Millgate* (2006).

Index

About the Author

ROSEMARIE MORGAN, editor and publisher of the annual *Hardy Review*, has taught at Yale University since 1984 and is currently holding a research fellowship. She is president of the Hardy Association, vice president of the Hardy Society, editorial consultant to *Rivista di Studi Vittoriani*, "Years Work" essayist for *Victorian Poetry* and has published the holograph manuscript of *Far From the Madding Crowd* as well as essays on Charlotte Brontë, Toni Morrison, Mary Chestnut, and women writers of the American Frontier. Her major works are *Women and Sexuality in the Novels of Thomas Hardy* (1988) and *Cancelled Words* (1992).